PRAISE FOR
THE NEW ASIAN HEMISPHERE

"Mahbubani provides a compelling case for a Western strategy of power sharing with Asia."

—*Foreign Affairs*

"There are lessons to be learned from *The New Asian Hemisphere*. . . . Aspiring presidential nominees and congressmen should take note."

—*Wall Street Journal*

"Kishore Mahbubani is a historian of ideas whose starting point is the present and whose horizon is a visible, startling future. This remarkable book is a fact-based projection of Asia's rising trajectory. The West has been synonymous with modernity for perhaps the last three centuries. Asia is the New Modern. Vision and clarity make this book a sparkling history of the Age of Asia."

—M. J. AKBAR, editor-in-chief, *Asian Age*,
and author of *The Shade of Swords*

"The Western, particularly the American, response to the rise of Asia has been petulant, degenerating into protectionism and panic. Japan-bashing of the 1980s was succeeded by India-bashing over outsourcing in the 1990s and now we have China-bashing in the 2000s. Mahbubani, one of the most perceptive and influential Asian intellectuals today, shows the folly of these reactions and the wisdom of applauding and working with the reality of Asia's remarkable success. His splendid book must be read by every Western policymaker; it is a tour de force."

—JAGDISH BHAGWATI, University Professor,
Economics and Law, Columbia University and
author of *In Defense of Globalization* (Oxford)

"Kishore Mahbubani understands better than most that the relationship between East and West, established after 1945, is no longer sustainable. This book even thrillingly explains why global power politics is at a crucial change, where the East and most especially the West must decide if er can be shared more equally or will be disputed more destructively."

—SHEKHAR KAPUR, director of the
Academy Award–winning film *Elizabeth*

"Once again, Kishore Mahbubani proves himself a global thought-leader. In *The New Asian Hemisphere*, he combines a prodigious knowledge of history, a flair for lucid, often witty analysis and advocacy, and the pragmatism of an experienced diplomat. The result is a set of prescriptions that leaders and citizens of the world in both hemispheres would do well to heed."

—STROBE TALBOTT, president of the Brookings Institution
and author of *The Great Experiment*

"Kishore Mahbubani, experienced diplomat, deeply immersed in the West and in Asia, is arguably the most articulate Asian voice bluntly telling the West how informed Asians see it. The tide is shifting and while Mahbubani's message will not be easy to take, Western leaders will ignore it at their peril."

—EZRA F. VOGEL, research professor, Harvard University

"Kishore Mahbubani has a global mind with a unique Singapore perspective and this comes out clearly in this forcefully argued book. He grew up in a Hindu family, among Muslim and Chinese friends and was shaped by British colonial education, the key ingredients of a proto-Singaporean. By studying Western philosophy and through working as a diplomat for a pragmatic city-state that has survived both hot and cold wars, he also caught the one-world spirit identified with the United Nations ideal. Thus has emerged the worldly Singaporean determined to dissect how a resurgent China, India and Islam might force the old West to change. He also challenges a new Asia to respond if and when this change in the West happens."

—WANG GUNGWU, chairman, East Asian Institute

"His view is that he, and Asia, sees the world differently than the U.S. does. In many respects he is right."

—JOSEPH E. STIGLITZ, Nobel Laureate and
author of *Globalization and its Discontents*

THE NEW ASIAN
HEMISPHERE

THE NEW ASIAN
HEMISPHERE

THE IRRESISTIBLE SHIFT
OF GLOBAL POWER TO THE EAST

KISHORE MAHBUBANI

PUBLICAFFAIRS
NEW YORK

Published in the United States by PublicAffairs™,
a member of the Perseus Books Group.

PublicAffairs books are available at special discounts for bulk purchases
in the U.S. by corporations, institutions, and other organizations. For more information, please contact the Special Markets Department at the Perseus Books Group,
2300 Chestnut Street, Suite 200, Philadelphia, PA 19103, call (800) 810-4145,
ext. 5000, or e-mail special.markets@perseusbooks.com.

Library of Congress Cataloging-in-Publication Data
Mahbubani, Kishore.
The new Asian hemisphere : the irresistible shift of global power to the East /
Kishore Mahbubani. — 1st ed.
p. cm.
Includes bibliographical references and index.
HC ISBN 978-1-58648-466-8 (hard cover : alk. paper)
PB ISBN 978-1-58648-671-6
1. Asia—Foreign relations.
2. International relations.
I. Title.
JZ1670.M34 2008
327.5—dc22
2007041265

10 9 8 7 6 5 4

To Kishore, Shelagh, and Jhamat

Contents

Acknowledgments

It was an act of sheer folly to agree to write a book while trying at the same time to build a new school of public policy. The only way to get it done was to burn months of weekends with writing. My family paid the price. This is one reason why I am dedicating this book to my three children.

But there is another, more important reason. I believe that they can live in a better world than my generation (which has had a good run for six decades). This will only happen if we take advantage of the remarkably plastic moment in world history we are experiencing now. If the right decisions are made today, my children's generation will be better off. The purpose of this book is to influence such decisions.

Since I have to work full-time, I relied on research assistants. One in particular, Kaajal Wallia, helped a great deal. Each Monday morning I would return to the office with a handwritten monograph. She would decipher the notes, fill in the blanks, and, quite remarkably, find the right statistics and anecdotes to bolster many of the points I made. She did brilliant work. This book owes a lot to her.

Kaajal left before the book was completed. To get the book to the finishing line, I obtained the help of Asya Anderson, Vrutika Mody, Denni Jayme, and Gillian Goh. Denni, Gillian, and my colleague, T. S.

Gopi Rethinaraj, also helped a great deal with the substantive research. Carol Chan and Wong Wee Cheng helped a great deal with the production work. An enormous amount of work goes into producing a credible manuscript. It would have been impossible without their help. I want to thank my editor, Clive Priddle, for once again shaping the manuscript so beautifully. This book has benefited from his touch. In addition, my thanks go to Annie Lenth and Beth Wright for editing this book so well.

I also want to thank my friends for giving me helpful advice and suggestions on the book. However, as some of them also advised me not to go to print with the book in its current form, I have decided not to mention their names in this section so as to avoid embarrassing them. I took seriously their advice that this book could alienate a significant audience, especially in the West. I respect and value their advice. However, after reflecting carefully, I decided to proceed. If I had written this book to fall within the "comfort zone" of my friends in the West, it would have a better chance of getting a positive reception there. But the new world that is emerging will be one that will be outside this "comfort zone." We need to prepare ourselves for this radically different world. The discomfort felt on reading the book is, unfortunately, part of the process.

Against this backdrop, you will understand why I deeply appreciate the generous gesture of some friends of mine to offer "blurbs" for this book. In particular, I would like to thank: Mr. M. J. Akbar, Prof. Jagdish Bhagwati, Prof. Zbigniew Brzezinski, Mr. Shekhar Kapur, Dr. Amartya Sen, Prof. Lawrence H. Summers, Mr. Strobe Talbott, Prof. Ezra Vogel, and Prof. Wang Gungwu.

Finally, I want to thank my wife, Anne, for her forbearance. I stretched her patience and understanding to the limit. I look forward to resuming my normal life now and to playing golf again on weekends.

Kishore Mahbubani

PREFACE TO THE PAPERBACK EDITION

The global financial crisis of 2008–2009 has significantly confirmed and bolstered some of the main theses of this book. First, it has resulted in a global demystification of the notion of Western competence. Any illusion that the Western economies are better prepared to handle great crises has vanished. This, in turn, has accelerated the end of the era of Western domination of world history that this book confidently predicted.

Second, the crisis has confirmed the wisdom of Asian countries in adopting a pragmatic rather than ideological approach to economic growth and development. Fortunately, few Asian policymakers were seduced by Alan Greenspan's ideological belief that markets knew best and that governments did best by stepping aside. Instead, most Asian governments believed that the virtues of the invisible hand of the markets had to be balanced by the virtues of good governance. Asian economies have been badly hit by the global financial crisis but they do not have to do an ideological U-turn to cope with it.

Third, the book also advocated the termination of the practice of Western domination of global institutions and its replacement by more globally representative institutions and processes. In this regard, it was hugely ironic that the last act of the most unilateralist contemporary American President, George W. Bush, was to convene a meeting of the G-20 to deal with the financial crises. This sheer act of convening the G-20 proved a point that this book had strongly argued: The G-8 had become both irrelevant and ineffective in dealing with global challenges.

The major mistakes made by Western economies do not however mean that the Asian economies are ready to displace them. They will also be seriously challenged by this crisis. China, India, and several other Asian economies were dependent on the American consumer to power their growth. American economic power will be seriously subdued in the coming years. The big challenge that Asian economies face is to maintain a growth rate of 5–7 percent in the coming years. The latest IMF and ADB predictions indicate that they may be able to scrape by the targets. The 7 percent figure is key. If they can sustain 7 percent growth over several decades, the Asian populations will still achieve the 10,000 percent improvement in standard of living in one lifetime that Lawrence Summers has predicted.

Another major challenge that the Asian economies, especially China and India, face is that they will be expected to provide greater global leadership to help steer the world through the emerging global challenges. In this book, I have tried to explain why both China and India will face difficulties in doing so. However reluctant they may be to exercise global leadership, there is also no doubt that no major Asian economy can afford to be a free rider on the global multilateral system. Hitherto, both the United States and the European Union have been good custodians of the open global multilateral systems. But will they remain good custodians when their populations no longer believe that they will benefit from open globalization? Hence, Asians too need to engage in new thinking to prepare for a different world.

The sharp contrast in the Anglo-American and Asian reactions to this book do indicate that Asians are developing their own perspective on global challenges. I have deliberately used the word "Anglo-

American" instead of Western because one of the most pleasant surprises I have had has been the positive continental European reactions to the book. Three European editions of this book have emerged, in Dutch, French and German. Indeed the Dutch edition had four print runs in the first two months of its publication, exceeding all of our expectations.

The Anglo-American intellectual community however remains, by and large, resistant to the arguments of this book. With a few exceptions, their reviews of the book have been relatively negative. The *Economist* labeled it as "an anti-Western polemic." Ironically, this has proved one of the theses of the book—that some Western societies are open in their political systems and closed in their minds.

The Asian reactions to this book have been remarkably positive. In general, one common point they make is that this is the one book that explains the Asian point of view to the world. The *Hindustan Times*, India's leading national daily, found that "very few Asian thinkers have closely studied and highlighted the changing rules of engagement between the West and the rest as Mahbubani. He has not only dwelled deep into the insecurities of the West and its ills, but also appreciated the Western practices that he says have played a big role in changing Asia's pace of political and economic growth." The Chinese journal *Around Southeast Asia* commented, "It is because of his global outlook and unique Singapore perspective that Kishore Mahbubani can write a work of such weight."

My hope is that this paperback edition will now reach a wider audience, especially a younger audience. Many of the most optimistic young people in the world today are young Asians. This volume will explain their optimism and also, hopefully, infect the other young people of the world. America is the early days of a new presidency, and perhaps its leader had a taste of Asian optimism when he was educated in Indonesia. We should all hope so. America seems to have decisively turned away from the unfettered market capitalism of the previous

decade, but it's too soon to know if this is a temporary rejection or a significant change of course for the long term. I have always argued that the word owes much to America and needs it to play a vital and constructive role. Americans need to understand better the new world that is emerging so that we can all work together to create a better world. This book explains how.

THE NEW ASIAN
HEMISPHERE

---

*The difficulty lies, not in the new ideas, but in escaping from
the old ones, which ramify, for those brought up
as most of us have been, into every corner of our minds.*

—JOHN MAYNARD KEYNES,

ENGLISH ECONOMIST (1883–1946),

IN *THE GENERAL THEORY OF EMPLOYMENT, INTEREST AND MONEY*

The rise of the West transformed the world. The rise of Asia will bring
about an equally significant transformation. This book describes why
Asia is rising now, how it will alter the world, and why the West, even
though it should celebrate Asia's rise, will have great difficulties adjust-
ing to these changes. It will also suggest some prescriptions for managing the obvious new challenges coming our way.

The rise of Asia will be good for the world. Hundreds of millions of
people will be rescued from the clutches of poverty. China's modernization has already reduced the number of Chinese living in absolute
poverty from six hundred million to two hundred million. India's
growth is also making an equally significant impact. Indeed, one key

reason why the United Nations (UN) will actually meet one of its Millennium Development Goals of reducing global poverty by half by 2015 will be the success of China and India in reducing poverty significantly. By the standards of any Western moral philosopher, from the British utilitarian philosophers of the nineteenth century to the moral imperatives of Immanuel Kant, it is clear that the rise of Asia has brought more "goodness" into the world. In purely ethical terms, the West should welcome the transformation of the Asian condition.

But the benefits of Asia's rise are more than ethical. The world as a whole will become more peaceful and stable. In September 2005 Robert Zoellick, the new president of the World Bank, called on China to become a "responsible stakeholder" in the international system. Since then, China has responded positively to this call. Indeed, most Asians want to become responsible stakeholders in the international system. Recent decades have demonstrated that Asians have become among the greatest beneficiaries of the open multilateral order created by America and the victors of World War II in 1945. Few Asian societies today want to destabilize a system that has helped them.

The word "modernization" will be used frequently in this book and will be defined fully in chapter 1. But any Western reader should intuitively understand what this term means. It describes both the physical and the ethical universe of Western societies. The really good news for the world is that the modernization of Asia is beginning to spread to all corners of the continent. Half a century ago, there appeared to be only two modern societies in Asia, at its eastern and western extremities: Japan and Israel. Between them lay a sea of humanity that seemed indifferent to modernization and growth. But Japan's example triggered a whole series of Asian success stories. First Japan was emulated by the four economic tigers: South Korea, Taiwan, Hong Kong, and Singapore. When China began to be aware that countries on its periphery were doing better than it was, it decided to join them by launching its own "Four Modernizations" program. For the past three decades, China has had the fastest growing economy in the world.

China's success has in turn also inspired the rise of India. Now, billions of Asians are marching to modernity.

The even better news for the world is that this March to Modernity is poised to enter the Islamic world of Western Asia too. It is only a matter of time before it spreads from India to Pakistan and then to Iran. All of Asia may well be modernized in the twenty-first century. If this happens, Israel will not be left as a lonely outpost of modernity in Western Asia. It could eventually have equally modernized neighbors. This may seem like a wild dream, but it is vital to understand that Asia's growth and success in the past few decades have exceeded most Asians' wildest dreams. This book, written by a realist, is underpinned by optimism about Asia's role in the global future. Generally Asians today do not have to be convinced to be optimistic. This creates a new global paradox: up until recently the most optimistic societies of the world have been Western societies, but they seem to be losing their optimism, at a point in time when they should be celebrating the galloping modernization of the world.

The term "the West" will be used frequently in this book. Often, when I refer to Western policies, some will respond that I am speaking primarily of American policies. Given the enormity of US power, American policies naturally dominate. But there is also an implicit compact between America and Europe as well as with the Anglo-Saxon states of Australia, Canada, and New Zealand on global policies. One of the least understood (and surprisingly least studied) phenomena is how the West often functions as a single entity on global issues. On fundamental challenges Western nations work together. Witness, for example, how the West came together on Afghanistan. Canadian and European soldiers are dying in defense of policies initiated by America. This is powerful solidarity.

When many Western eyes peer into the twenty-first century, they see only dark images, not a new dawn in the history of human civilization. This is a strange development. For the past few centuries, the West has been by far the most open and resilient civilization, during which it has largely carried the world on its shoulders. It was the West that triggered the Asian March to Modernity, so it should be cheering this positive new direction of world history. Instead, leading Western minds are filled with dread and foreboding. I hope to explain this reversal.

Evidently, Asia and the West have yet to reach a common understanding about the nature of this new world. The need to develop one has never been greater. We are now entering one of the most plastic moments of world history. The decisions we make today could determine the course of the twenty-first century. Never before have we had as much potential as we have today to create a better world for the 6.5 billion people who inhabit our planet. The explosion of knowledge, especially in science and technology, has delivered this opportunity. It is also clear that the mental maps of the leading minds of the world, especially in the West, are trapped in the past, reluctant or unable to conceive of the possibility that they may have to change their worldview. But unless they do, they will make strategic mistakes, perhaps on a disastrous scale.

The decision by the United States and the United Kingdom to invade Iraq in March 2003 was one such mistake. It is possible to argue convincingly that the Americans and British intended only to free the Iraqi people from a despotic ruler and to rid the world of a dangerous man, Saddam Hussein. Neither Bush nor Blair had malevolent intentions, yet their mental approach was trapped in a limited cultural context: the Western mindset. Many leading American minds truly believed that invading American troops would be welcomed with rose petals thrown on the streets by happy Iraqis. Yet the grain of history had been irrevocably changed in the second half of the twentieth century: no country today welcomes foreign invaders. The notion that any Islamic nation would welcome Western military boots on its soil is ridiculous. The invasion and especially the occupation of Iraq will be remembered as a colossally botched operation. Even if it had been well-executed, it was doomed to failure because while the British could successfully invade and occupy Iraq in the early twentieth century (in

1921 to be exact), no Western army could successfully repeat this in the early twenty-first century. In 1920, as secretary for war and air, Winston Churchill had responsibility for quelling the rebellion of Kurds and Arabs in British-occupied Iraq, which he achieved by authorizing the use of poison gas. Churchill said, "I am strongly in favor of using poisoned gas against uncivilized tribes."[1] If Blair had tried the same actions in 2003, he would have been crucified. The world has moved on from this era. Western mindsets have not abandoned the old assumption that an army of Christian soldiers can invade, occupy, and transform an Islamic society.

For most of the previous three centuries, the peoples of Asia, Africa, and Latin America were objects of world history. The decisions that drove history were made in a few key Western capitals, most often London, Paris, Berlin, and Washington, DC. The misnamed World War I and World War II were carried out without consulting the majority of the world's populations. They were co-opted into fundamentally European wars—at least until Japanese aggression appeared in China and the Pacific. Today, the 5.6 billion people who live outside the Western universe will no longer accept decisions made on their behalf in Western capitals.

So, will the twenty-first century be seen as a moment of historical triumph for the West or a moment of historical defeat? The answer cannot be given now. It will depend on how the West reacts to the rise of Asia. The number of people in the world who are seeking the Western dream of a comfortable middle-class existence has never been higher. For centuries, the Chinese and Indians could not aspire to it. Now more and more believe that it is within their reach. Their ideal is to achieve what America and Europe achieved. They want to replicate, not dominate, the West.

The universalization of the Western dream should therefore represent a moment of triumph for the West. Yet many Western leaders begin their speeches by remarking how "dangerous" the world is becoming. President Bush said in August 2006, "The American people need to know we live in a dangerous world."[2] Other Western leaders have made similar statements. The French minister of foreign affairs, Michel Barnier, stated in February 2005, "We have so many challenges to take up at the same time, in this world which is dangerous, unstable and in disarray."[3] The Canadian ambassador to the United States, Michael Wilson, said, "In an age where the world has become a smaller, more dangerous place, Canada is stepping up to the plate, refocusing our efforts on the new threats facing our people."[4] These statements reflect a new Western zeitgeist: the belief that the world is becoming more dangerous.

One of the great strengths of Western civilization is its belief that societies progress best when they do not become trapped in any ideology. This is how the West believed it achieved one of its greatest triumphs: the Soviet Union imploded because it was trapped in a dead ideology. Western societies, by contrast, were more rational and open to new ideas, never trapped in any ideological straitjackets.

Paradoxically, in the post–Cold War era, the West seems to have become an ideologically driven entity. The iconization of democracy—an unquestionably virtuous idea—became an ideological crusade that insisted democracy could be exported to any society everywhere in the world, regardless of its stage of political development. Disasters followed in Lebanon, Palestine, and Iraq. A conservative Republican, Congressman Henry Hyde, bluntly pointed out that ideological ambition had been allowed to trump common sense and experience: "We also have a duty to ourselves and to our interests, the protection and advancement of which may sometimes necessitate actions focused on more tangible returns than those of altruism. Lashing our interests to the indiscriminate promotion of democracy is a tempting but unwarranted strategy, more a leap of faith than a sober calculation." He further added, "We can and have used democracy as a weapon to destabilize our avowed enemies and may do so again. But if we unleash revolutionary forces in the expectation that the result can only be beneficent, I believe we are making a profound and perhaps uncorrectable mistake. History teaches that revolutions are dangerous things, more often destructive than benign, and uncontrollable by their very nature."[5]

The great paradox about failed Western attempts to export democracy to other societies is that in the broadest sense of the term, the West has actually succeeded in democratizing the world. One key goal of democracy is to empower its citizens and make them believe that they are the masters of their own destiny. The number of people in the world who believe this has never been higher. Even in the "undemocratic" society of China, citizens have seized the opportunities provided by the new economic freedoms they enjoy to completely change their lives. The same is true in India: the government has now increased the list of economic freedoms. In global terms, there has been a huge democratization of the human spirit. The West should be celebrating this, not berating countries about imperfect voting practices.

One reason above all explains why the West hesitates to celebrate the great democratization of the human spirit. It is keenly aware that if this trend continues, a great day of reckoning must come. As the spirit of democratization gathers strength and more and more human beings take charge of their own destinies, they will increasingly question the undemocratic world order they live in. Samuel Huntington effectively described this world order. Two sentences from his famous essay "The Clash of Civilizations" explain the current situation: "In the politics of civilization, the peoples and governments of non-Western civilization no longer remain the objects of history as targets of Western colonization but join the West as movers and shapers of history." He then adds, "The West in effect is using international institutions, military power and economic resources to run the world in ways that will maintain Western predominance, protect Western interests and promote Western political and economic values." He's right. The rest of the world is beginning to realize it. Left unchanged it's a recipe for disaster.

The reluctance of leading Western minds to acknowledge the unsustainability of Western global domination presents a great danger to the world. Western societies have to choose whether they will seek to nd Western values or Western interests in the twenty-first century. Most Western minds like to think that they are primarily promoting Western values, democracy high among them. But the rest of the world notices how the West promotes democracy selectively. No Western society is keen to promote democracy in Saudi Arabia for fear of endangering oil supplies to the West, for example.

That is why the primary purpose of this book is to explain the world as it is seen through non-Western eyes, so that the 900 million who live in the West appreciate how the remaining 5.6 billion people view the world. The language and concepts that will be used to describe non-Western perspectives will be Western in origin and context. This is one of the many great tributes that this book readily pays to the West. Most of the concepts we use to describe contemporary realities are Western. The willingness of the rest of the world to absorb and use Western concepts is one of the strongest foundations for global optimism. The vast majority of societies who want to succeed and prosper in the modern world do not want to do so by rejecting the West or its values. Instead they would prefer to work with the West. It is a huge sign of the new cultural confidence of many Asian societies, especially China and India, that they are prepared to learn from and absorb Western best practices in developing their societies.

The simplest way of describing how this book is different from Western discourse is that it points out how the West is both a large part of the solution and a large part of the problem in our efforts to restructure the world order. The latter, though, is hardly mentioned in most Western discourse. Indeed, as a frequent traveler to Western intellectual gatherings, I often come away from them astonished that at a time when Western minds should be opening themselves to completely new realities, they are actually becoming more closed. I often despair when I read the op-ed pages of the *New York Times* and the *Financial Times*. Newspapers are filled with an incestuous discourse among minds who believe that the 12 percent of the world's population who live in the West can continue to dominate the remaining 88 percent who live outside the West.

Few in the West have grasped the full implications of the two most salient features of our historical epoch. First, we have reached the end of the era of Western domination of world history (but not the end of the West, which will remain the single strongest civilization for decades more). Second, we will see an enormous renaissance of Asian societies. The strategic discourse in the West should focus on how the West should adapt, but this has not happened. To make matters worse, the West has gone from being competent to becoming incompetent in its handling of many key global challenges, from the threat of terrorism to climate change to keeping the nuclear nonproliferation regime alive. This incompetence, with naturally disastrous consequences, aggravates the Western sense of insecurity.

We are therefore moving toward a real crisis in the management of our world order unless the West changes course. In reflecting on future strategic options, Western minds should reflect on the Chinese wisdom in translating the Western word "crisis" by combining two Chinese characters, "danger" and "opportunity." Too many Western minds are looking at dangers; few are looking at opportunities. One key message of this book is that the Asian March to Modernity (which the next chapter will describe) represents a new opportunity both for the West and for the world. If the West could learn to work with, rather than against, this march, it can help make the twenty-first century one of the happiest centuries of human history.

My goal is to leave Western (and non-Western) readers feeling optimistic about the future of the world after reading this book. I am optimistic: I believe that my children will have a much better future than I. This is why I dedicated this book to them. But I also know that optimistic outcomes do not happen on their own. They require decisive human intervention. The time to act is now.

Finally, let me end this introduction with a shocking statistic. I did not uncover this statistic; Larry Summers did. When I sent him this manuscript for review, he responded with a paragraph that he uses to describe the rise of Asia: "They called it the Industrial Revolution because for the first time in all of human history standards of living rose at a rate where there were noticeable changes in standards of living in a human life span—changes of perhaps 50 percent. At current growth rates in Asia standards of living may rise 100 fold, 10,000 percent within a human life span. The rise of Asia and all that follows it will be the dominant story in history books written 300 years from now with the Cold War and rise of Islam as secondary stories."

When I first read this, I was skeptical of his claim that the standard of living of Asia could improve by 10,000 percent in one human life span. Fortunately, I ran into James Wolfensohn, the former President of the World Bank. He had read the same statistic from Larry Summers and he was equally skeptical. He therefore asked his research assistants to check. They checked and discovered, of course, that Larry Summers was right. Skeptical readers of this book may want to do a similar check. If their research confirms this, then the dramatic story of Asia's rise will sink in.

1

THE THREE SCENARIOS

On 30 December 2006, the Singapore paper *Straits Times* reported that a major political party in the southern Indian province of Tamil Nadu, Dravida Munnetra Kazhagam (DMK), in an effort to gain votes, had promised to give away free color televisions. It had handed out sixty thousand TV sets and planned to give away thirty thousand more. DMK's party secretary, Mr. T. K. S. Elangovam, explained the move by saying that color TVs had become a necessity. "Nowadays, it is not just entertainment, it is more, it informs about health, politics and public awareness issues," he said.[1]

What is so remarkable about a story of a Tamil politician giving away free color televisions? Try substituting the word "Tamil" with "Palestinian." A story about a Palestinian politician giving away TVs would be astonishing because Palestinian politics has become inter-twined with violence and conflict. Palestinians who live under Israeli occupation have more basic issues to address.

But suicide bombings were not invented in our modern era by the Palestinians. They were first practiced by the Tamils. The suicide bombings began not in Tamil Nadu but across the narrow Palk Straits in Sri Lanka. In response to demagogic Sinhalese politicians, who tried to take away language and other rights from the minority Tamil population in 1956, a violent resistance movement began among the Tamils, called the LTTE (Liberation Tigers of Tamil Eelam). The famous Tamil Tigers carried out suicide bombings mainly in Sri Lanka, but they also killed an Indian prime minister, Rajiv Gandhi, on 21 May 1991 in Sriperumbudur, a city in Tamil Nadu.

There are 3.1 million Tamils in Sri Lanka and 62 million Tamils in Tamil Nadu, India. Initially, many Indian Tamils were sympathetic to the LTTE struggle, just as Palestinians overseas supported Yasser Arafat and the Palestine Liberation Organization (PLO). However, soon the LTTE's violent tactics, especially the killing of Rajiv Gandhi, repelled the Tamils in India. Also, as India modernized, the Tamil community in Tamil Nadu began to focus their efforts on modernization and acquiring the comforts of modern life. Now the politicians who get elected in Tamil Nadu are not fiery supporters of the Tamil liberation struggle in Sri Lanka but those, like Elangovam, who promise free TVs.

Tamil Nadu is moving in the same direction as much of Asia. India is blessed with many talented and gifted ethnic groups. The Tamils have been among the most successful. Many famous mathematicians come from Tamil Nadu, including Srinivasa Ramanujan, the brilliant twentieth-century mathematician; Subbayya Sivasankaranarayana Pillai, well-known for his work in number theory; Kollagunta Gopalaiyer Ramanathan, also known for his well-recognized achievements in number theory; C. P. Ramanujam, who worked on number theory and algebraic geometry; T. S. Vijayaraghavan, who worked on Pisot-Vijayaraghavan numbers; and Ravindran Kannan, professor of computer science and mathematics at Yale University and joint winner of the 1991 Fulkerson Prize in discrete mathematics for work on the volumes of convex bodies. Two Tamils have won the coveted Nobel Prize in physics: Sir C.V. Raman in 1930 and Subrahmanyan Chandrasekhar in 1983. Chennai-born S. R. Srinivasa Varadhan, a professor at New York University, won the 2007 Abel Prize—which is considered the equivalent of the Nobel Prize in the field of mathematics—for his "fundamental contributions to probability theory, in particular for creating a unified theory of large deviation." Many other talented Tamils have also done well in the West. The most famous female Tamil in the world is an American: Indra Nooyi, the chair and CEO of PepsiCo.

Why list so many brilliant and successful Tamils in one paragraph? It highlights one of the key themes of the book. Asia is exploding because so many Asian minds, underused for centuries, are now exploding with creativity. If a relatively small state like Tamil Nadu (with about 5 percent of India's population) can produce so many talented and gifted individuals despite its relatively low per capita income, just imagine the impact that India will have on the world as the entire country modernizes. Within one country, India could replicate many European success stories. Tamil Nadu alone (population of 62 million) could match France (population of 60.9 million), Gujarat (50.6 million) Spain (43.4 million), West Bengal (83 million), and Italy (58.6 million). The impact on global productivity and creativity could be explosive.

An old Arab proverb declares: he who speaks about the future lies even when he tells the truth. No one can predict the future. But in one respect, at least, we can speak a little more confidently about the future: we can make reasonable extrapolations from known facts. If you could measure the amount of snow that falls on the Himalayas in any winter, you could make reasonable predictions about the flood levels in the river Ganges six months later, or so the saying goes. The snow that has already fallen will determine the flood levels.

In many ways, a lot of "snow" has fallen on the world. This chapter offers three possible scenarios of how the world will develop over the next fifty years. Each is an extrapolation of trends that have already surfaced. The first and most likely, indeed probable, scenario is the March to Modernity. It is truly our good fortune that the odds favor its realization. The second scenario is much less happy, but less likely: the

Retreat into Fortresses. The third scenario is the most unlikely, but I discuss it at length because it represents the wishes of many leading Western minds on how the world should evolve. They continue to believe and hope that Western civilization will triumph and eventually westernize the world. Its spirit is best captured in Francis Fukuyama's famous essay "The End of History." The enormously enthusiastic response the essay received in the West reflected the deep desire of the West to believe that history had concluded with the West's triumph and therefore the rest of the world faced no choice but to become cultural clones of the West. The scenario, then, is of Western Triumphalism.

THE MARCH TO MODERNITY

The March to Modernity is probably going to be the single most important trek in human history. If it succeeds, it will ensure a far more peaceful, stable, and prosperous world.

"Modernity" is a strange notion. In the West the more basic aspects of modernity—or modern living—are taken for granted. "Modernity" is often associated with a peculiar cultural or artistic strain: modern painting is linked to Picasso, modern literature to James Joyce, modern living to *Vanity Fair*. It represents—in American minds at least—a new and particular cultural stream. This, however, is not the March to Modernity that billions are aspiring to make.

To understand the destination of "modernity" that they aim for, it is important to understand the "premodern" world that they hope to leave behind, a world I know well because I grew up in it. My childhood circumstances were modest (some would say poor). Until the age of ten, I lived with four other family members in a one-bedroom home. We had no refrigerator, no telephone, no television. But the real inconvenience we suffered was that we had no flush toilet (even though we had clean piped water and electricity).

Each morning, a group of men would come to take away the metal bin in our toilet and replace it with a fresh one. There it would stay for

All pg. 11-14

⓪ pg. 14-26
March to
modernity

② pg. 26-42
Retreat to
For tress

③ pg. 42-50
Triumph of the
West

twenty-four hours, filling up over the course of
I discovered we were lucky. When I went to
some relatives, I discovered that their metal bir
three to four days. Using those toilets has prov
the more excruciating memories of my life.)

I do not remember exactly when our metal b
flush toilets. It probably happened when I was
And if I were asked to name the date when my life entered the modern world, I would date it to the arrival of the flush toilet. On that day I felt that there had been a magical transformation of my life. Suddenly, I felt that I could lead a life of greater dignity, suffering from less embarrassment when visitors came to our house. Few people of my generation in the West can appreciate this transition, for they have never experienced it, though many of their parents and grandparents did. Asians can. Perhaps blacks in America may understand this Asian experience. Vernon Jordan tells the story of his grandfather who, at the end of his very poor life, was asked what he would most like. Instead of a trip to Venice or a Cadillac, he replied, "I'd like to have a bathroom inside my own home." In his book *Dangerous Nation*, Robert Kagan describes the list of things that fascinated the young Meiji reformers from Japan who visited the United States in 1860, almost a hundred and fifty years ago. He says, "They came back impressed by American science and technology, marveling at everything from railroads and weaponry to gaslights and flush toilets."[2]

Daily access to flush toilets may well be the best indicator of how many of the 6.5 billion people in our world live in the premodern world and how many have transcended it. One unofficial estimate claims that only about 15 to 20 percent of the total world population has flush toilets. The UNDP Human Development statistics reveal that nearly 42 percent (or 2.6 billion) of humanity is without toilets—most of whom live in Asia and Africa. Less than one-half of all Asians have access to toilets. A young Singaporean, Jack Sim, has set up the World Toilet Organization, which currently has forty-seven international members. This "WTO" communicates the need for better toilet standards in both developed and developing economies, and provides a service platform for all toilet associations, related organizations, and committed individuals to facilitate an exchange of ideas and health and cultural issues. It is easy to laugh at or pour scorn on the work of a World Toilet Organization, but for his courageous efforts Jack Sim was recognized as a global social entrepreneur by the Davos World Economic Forum in 2006.

After the flush toilet, our little home in Singapore began to acquire other conveniences: the refrigerator, the TV set, the gas cooker (which replaced the charcoal fires my mother used), and the telephone. Each new modern convenience made a huge difference. I have vivid childhood memories of watching shows like *I Love Lucy* and *My Three Sons* on TV, which had a profound impact on me. I didn't really watch them for their stories. Instead I watched in amazement as the TV scenes showed row after row of suburban homes, each with a lawn and a driveway. All homes were equipped with refrigerators, TVs, telephones, and washing machines (I had not even heard of them), and miraculously each home had one or two cars. Those scenes of suburbia, which stood in sharp contrast to my own living circumstances, provided me with a vision of what an ideal world could be.

It is this "heaven" of modernity that the vast majority of the world's population is aspiring to enter. They want to create a better world where they can enjoy many of the conveniences of modern living. The greater the number of people who enter the modern world, the safer and more secure our world will become.

The virtues of modernity are not purely material. Though the material gains are important, populations deprived of shelter, water, and electricity (to name just three basic needs) feel an enormous psychological boost and a surge of hope when they gain access to these improvements. Take the case of India, where more than three hundred ninety million people still live on US$1 a day or less. However, according to the National Council for Applied Economic

Research, the leading collector of data on rural India, seven hundred million Indian villagers now account for the majority of consumer spending in the country, more than US$100 billion a year. "Basically, what we are observing is the impact of liberalization which started in 1991," said Rajesh Shukla, an economist and senior fellow at the research council. "The impact on the smaller towns and rural areas is happening now." Pradeep Kashyap, a marketing expert in Delhi who heads MART, the country's leading rural marketing consultancy, said: "There is much more hope for the future than ever before in rural India."[3]

The other benefits of modernity are even more far-reaching. Entering the modern universe almost inevitably leads to a greater adherence to the rule of law. Those who live in a premodern society often live under various kinds of arbitrary regimes. Their material belongings (even though meager) can be confiscated. The presence of laws enhances the sense of certainty and the reality of ownership.

Even though modernity is a gift from the West to the rest of the world, many Western minds fail to appreciate its multidimensional benefits. The Western media has from time to time reported the explosive growth in demand for consumer goods in Asia. If any theme emerges from such reporting, it is that Asians, like many in the West, are falling prey to consumer culture. Such reporting essentially misses the big story here: as Asians acquire more consumer goods, they are not merely becoming materialistic. More importantly, they are becoming responsible stakeholders in the modern world. When billions of people become stakeholders in peace and prosperity, they steer world history in a positive direction. This simple fact is often ignored by intellectual analysts. The direction of world history is settled by the people of the world, all 6.5 billion of us. If we become more optimistic, the world becomes a more optimistic place.

At the heart of Asia's story—often overlooked—is the empowerment of hundreds of millions of individuals who previously had felt a total sense of powerlessness in their lives. Growing up as a young boy in a Hindu family in Singapore (while living with Chinese and Malay neighbors), I naturally absorbed a belief—one strongly held by many Asian minds—that our lives were determined by fate. It was therefore futile to strive or work hard. Whatever would happen happened. The acceptance of poverty is much easier if it is seen as a result of destiny.

Gradually, this belief in the inevitability of destiny is being corroded by the growing application of Adam Smith's principles and the sense of empowerment they create. When many Western observers look at China, they cannot see beyond the lack of a democratic political system. They miss the massive democratization of the human spirit that is taking place in China. Hundreds of millions of Chinese who thought they were destined for endless poverty now believe that they can improve their lives through their own efforts. It is remarkable that a Scottish moral philosopher of the eighteenth century could see more clearly the moral consequences of the application of his economic principles than most contemporary Western economists and political scientists. The real value of free-market economics is not just in the improvements in economic productivity. It is about how it uplifts the human spirit and liberates the minds of hundreds of millions of people who now feel that they can finally take charge of their destinies. This is why Asia is marching forward.

So the March to Modernity will lead to a more ethical universe in several ways. First, the move out of an existence of grinding poverty is inherently morally desirable. Most focus on the material benefits. In reality, the increased sense of self-worth and the increase in personal freedom are even more meaningful. People feel liberated when they have increased choices and access to all kinds of possibilities. Most people today perceive South Korea as a successful modern society, but few are aware of the scale of poverty it endured fifty years ago. In *The Koreans* Michael Breen describes a foreign scholar's conversation with Korean students in the 1980s: "There weren't many foreigners on campus and people always asked me where I was from and what I was studying. I'd say, 'I'm studying Korean thought' and they'd give me a puzzled look and say, 'But we have no thought.'"[4] Few Koreans would say this today.

Second, society benefits when people step out of poverty. Crime rates decline. Health standards improve. Infant mortality decreases. Life expectancy increases. Education standards rise. Compare the education choices made in two of the leading civilizations of the world: the Chinese civilization and the Islamic civilization. In China, there is a deep and profound hunger for education. Parents invest a huge amount of their savings to send their children to regular schools and to provide private tuition. The education they aspire to for their children is a modern Western secular education with a heavy bias toward science and technology. Almost every Chinese parent wants to produce an Einstein or a Bill Gates—both are equally revered in China. A testimony to this fact are the new world history textbooks now being taught in Shanghai schools, later to be introduced across China, that focus on ideas such as economic growth, innovation, foreign trade, political stability, respect for diverse cultures, and social harmony. J. P. Morgan, Bill Gates, the New York Stock Exchange, the US space shuttles, and Japan's bullet train are all highlighted. Wars, dynasties, and communist revolutions have been dropped in favor of colorful tutorials on economics, technology, social customs, and globalization. Socialism has been reduced to a single, short chapter in the senior high school history course. Chinese communism prior to economic reform in 1979 is covered in a sentence, and the text mentions Mao only once, in a chapter on etiquette. "Our traditional version of history was focused on ideology and national identity," said Zhu Xueqin, a historian at Shanghai University. "The new history is less ideological, and that suits the political goals of today."[5]

By contrast, in the neighboring Islamic state of Pakistan, approximately 1.5 million students are believed to be studying in the estimated thirteen thousand madrassas or Islamic religious schools (unofficial estimates range between fifteen thousand and twenty-five thousand and in some cases as high as forty thousand). In August 2005, the Supreme Court of Pakistan observed that these madrassas were not providing students with a general education that could enable them to enter mainstream society and compete with the educated class for employment or other purposes, including elections. The court further noted that not a single religious educational institution had included such subjects as English, Urdu, and Pakistan studies in its curriculum, even though the Inter-Board Committee of Chairmen had recommended this. As Pakistan's reputed *Daily Times* said in its editorial on 1 September 2005: "The seminaries in Pakistan enlist a million pupils and throw up thousands of 'graduates' every year with nothing much to do except set up new mosques to earn their livelihoods. . . . Pakistan cannot produce young people who can propel the economy forward. What kind of young men does Pakistan produce? In a word, warriors. The truth is that there is nothing secular in Pakistan studies, English and Urdu either if you take a close look at the textbooks that the students have to mug up."[6]

Despite the explosion of madrassas in Pakistan, it is vital to stress here another equally important fact. Many Muslims want to join the Asian March to Modernity. One Indian Muslim doctor, Mohammed Haneef, was wrongfully accused of involvement in the failed car bombings in London and Glasgow in July 2007 (and the Australian government treated him shabbily). In defense of Dr. Haneef, his brother said, "He is a good Muslim and a clean man. We practice Islam, we believe in Islam. We live in modern Indian culture. Haneef is a modern religious person. He has not done anything wrong and will be released with respect and honor."[7] Note his use of the word "modern." It captures the new Asian zeitgeist well.

Similarly, when a Muslim minister in Singapore wanted to point out the contributions made by the 2006 Nobel Peace Prize winner, Prof. Muhammad Yunus, he said, "Prof Yunus' contribution . . . comes at a time when Muslim societies are being questioned whether our faith is compatible with the modern world and whether Muslims can co-exist harmoniously with other communities in secular societies. Prof Yunus has proven that modern Muslims can play a constructive role towards the betterment of mankind."[8] In most Asian minds there is a clear correlation between modernity and virtue.

The most important ethical result of the March to Modernity may well be a more stable and peaceful world. To get a glimpse of what we can achieve, we do not have to look very far. The greatest peak of human civilization is reached not just when nations stop war but when nations achieve zero prospect of war. Some nations have achieved it. The United States and Canada have zero prospect of going to war with each other. So too do the current member states of the European Union. One simple thesis of this book is that what North America and the European Union have achieved today can also be achieved by the rest of the world tomorrow. In short, world peace is not a pipe dream. We have seen how it can be done.

At the root of the reason why North Americans and Europeans do not wage war among themselves is a powerful middle class that has little desire to sacrifice its comfortable life. A new ethos that has progressively delegitimized war has sunk deeply into most modern societies. Disputes will always emerge between individuals and between societies. But one key aspect of our modern world is the near universal consensus that dispute settlement should be done on the basis of agreed rules and procedures, not by warfare. So the March to Modernity also aids the spread of the rules-based order—domestically, regionally, and globally.

There is a profound reason why most human beings like to live in a fair rules-based order. It creates a more secure environment. Larry Summers emphasizes that there can be no personal freedom without personal security.[9] Most Western writers have focused on freedom that individuals need to fight for against an authoritarian or totalitarian state. But it is equally important to secure freedom by preventing chaos and anarchy. These extreme conditions also deprive human beings of freedom. This is why the Chinese mind has a strong revulsion against chaos (in Chinese, *luan*). Having suffered disorder for centuries, the Chinese have a deep longing for order and stability.

One of the world's great modernizers was Deng Xiaoping. He bravely showed the Chinese people where their future lay: in the March to Modernity. He opened the eyes of the Chinese people in the same way that my eyes were opened as a child: by allowing the state-controlled Chinese TV stations to show scenes of American middle-class homes, large and comfortable, full of modern appliances and a car or two in every garage. Deng showed the practical and down-to-earth Chinese people that all this was within their reach.

While the term "modernization" is increasingly out of vogue in the West, it still has a powerful resonance in China. The Chinese carefully measure their relative successes in terms of modernization. The China Modernization Report is prepared by the China Modernization Strategic Studies Group, under the Chinese Academy of Sciences, and studies industrialization, urbanization, secularization, and the improvement of social welfare and democracy. To measure the modernization levels of countries and regions, the China Modernization Strategic Studies Group established assessment criteria for first- and second-stage modernization drives. The first stage of modernization typically features industrialization and urbanization, while the typical features of the second stage include a knowledge-driven and information-driven society.[10] The 2007 China Modernization Report predicts that on the basis of China's rate of growth between 1980 and 2004, another eight years will pass before it realizes its first stage of modernization. This means that by 2015 China will have modernized to the level of developed nations in 1960. By 2005 China had realized 87 percent of its goals for the first stage of modernization, one percentage point higher than the previous year.

It is easy for our eyes to glaze over such statistics. Most people relate to human stories, not to statistics. One way of describing the great human impact of modernization is to look at the impact that just one modern instrument has had on India: the cell phone. The well-known Indian writer Shashi Tharoor describes how the cell phone revolutionized

India. He notes that in December 2006, for the first time, seven million Indians subscribed to new mobile phones in one month. He adds, "That's a world record. In September 2006, India overtook China for the first time in the number of new telephone subscribers per month. We're still way behind China in the total number of cell phone users (just over 140 million against their 450 million), but each month the gap is narrowing. By 2010, the government tells us, we'll have 500 million Indian telephone users. China will probably still be ahead, but on a per capita basis there will be little to choose between us."

This spread of mobile cell phones in India showed how much the Indian mindset had changed on modern instruments. Tharoor quoted the views of former Indian Communication Minister C. M. Stephen, who declared in Parliament in the 1970s, in response to critics who decried the rampant telephone breakdowns in the country, that telephones were a luxury, not a right, and that any Indian who was not satisfied with his telephone service could return his phone—since there was an eight-year waiting list of people seeking this supposedly inadequate product.

Shashi Tharoor emphasized that the real beneficiaries of this mobile revolution are not the capitalists. Instead,

> What is truly wonderful about the "mobile miracle" (and I'm not embarrassed to call it that) is that it has accomplished something our socialist policies talked about but did little to achieve—it has empowered the less fortunate. The beneficiaries of the new mobile telephones are not just the affluent, but people who in the old days would not even have dreamt of joining those 20-year-long waiting lists. It's a source of constant delight to me to find cell phones in the hands of the unlikeliest of my fellow citizens: taxi drivers, paan wallahs [those who sell sweetened betel leaves], farmers and fisher folk. As long as our tax policies keep telecommunications costs low and it's cheap for people to call on their cell phones, the greatest growth in

the use of mobile phones will be in this sector. Communications, in the new India, is the great leveller.[11]

An article published in the *Washington Post* in October 2006 reinforces Tharoor's key point: that the impoverished masses of India have been among the prime beneficiaries of the spread of the cell phone revolution.

> For less than a penny a minute—the world's cheapest cell phone call rates—Indian farmers in remote areas can check prices for their produce. They call around to local markets to find the best deal. They also track global trends using cell phone–based Internet services that show the price of pumpkins or bananas in London and Chicago. Indian farmers use camera-phones to snap pictures of crop pests, then send the photos by cell phone to biologists who can identify the bug and suggest ways to combat it. In cities, painters, carpenters and plumbers who once begged for work door-to-door say they now have all the work they can handle because customers can reach them instantly by cell phone. "This has changed the entire dynamics of communications and how they organize their lives," said C. K. Prahalad, an India-born business professor at the University of Michigan who has written extensively about how commerce—and [the] cell phone—is used to combat poverty. "One element of poverty is the lack of information," he added. "The cell phone gives poor people as much information as the middleman." For Rajan, one of the millions of fishermen who work off India's 4,350 miles of coastline, monthly income has at least tripled to an average of US$150 since 2000 when cell phones began booming in India. "The dealers are now forced to give us more money because there is competition," he said, adding that he is providing his family in ways that his fisherman father never could, including a house with electricity and a television.[12]

A 2005 study by Leonard Waverman, of the London Business School, shows that an extra ten mobile phones per hundred people in a typical developing country leads to an additional 0.59 percentage point of growth in GDP per person. (He recently repeated this earlier study using a more elaborate model and found that an extra 10 percentage points in mobile-phone penetration led to an extra 0.44 percentage point of growth, a difference he says is not statistically significant.)[13]

In many Western minds, one Asian country that seems to have an automatic association with poverty is Bangladesh. Nevertheless, Bangladesh has benefited from the spread of cell phones. In 1993 this country of 142 million people had a scant US$3 million of foreign investment. But that was before the country witnessed the launch of the first cellular phone operator, GrameenPhone, Bangladesh's largest telephone company, and the ensuing cellular revolution. In 2007 Bangladesh had five cellular phone companies and US$2 billion in foreign investment. "Adding one cell phone to Bangladesh would add US$6,000 to the national GDP," according to Nick Sullivan, author of *You Can Hear Me Now: How Microloans and Cell Phones are Connecting the World's Poor to the Global Economy*. Sullivan cited a World Bank projection that if countries in South Asia continue growing at a 7 percent rate, the incidence of poverty would be reduced from 50 percent to 20 percent. "In addition to becoming a talking device, the cell phone has fast-forwarded to acting as a mini-PC, which is used for mobile banking. People who did not have bank accounts two years ago are now transferring money via mobile phones," Sullivan said, adding, "This is a silent revolution as dramatic as the Industrial Revolution. . . . You can see the lines crossing between foreign direct investment going up and foreign aid going down. We're at an extraordinary tipping point actually."[14]

According to Iqbal Quadir, cofounder of GrameenPhone, "Connectivity is productivity. If you connect people, they are more productive. You can see throughout the developing world that the people are not dependent on aid, their governments are. What we have done with aid is empowered the governments in poor countries, put them on their high horses, so they don't have to be concerned with their citizens, because they don't rely on them for funding. The Bangladeshi economy has gone up because of mobile phones by 2 percent. That surpasses the money given to Bangladesh through aid."[15]

When India eventually goes from eight million people connected to telephones in the 1990s to over five hundred million people with cell phones by 2010, the world will have been truly transformed. China will no doubt match the figure. In addition there are a billion other Asians outside China and India aspiring to join the mobile revolution. Effectively this means that in the space of two decades, over a billion to a billion and a half people will have been connected to the modern world. That is the scale of the March to Modernity in Asia.

THE RETREAT INTO FORTRESSES

The course of world history will be determined by how the West reacts to this great Asian March to Modernity. The West has two clear alternatives. It could welcome and embrace the spread of modernization and continue to work with Asia toward opening the world order. Alternatively, it could feel increasingly threatened by the success of Asia and begin to retreat into fortresses, political and economic. As of 2008 the Western reaction contains both strands, but it is the second regressive strand that is becoming stronger. During the June 2007 European Union (EU) summit, Nicolas Sarkozy, the French president, famously said, "The word 'protection' is no longer taboo." Sarkozy's words finally injected some honesty into the trade debate. The truth is that large parts of the West are losing faith in free trade, though few leaders admit it. In theory, the West has been vehemently opposed to protectionism, especially after having witnessed the disastrous Depression that resulted from the Smoot-Hawley Tariff Act of 17 June 1930. In practice, the West has often been protectionist. For example, on 13 June 2007, four US senators—Max Baucus, Charles Grassley, Charles

Schumer, and Lindsey Graham—introduced a new trade bill that would require the Treasury Department to identify misaligned currencies based on International Monetary Fund criteria. This amounts to protectionism, since it would allow US companies to appeal for anti-dumping duties on Chinese goods based on the distorted value of the yuan.

Johan Norberg, author of *In Defense of Global Capitalism*, writes, "According to the United Nations Conference on Trade and Development, EU protectionism deprives developing countries of nearly US$700 billion in export income a year. That's almost 14 times more than poor countries receive in foreign aid. EU protectionism is a continuing tragedy, causing unnecessary hunger and disease. The Cold War 'iron curtain' between East and West has been replaced with a customs curtain between North and South." He further adds, "EU protectionism takes a toll on Europeans, too. The rich countries' protectionism costs their citizens almost US$1 billion every day. At that rate, you could fly all the cows in the OECD [Organization for Economic Cooperation and Development], 60 million of them, around the world every year in business class. In addition, the cows could be given almost US$3,000 each in pocket money to spend in tax-free shops during their stopovers."[16] The United States is equally protectionist in agriculture. Millions of poor West African cotton farmers suffer because twenty-five thousand rich American cotton farmers get billions in subsidies.

When the West first endorsed the virtues of free trade to Asian countries, it was received with skepticism. But the great economic successes of Japan and the four Asian tigers eventually convinced other Asian countries that they should follow suit. Starting from the first trade round in Geneva in 1947 through the successor rounds until the Uruguay Round in April 1994, the West remained true to its principles and kept the global trading system open.

As a result, in the twenty-first century the world possesses one of the most open trading systems ever seen. Global trade has exploded from 7 percent of the world GDP in 1940 to 30 percent in 2005[17] because of the rules-based multilateral trading order that came with the creation of the General Agreement on Tariffs and Trade (GATT) in 1947. Total global exports have ballooned from US$58 billion in 1948 to US$9 trillion in 2004.[18] GATT was essentially an American gift to the world, given on the assumption that as nations progressively opened and traded more with the world, goods and services would be produced according to countries' comparative advantages, resulting in higher levels of prosperity. The past sixty years have shown the American assumption to have been correct: total global trade in 2000 was fifty times what it was in 1950, according to the 2007 World Bank report on Globalization.[19] The report further states, "Between 1970 and 2004, the share of exports relative to global output had more than doubled and were over 25 percent. The output of the global economy is expected to rise from US$35 trillion in 2005 to US$72 trillion (at constant market exchange rates and prices) in 2030, an average annual increase of about 3 percent—2.5 percent for high-income countries and 4.2 percent for developing countries."

Countries that have embraced open trade have benefited tremendously: according to a study by the Institute for International Economics (IIE), US annual incomes are US$1 trillion higher, or $9,000 per household, as a result of trade liberalization since 1945. If remaining global trade barriers are eliminated, US annual incomes could increase by an additional US$500 billion, adding roughly US$4,500 per household, says IIE.[20] The World Bank estimates that the full elimination of trade barriers can lift tens of millions more out of poverty. Moreover, while debt relief and foreign aid can make an important contribution to development in poor countries, trade and trade liberalization are likely to be even more powerful tools for alleviating poverty and providing societies with the economic resources to address their most pressing needs. According to the World Bank, the annual income gain to developing countries from the elimination of trade barriers to goods alone is US$142 billion, conservatively measured. This amount exceeds the US$80 billion in foreign economic assistance by the major industrialized countries in 2005 and the proposed US$42.5 billion for developing country debt relief combined.[21]

In the same period, the West (especially America) has accepted trade deficits with Asian countries. In the 1980s the United States had major trade deficits with Japan (a close political ally in the Cold War). There was a political backlash against these trade deficits, but the Reagan administration held firm and refused to buckle under protectionist pressures. In more recent years, the US trade deficit with China has ballooned from US$34 billion in 1995 to US$202 billion in 2005.[22] This too has created a political backlash. But the Clinton and Bush administrations have held the line most of the time.

Governments all over the world have to be sensitive to political trends. Political support for protectionism is increasing in both Europe and America. With the end of the Cold War, there has been a little noticed but effective decoupling of the United States and the European Union on the issues of openness to trade and investment. Immediately after the Cold War ended, America continued to practice what it preached. By contrast, almost immediately after the end of the Cold War, the EU began to retreat into a "Fortress Europe" mentality. This was clearly demonstrated in the European attitude toward the discussions in the Uruguay Round (UR). The round began in September 1986. They should have been completed by 1990. However, the end of the Cold War intervened. With its end, the EU lost its incentives to keep its borders open and allow for greater relaxation in trade barriers.

In the UR of trade negotiations, agriculture largely determined the pace and progress of the talks, and the unwillingness of the European Union to make significant concessions on agriculture blocked agreement for a long time. The EU tried to defend its Common Agricultural Policy (CAP), as it had in previous discussions on GATT, and to minimize any changes that might result from the UR agreements. For a long time, the EU was not prepared to accept trade-related discipline on export subsidies in particular, and the

1990 Brussels ministerial meeting, which was expected to conclude the UR after four years of negotiations, broke down over the EU's resistance to cuts in agricultural export subsidies. It took another three years of talks to find agreement on agriculture.

In 1993, the United States forced the European Union to end its opposition to the closure of the UR. For the first time, President Clinton organized a meeting of the Asia-Pacific Economic Cooperation (APEC)[23] Forum at the summit level in Seattle, Washington, in November 1993, at which all the major economic powers of the world were represented, except the EU. I participated in this meeting. The clear message was that unless the EU cooperated, America would turn from the Atlantic to the Pacific. This trick worked. German Chancellor Helmut Kohl called President Mitterrand and persuaded him to compromise. When asked to explain the abrupt change in their position, top European negotiators replied that the decisive element was the APEC decision because it "showed us you had an alternative that we did not."[24] The UR was ratified in the Moroccan town of Marrakesh in April 1994.

Behind the bare bones of this story of the Uruguay Round lies a complex story, full of intrigue and double-deals. Trade negotiations are inherently difficult to explain to a lay audience. They are full of technical jargon and formulae. The American and European negotiators have become very adept at this game. Let me illustrate how arcane it can become with one concrete example: the agricultural sector in the UR negotiations.

There were three key players in these agricultural negotiations: the US, the EU, and the Cairns Group (a group of seventeen developed and developing countries: Argentina, Australia, Bolivia, Brazil, Canada, Chile, Colombia, Costa Rica, Guatemala, Indonesia, Malaysia, New Zealand, Paraguay, the Philippines, South Africa, Thailand, and Uruguay). The US was enthusiastic about promoting greater liberalization in agricultural trade, and was keen to reduce the protection and support granted to EU producers under the Common Agricultural Policy. The EU was much less amenable to far-reaching liberalization but was eager to reach a workable com-promise that could be enshrined in GATT, in order to minimize fu-ture trade friction between itself and the US. The Cairns Group, as net exporters of agricultural commodities, generally shared a com-mon interest in greater liberalization of farm trade; it argued strongly for a reduction in protectionism and support measures in developed countries.

After several rounds of negotiations failed in GATT, the US and the EU reached a bilateral "Blair House" agreement on agricultural reform. In essence, the US and EU negotiators agreed at Blair House that the volume and value of directly subsidized farm exports were to be reduced by 21 percent and by 36 percent, respectively, over the six-year life of the agreement, from the base levels that had prevailed in 1986–90, and that products not subsidized during the base period were not to be subsidized at all during the implementation period. This was much less than the 100 percent reduction in subsidized exports originally sought by the Cairns Group, less than the 90 percent reduction the United States had called for in its modified proposal of October 1990, and even a bit less than the modest 24 percent (volume) reduction called for in the Decem-ber 1991 "Draft Final Act" submitted by GATT Director General Arthur Dunkel.

Even though the Blair House accords fell far short of what the rest of the world expected in agricultural reform, the EU introduced further safeguards to limit the actual changes it would have to make. Parties to the final agreement committed to reducing a specially constructed index of their "trade distorting" internal support to farmers—their Aggregate Measurement of Support (AMS)—by 20 percent from a 1986–1988 base, over the six-year implementation period of the agree-ment (1995–2000). The EU insisted upon using a 1986–1988 base period for calculating AMS reductions so that it could count toward its final GATT obligation the internal support reductions it was already in the process of attaining unilaterally outside of GATT, under the 1988 "stabilizer" reforms. Once credit for this earlier set of reforms was

given, existing EU wheat and feed-grain policies would automatically
be in compliance with a modest 20 percent AMS reduction commitment in GATT and would require no additional reform.

Already modified by this granting of credit for earlier reforms, the
AMS index for calculating internal support disciplines was further
weakened during the final stages of the round, when the 1992 Blair
House agreement effectively set aside two large domestic cash subsidy
policies (US deficiency payments to farmers and EU compensation
payments) as not counting in AMS calculations. Deficiency payments
are a principal instrument of US domestic farm support (they totaled
US$8.6 billion in 1993, the year the GATT agreement was concluded),
and compensation payments were just then becoming a principal means
of domestic farm support in the EU, under the terms of the 1992 Mac-
Sharry reform plan for CAP. The final terms of the internal support
reduction commitment were so weak that they obliged neither the US
nor the EU to contemplate any additional internal policy liberalizations
for the duration of the upcoming six-year implementation period. All
this led the OECD, in 1995, to reach the disappointing conclusion that
"the Uruguay Round agreement may not necessarily lead to a reduction
in the level of support" to farmers. More recent data from the OECD
shows that total transfers to agriculture in OECD countries amounted
to US$327 billion in 2000, compared with US$298 billion in
1986–1988, and exceeded the value of world trade in agricultural products. The EU gave larger domestic agricultural subsidies than any other
country or group in the world.

This tangled tale of how the US and the EU cleverly avoided making any real concessions in the agricultural negotiations is worth
reporting in some detail because it vividly demonstrates a powerful
political reality in the West. Given a choice of promoting larger global
interests (which would eventually also benefit the West by creating a
more stable and peaceful world) and protecting short-term and narrow
sectoral interests, the West has increasingly shown a dismal record of
dumping the world in favor of small but powerful lobbies.

This tale is now going to become a horror story. In 2008 and 2009, there will be the biggest release of information held by governments since the creation of the EU. All twenty-seven EU countries will disclose data revealing details of some €100 billion given in subsidies by the European taxpayer every year to farmers, food companies, industrial regeneration schemes, and the fishing industry, from the Black Sea resorts in Bulgaria and Romania to the Canary Islands and Madeira.

The decision to release this information is the result of a rare example of EU journalists cooperating with each other to bring pressure on the governments of member states using national freedom of information laws. The data to be released in 2008 and 2009 has been among the secrets most strongly guarded by national governments, who have used privacy and data protection laws to prevent people from finding out the main recipients of European largesse. The reason—as has become clear as the information has dribbled out—is to protect from unwanted publicity not poverty-stricken hill farmers but huge multinationals such as Tate & Lyle and the Danish Arla group (which owns Express Dairies), powerful politicians, and royals from Queen Elizabeth and Prince Charles to the Grimaldis in Monaco. For they are emerging as the biggest beneficiaries under the information already released.[25]

If indeed these accounts are confirmed and the true beneficiaries of the massive European agricultural subsidies are found to be the most privileged citizens of the EU, this will once again provide powerful proof that when Western societies are confronted with the choice of protecting their own interests or protecting values, interests trump values, even if these are the interests of a select few. In so doing, the West could endanger the world at one of its most propitious moments.

The drift toward "Fortress Europe" will be aggravated by the lack of honesty in European discourse about both its internal directions and its relations with the world. While the formation of the EU has overall been good for Europe and the world, its rapid expansion after the end of the Cold War has taken place almost unthinkingly, without proper thought to rationalizing its organizational structure or the sheer expense of its hugely wasteful subsidies. It is absurd that a united Europe needs to speak to itself in twenty-three languages. EU's vast administrative machine employs over 3,400 interpreters and translators, and costs the EU 1 percent of its budget, €990 million (US$1,431 million) a year—around €180 million (US$250 million) for interpreting and €810 million (US$1,171 million) for translation. In the European Parliament a full-day meeting costs €118,000 (US$170,552) if twenty languages are in use, but with only English, German, and French, the expenditure would fall to €8,900 (US$12,865). Alexander Stubb, the Finnish member of European Parliament, wrote a report on the financial implications of the EU's language regime, criticizing unnecessary expenditure. In September 2006, he highlighted the €26 million (US$37.6 million) wasted on interpretation costs that were never used or were cancelled at the last minute. "I am talking about taxpayers' money being squandered," he said.[26] In short, the European discourse is dominated by competitive populism. Each segment of Europe looks at its narrow interests. There is no countervailing force to evaluate the damage Europe's policies do to global interests.

The European backsliding from open trade did little damage as long as America held firm. The real danger that the world faces today is that protectionist sentiment is growing in America too. Lou Dobbs represents an extreme version of the new protectionist spirit in America. Viewers of his show are likely to be convinced that India is now the single biggest threat to the US economy because of its strength in attracting outsourcing. (Paradoxically, Dobbs's shrill diatribe against Indian outsourcing has only helped to make small- and medium-sized enterprises in America more aware of the virtues of outsourcing.[27]) Even relatively moderate voices like Senator John Kerry, a former presidential candidate, have compared American companies investing overseas to "Benedict Arnold." Politicians are known to pander to lobbyist and populist sentiments, but it is somewhat unusual for independent intellectuals to bend to populist winds. Until a decade ago, it would have been rare for a leading American intellectual to lend his weight and respectability to protectionist causes. Today, it has become less rare. Paul Krugman is universally regarded as one of America's leading economists. In his recent writings, he has argued that the concerns of protectionists need to be addressed. He says:

> Yet, it's bad economics to pretend that free trade is good for everyone, all the time. "Trade often produces losers as well as winners," declares the best-selling textbook in international economics (by Maurice Obstfeld and yours truly). The accelerated pace of globalization means more losers as well as more winners; workers' fears that they will lose their jobs to Chinese factories and Indian call centers aren't irrational. Addressing those fears isn't protectionist. On the contrary, it's an essential part of any realistic political strategy in support of world trade.[28]

Krugman's remarks about "realistic political strategy" shows how far America has drifted away from its earlier steadfast advocacy of free trade. In his special message to the US Congress on foreign trade policy in January 1962, President John F. Kennedy said,

> A more liberal trade policy will in general benefit our most efficient and expanding industries—industries which have demonstrated their advantage over other world producers by exporting on the average twice as much of their products as we import—industries which have done this while paying the highest wages in our country. Increasing investment and employment in these growth industries will make for a more healthy, efficient and expanding economy and a still higher American standard of living. Indeed, freer movement of trade between America and the Common Market would bolster the economy of the entire free world, stimulating each nation to do most what it does best and helping to achieve the OECD target of

a 50 percent combined Atlantic Community increase in Gross National Product by 1970.[29]

In his remarks, Kennedy was drawing upon a well-established consensus that rested on the conclusions Franklin Roosevelt drew from the collapse of trade between 1929 and 1931. Roosevelt believed this event, sparked by a worldwide cycle of tariff hikes and retaliations beginning in the United States, had deepened the Depression, closed avenues of escape, and ultimately helped open politics to radical nationalists in Europe and Asia. Roosevelt's 1936 speech explains:

> Every Nation of the world has felt the evil effects of recent efforts to erect trade barriers of every known kind. Every individual citizen has suffered from them. It is no accident that the Nations which have carried this process farthest are those which proclaim most loudly that they require war as an instrument of their policy. It is no accident that, because of these suicidal policies and the suffering attending them, many of their people have come to believe with despair that the price of war seems less than the price of peace.

In 1945, Roosevelt hoped reopening trade could do this in reverse: restore growth; guard against a second crisis and Depression; and ultimately, as he suggested in announcing the first multilateral trade negotiations, give nations a greater stake in one another's security and prosperity and help create "the economic basis for the secure and peaceful world we all desire."[30] If Roosevelt were alive today, he would be surprised to see America turning away from its ideals at the precise moment of history when this dream was so close to being realized.

Writing in the *Wall Street Journal* on 31 July 2007, David Hale noted the extraordinary prosperity that the world was enjoying:

> The world economy is currently experiencing a level of growth unsurpassed in human history. World growth has been running at close to 5% for over three years—the highest level since the

late 1960s. But the current situation is profoundly different from that era: In the 1960s, over two-thirds of the world's people were excluded from the global economy because of their political regimes. During the past 20 years, China, India, the former Soviet Union, Eastern Europe and Africa have rejoined the global economy. Their re-entry has unleashed a tremendous burst of entrepreneurial energy and set the stage for extraordinary economic growth. China has been growing at double digit rates since 2002. India's growth rate has risen to 9% from only 2%–3% 25 years ago.[31]

Hale then goes on to point to the greatest danger to the extraordinary global economic prosperity we are enjoying:

The great threat to the boom is that the U.S. will lose confidence in the free market ideology which allowed the global economy to take off during the 1990s. All the Democratic presidential candidates are proposing protectionist trade policies. Congressional Democrats and Republicans are threatening China with trade sanctions if it does not revalue its currency more quickly. Other Democrats want to block the proposed free trade agreement with South Korea. If the U.S. moves in protectionist direction, it will jeopardize both the import of low-cost manufactured goods which restrains U.S. inflation and the large flows of capital compensating for America's budget deficit and low household savings rate. Such shocks would threaten both America's prosperity and the new global economic equilibrium now sustaining high growth in the developing countries.[32]

The growth of such protectionist sentiments in both Europe and the United States explains why the world faces—for the first time since the end of World War II—a real danger that the latest round of trade negotiations (the Doha Round, which was launched in November 2001) may actually fail. Many leading voices, including Pascal Lamy, the head of the WTO (World Trade Organization), say the situation is desperate. All previous trade rounds have reached a successful conclusion because the chief custodians of the open global trade system, the United States and Europe, have seen it to be in their interest to continue opening up the international trading system. Now the chief custodians of the open global trading system are increasingly becoming the main opponents of further trade liberalization. The Doha Round is not making progress ostensibly because both the EU and the US refuse to adhere to their previous commitment and end the massive subsidies to their agricultural sectors. Each year, the EU spends an average €49 billion euros (US$67.5 billion)[33] and the US more than US$20 billion on agricultural subsidies.[34] Between 1995 and 2005, federal farm subsidy payments totaled more than US$164 billion.[35] Even though it is hard to justify their subsidies on economic grounds and many subsidies do massive damage to developing countries, no American or European politician can afford to lose the support of agricultural lobbies. But the heart of the problem is that American policymakers are gradually losing confidence in the ability of their societies to compete with the newly emerging economies of China and India. It takes confidence to open up to international competition. Diminishing confidence results in less openness.

If both America and Europe retreat from their strong support for a global trading system, protectionism may in fact rise. Open markets will become progressively less open. Today more than twelve bills in the US Congress aim to punish China. So far most American administrations have vetoed bills that are clearly unreasonable. But if the protectionist mood continues, some protectionist bills will inevitably be passed.

The new American protectionist streak is not confined to trade but is spreading to the investment field. For almost four decades after World War II, the United States was the strongest global voice in favor of open doors to foreign investment. This strong voice was a result of two factors: deep ideological faith in the virtues of foreign investment and the fact that the largest overseas investors in the world were American corporations. When both self-interest and values point in the same direction, it is easy to espouse the virtues of an idea. Even though the US did not succeed in creating a GATT-like equivalent in the field of investment, it pushed hard within the OECD to create a global consensus in favor of unrestricted foreign investment. The US had a credible position because it kept its own doors open to foreign investment.

Against this backdrop, it came as a surprise to see America open the twenty-first century by restricting some foreign investment, ostensibly on national security grounds. In 2003, the state-owned Chinese oil company, CNOOC, tried to purchase UNOCAL in competition with an American oil company, Chevron. Under American-drafted rules on investment, this should have been seen as a purely commercial transaction, which the US in particular should have welcomed since it championed the right of major American oil companies to purchase oil companies all around the world. Instead, in a dramatic reversal of its espoused position, the American government intervened to block the sale of UNOCAL to CNOOC. This made a deep impression on the Chinese leadership.

The American opposition to CNOOC's purchase of UNOCAL was followed by enthusiastic popular opposition to the purchase of P&O (a British company) by Dubai Ports World (DPW), a state-run business in the United Arab Emirates. The problem here was that P&O managed several American ports. A wave of national hysteria emerged. In the House Appropriations Committee the vote was 62–2 to stop the DPW takeover of American port operations, a tally that would seem to indicate virtually universal rejection of the whole project. Normally sober politicians like Hillary Clinton and Charles Schumer lent respectability to what was obviously pure protectionism. These American ports, even when run by a British company, were regulated and controlled by American governmental agencies. On the ground, there would have been no changes. No Arabs were going to walk in to take over American ports (even though this was the hysterical speculation).

The security of US ports is the responsibility of the Coast Guard and of the US Customs and Border Protection (both components of the Department of Homeland Security) rather than the port operator. Ironically, the deputy CEO of DPW is Ted Bilkey, an American citizen. In the face of this national hysteria, DPW had no choice: it was allowed to purchase P&O on the understanding that it would have to sell off the American interests of P&O to American companies.

The link between national security and foreign investment has long been debated in the United States. During and after World War I, Congress passed legislation that restricted foreign ownership in specific sectors such as broadcasting, civil aviation, and shipping. These restrictions were established in reaction to perceived national security threats at the time. In some cases, such as in the telecommunications sector, restrictions on foreign ownership and control have gradually been eased. In sectors such as transportation, shipping, and broadcasting, restrictions remain in place. In the 1970s, alarm over petrodollar investments from oil-producing nations led to congressional hearings and the creation of the Committee on Foreign Investments in the United States (CFIUS), a twelve-agency committee chaired by the Department of the Treasury, which would be charged with reviewing acquisitions that could potentially threaten US national security interests.

In the late 1980s, serious public concerns arose about the growing level of Japanese investment in the United States, concerns driven by high-profile acquisitions of American-owned and -controlled firms and cultural icons like Rockefeller Center. In cases like the semiconductor sector, the transfer of ownership and control from American corporations (e.g., Fairchild) to Japanese firms (e.g., Fujitsu) was widely viewed as a threat to American competitiveness. Existing export-control laws and regulations governing dual-use technologies were criticized as inadequate. However, as Congress deliberated on these issues, the focus of the debate gradually shifted from concerns about economic competitiveness toward those acquisitions by which foreign ownership might threaten national security. This series of events was the background against which Congress enacted the Exxon-Florio Amendment to the Defense Production Act of 1950 as part of the Omnibus Trade Act of 1988. Exxon-Florio empowered the president to block mergers and acquisitions of US companies by foreign firms when such takeovers threatened national security and when that threat could not be addressed effectively through other laws and regulations.

Thus, while America has traditionally remained bold and open in its rhetoric when it calls for greater liberalization in trade and investment fields, its record has in fact been mixed. All societies have protectionist elements; the United States is no exception. But in the past, the various protectionist elements were kept in check by a powerful combination of ideological conviction (when the American intellectual establishment was convinced that free trade was an inherent good and that America would always benefit from free trade) and Cold War national security interests. Since 1990 both of these powerful forces have eroded.

Protectionism in trade and economic fields may not be the only way in which the West could endanger the open global system it had created at the end of World War II. Europe could also become the single biggest obstacle to changing the global order to adjust to new economic and political realities. Although European countries are still significant, their economic and demographic growth does not match those of either the emerging powers (including China and India) or the United States. Daniel Drezner writes in his *Foreign Affairs* article "The New New World Order":

Having been endowed with privileged positions in many key postwar institutions, European countries stand to lose the most in a redistribution of power favoring countries on the Pacific Rim. And since they effectively hold vetoes in many organizations, they can resist US-led changes. The Europeans argue that they still count thanks to the EU, which lets them command a 25-member voting bloc in many institutions. But if the EU moves toward a common policy on foreign affairs and security, it will be worth asking why Brussels deserves 25 voices when the 50 states comprising the United Sates get only one.[36]

Under the UN Charter, the Security Council has the primary responsibility for handling threats to international peace and security. To achieve this goal, the major powers of the day were given a special place in the council: "permanent membership." The principle was a wise one: the great powers should become a part of the solution and not part of the problem. But the great powers represented in the UN Security Council are the great powers of 1945, not the likely powers of 2045. The logic of European unification should lead to the conclusion that there should be a single European permanent seat on the council. But the UK and France refuse to cede their places. They have become obstacles to change. In the same way, Europe has also become an obstacle to change in other key multilateral fora, like the IMF (International Monetary Fund) and the World Bank.

This growing inflexibility of Europe to accommodate change would well be replicated in the United States if Americans begin to share the same degree of insecurity as Europeans. It has not happened so far, but the trends point in this direction. If this were to happen, the painful scenario of "Retreat into Fortresses" may well be realized.

THE TRIUMPH OF THE WEST

The third possible scenario for the outcome of the world as we know it is the westernization of the world—and the ultimate triumph of the West. When the Cold War ended, the West had a very clear idea of how history would unfold. It was captured in several celebratory, often triumphant statements. James Baker, who was then the US secretary of state, expressed this mood by talking about a new community of democracies that would "stretch from Vancouver to Vladivostok." He revealed a great deal with this statement. The only country overlooked between Vancouver and Vladivostok was Japan, the first and until then the only Asian member of the Western club (having been admitted to both the OECD and the G–7). Also excluded from the discussion of this new community was India, the largest democracy in the world. Many in the rest of the world thought that James Baker—somewhat unthinkingly and inadvertently—had revealed what was deeply buried in Western minds: the desire to create a new and powerful white men's club. This was never said explicitly. It would have been politically disastrous to do so. But the message received by the rest of the world was clear and unmistakable.

This triumphant frame of mind could also be found across the Atlantic, in Western Europe. I remember attending a meeting between the foreign ministers of the EU and Association of Southeast Asian Nations (ASEAN) in the early 1990s. The Belgian foreign minister, Willy Claes, was then the president of the EU. He said matter-of-factly at this ASEAN-EU meeting that with the end of the Cold War, there were only two superpowers left in the world: the United States and the European Union. He did not have to say the rest: these two new superpowers would dominate the world, while other nations would have to adapt and adjust to their wishes.

The best evidence that this mood of triumphalism had enveloped both the United States and Western Europe was provided by their positive reactions to Francis Fukuyama's "The End of History." His sophisticated essay made many nuanced arguments. For example, he wrote, "The triumph of the West, of the Western idea, is evident first of all in the total exhaustion of viable systematic alternatives to Western liberalism. . . . What we may be witnessing is not just the end of the Cold War, or the passing of a particular period of postwar history, but the end of history as such: that is, the end point of mankind's ideological evolution and the universalization of Western liberal democracy as the final form of human government."[37] However, what many in the West gleaned from his essay was something they wanted to hear: that the world had reached the "End of History" with the triumph of Western civilization. Hence, the only way forward for the 5.6 billion people who then lived outside the West was simple: all they had to do was to become cultural clones of the West.

It is now clear that neither Fukuyama's nor Baker's vision is likely to come to fruition. No Belgian foreign minister would be foolish enough to suggest that the US and the EU are the two superpowers of the day. Nor would any American secretary of state speak of a "community" involving a Russia ruled by Putin. The Western post–Cold War vision has had to be drastically revised. Yet in the West there is little willingness to analyze what went wrong.

There were three fundamental flaws in the Western triumphalist themes that emerged after the end of the Cold War. The first flaw was the belief that the West had triumphed over the Soviet Union because of its values. The West had actually triumphed because of the strength of its economic system—free market economics—and *not* because of its political system. The new leaders of the Soviet Union unfortunately bought the Western story. Gorbachev prioritized glasnost (political openness) over perestroika (economic restructuring) in trying to reform the Soviet Union. He made the wrong choice for Russia. Gorbachev is lionized in the West for having the courage to transport Western values into the former Soviet Union. Many Americans also revere him because he removed the nuclear nightmare from their lives (and, in this sense, he did make a great contribution to human history). Yet most intelligent observers in the rest of the world still see Gorbachev as a fool: he gave away an entire empire to its erstwhile enemy and got nothing in return. Significantly, this is how most Russians view him.

In contrast to Gorbachev, Deng Xiaoping well understood the real sources of Western strength and power. He had no illusions that Western values were responsible for Western success. Hence, he focused his efforts on introducing free-market economics into China, while trying his best to preserve political stability during the difficult economic transitions. By any standards, this was no easy task. A lesser man would have failed. But Deng had a will of steel. One of the reasons why Deng would not allow the students protesting in Tiananmen Square to set the agenda for China was because they wanted to follow Gorbachev's example. Had they succeeded, China might have suffered as much as Russia. A billion Chinese people would have seen their livelihoods deteriorate as the Russian people's did. The Russian economy, which lost 45 percent of its output in 1989–1998, witnessed a sharp rise in death rates and crime rate. According to a *New York Times* article published on 3 December 2000, "Since 1990, according to the most recent figures, the death rate has risen almost one-third, to the highest of any major nation, and the birth rate has dropped almost 40 percent, making it among the very lowest. Mortality from alcohol-related diseases has jumped by a fifth; from suicides, a third; from alcohol-related causes, almost 60 percent; from infectious and parasitic diseases, nearly 100 percent."[38] Crime and murder rates saw an unprecedented surge after the collapse of the Soviet Union: by the mid-1990s, the murder rate stood at over thirty per hundred thousand inhabitants, as against one to two in Western and Eastern Europe, Canada, China, Japan, Mauritius, and Israel. The 1999 United Nations Human Development Report, which ranks countries according to quality of life, placed Russia seventy-second of 174 countries surveyed. Russia's Human Development Index (taking account not only GDP per capita, but also of life expectancy and levels of education) is still inferior to that of the USSR and even below that of China, where life expectancy is seventy-two years, against sixty-five in Russia.[39] The success of Deng and the failure of Gorbachev revealed the first flaw of the Western triumphalist thesis.

The people of Russia are truly unfortunate. They have been diverted down the wrong road of history twice in the twentieth century. At the beginning of the twentieth century, the Russian communist leaders ignored the specific advice of Karl Marx and tried to make the leap directly from feudalism to communism. Marx told them they would fail unless they pursued capitalism before communism. At the end of the twentieth century, the Russian people were misled again: they tried to make the leap from Communist Party rule to democracy without reforming the economic system first. Many Russians feel great bitterness toward the West, from a clear sense that they were betrayed. It is truly surprising that many in the West fail to understand Putin's attitudes toward the West. He reflects a strong Russian consensus.

The second flaw in the triumphalist post–Cold War thesis was the belief that any society anywhere in the world at any stage of social and economic development could be immediately transformed overnight into a liberal democracy. This belief had been encouraged by the quick and successful transition to democracy of Eastern European countries. But they had the advantage of a common history and culture with Western Europe. More importantly, having suffered Soviet domination for almost forty-five years, the Eastern Europeans had a vested interest in seeing democracy succeed. Joining the European Union (and in many cases NATO too) brought them additional security as well as real economic benefits.

Virtually everywhere else the democratic experiment failed in the post–Cold War era. Worse than Russia was what happened in the Balkans. The democratic elections in both Croatia and Serbia did not result in the election of new liberal democrats. Instead, tough and brutal nationalist demagogues were elected: Franjo Tudjman in Croatia and Slobodan Milosevic in Serbia. None of these new countries had effective checks and balances to restrain such demagogic leaders. To retain their power and influence, both appealed to visceral nationalist sentiments. Having unleashed these violent teachings, the young nations were soon drawn into war. One of the cherished beliefs of Western liberal democrats is that democracies prevent war. Not in Croatia and Serbia.

They provided vivid proof that unless the right conditions were in place, a transition to democracy could fail. Without the right institutions and political culture, long-smoldering ethnic, religious, and nationalist sentiments in many countries can be whipped up by opportunistic demagogues. Amy Chua, a professor of law at Yale University, has warned against viewing the free-market democratic system as the panacea for the developing world of today. In her book

World of Fire she writes of a "phenomenon—pervasive outside the West yet rarely acknowledged, indeed often viewed as taboo—that turns free market democracy into an engine of ethnic conflagration." She then cites three recent examples of this phenomenon: the ethnic cleansing of Croats in parts of the former Yugoslavia, the attacks on the Chinese minority in Indonesia, and the Tutsi slaughter in Rwanda. "In each case, democratization released long-suppressed hatreds against a prosperous ethnic minority," she says, adding, "In the many countries that have pervasive poverty and a market-dominant minority, democracy and markets—at least in the raw forms in which they are currently being promoted—can proceed only in deep tension with each other. In such conditions, the combined pursuit of free markets and democratization has repeatedly catalyzed ethnic conflict in highly predictable ways."[40]

It should not, therefore, have come as a surprise when the export of democracy to Rwanda in the post–Cold War era resulted in the most violent ethnic explosion of recent times. As Amy Chua says,

> In Rwanda, for example, the 14 percent Tutsi minority dominated the Hutu majority economically and politically for four centuries, as a kind of cattle-owning aristocracy. But for most of this period, the lines between Hutus and Tutsi were permeable. The two groups spoke the same language, intermarriage occurred, and successful Hutus could "become Tutsi." That ceased after the Belgians arrived and, steeped in specious theories of racial superiority, issued ethnic identity cards on the basis of nose length and cranial circumference. The resulting sharp ethnic divisions were later exploited by the leaders of the Hutu Power movement, especially after US and French pressure to democratize in the early 1990s.[41]

The minority Tutsi community and moderate Hutus suffered brutally. Eight hundred thousand were killed, many with machetes.

The story of Rwanda has seared the Western conscience, and despite the amount of assistance received by the new Rwanda, it raises a profound question of moral responsibility.

Some democratically elected Western politicians express little hesitation in promoting democracy in other countries. However, when promoting democracy leads to disaster and a choice emerges between sending troops overseas to help suffering victims or bringing them home, the liberal Western politicians almost inevitably pick the popular choice. The Dutch peacekeeping troops allowed a massacre to take place in Srebrenica in July 1995. Around seven thousand to eight thousand Muslim men are believed to have been killed by Bosnian Serb soldiers after the Dutch peacekeepers abandoned the United Nations "safe area" of Srebrenica. The Belgian peacekeeping troops abandoned Rwanda in its hour of need after ten Belgian soldiers were captured, tortured, and murdered by the Hutus in 1994.

The self-interest of Western politicians in getting elected trumps their moral responsibility for those whose lives they endanger with their actions in promoting democracy. In 2007, American politicians debated intensely whether American troops should come home from Iraq. Many took the popular route: let us bring our troops home. Few had the courage to say: we have to stay in Iraq and take responsibility for our actions in introducing democracy in Iraq. Yet this was exactly what the rest of the world felt.

The third major flaw in the triumphant post–Cold War thesis was the belief that differences in culture did not matter because Western liberal democratic society was universally applicable to all societies. Difference in culture did not matter because Christian and Muslim societies, Confucian and Hindu societies were all equally ready for liberal democracy. The curious aspect about this Western blindness to differences in culture is that it demonstrates simultaneously generosity and arrogance. The generosity comes through the belief that we are all the same. Hence, there is nothing inherently superior about the Western human species. All humans can achieve what the West has achieved. This assumption underlines the "End of History."

Yet the blindness also implies arrogance. It demonstrates an unwillingness to accept the simple human reality that other cultures *are* different. They may have different values and different perspectives on the world. J. M. Roberts revealed this when he said, "Paradoxically, we may now be entering the era of its greatest triumph, not over state structures and economic relationships, but over the minds and hearts of all men. Perhaps they are Westerners now."[42]

This Western blindness to the reality of other cultures has a deeper aspect. The West failed to see that the time when it was experiencing one of its most triumphant moments also coincided with the moment that long dormant cultures were undergoing a revival of cultural confidence and dynamism. The moment when the West was basking in the glow of Cold War triumph was also the moment when Confucian, Islamic, and Hindu civilizations (among others) were also stirring, each for its own reasons.

The surprising thing about this revival of cultural confidence in other civilizations is not that it happened but that it happened so late. The West leaped ahead in the late eighteenth and early nineteenth centuries. There was nothing inherently superior about the performance of Western societies until then. Indeed, in the period from 1 CE to 1820, as British historian Angus Madison has recorded, the two largest economies of the world were China and India. The past two centuries of Western domination of world history are the exception, not the rule, during two thousand years of global history.

The end of the Cold War brought a huge degree of complacency, and indeed a great degree of intellectual smugness in many Western minds, much of which remains despite more recent foreign policy debacles. This was probably the greatest damage done by the "End of History" thesis. It allowed many Westerners to believe that the West had "arrived" at the final destination of human history. All that the West had to do was to wait for the rest of the world to catch up.

The simple conclusion of this chapter is that the West should be celebrating, not mourning, this moment of history. Its wishful thinking —that with the end of the Cold War it had reached eternal triumph— has not been realized. But the West may have actually succeeded beyond its wildest imagination if the scenario of the March to Modernity is indeed finally successful. Instead of perceiving itself as a lonely group of responsible stakeholders, the West will be joined by billions of new responsible stakeholders. This will inevitably make the world more stable and peaceful, even for those who live in the West.

To understand what this new world will look like, more Western citizens should travel to Asian cities. If they went to Shanghai or Hong Kong, Singapore or Dubai, they would immediately understand the new islands of modernity springing up all over Asia. Asian cities and societies are also busy learning from each other, trying to understand the real ingredients for the long-term success of contemporary societies.

The lessons they have learned should give the West even more reasons to feel optimistic about the future. Asians have come to realize that to succeed over the long run, they will have to absorb key pillars of Western wisdom. This is what the next chapter will document.

2

WHY ASIA IS RISING NOW

In the first century CE, Asia accounted for 76.3 percent of global GDP. Western Europe at this time accounted for only 10.8 percent. In the year 1000 CE, Western Europe's share of global GDP was 8.7 percent. Asia's, in contrast, was 70.3 percent. This balance began to shift with the Industrial Revolution. In 1820, Western Europe's share had grown to 23.6 percent, while Asia's had shrunk to 59.2 percent. Around this time Western offshoots with significant levels of GDP, including the United States, Canada, Australia, and New Zealand, began forming as well. In 1820 this group made up for only 1.9 percent of global GDP, but by 1998 these "offshoots" accounted for a little more than 25 percent of the world's GDP. Western Europe's share was 20.6 percent in 1998, while Asia's global share was only 37.2 percent. The rise of the West, in other words, happened very quickly, within the last two hundred years. For the vast majority of recorded history, Asia, with the greatest share of the world's population, has had the greatest share of the world's economy.[1] Against this historical backdrop, we should not be surprised by the following prediction made by the Goldman Sachs BRICs study. By 2050, three of the four largest economies in the world will be Asian, and in this order: China, the United States, India, and Japan.[2]

Curiously, even though the world is returning to the historical norm in terms of the natural place of Asian societies in the hierarchy of societies and civilizations around the globe, Asian societies are *not* succeeding because of a rediscovery of some hidden or forgotten strength of Asian civilizations. Instead they are rising now because through a very slow and painful process they have finally discovered the pillars of Western wisdom that underpinned Western progress and enabled the West to outperform Asian societies for the past two centuries. The surprise is not that China and India are rising so fast, but that they (together with many other Asian societies) discovered these pillars so late. Japan surged ahead of the rest of Asia because it understood the message of Western success almost a hundred and fifty years earlier.

In the 1860s, a group of Meiji reformers—who were determined to save Japan from the fate of Western colonization or domination that had engulfed most of Asia—sailed to all the leading Western societies to discover the best practices of the West. The Japanese learned well: they found—as the four tigers found a century later, and China and India have realized during the past two decades—that there were at least seven pillars of Western wisdom that could have an almost miraculous effect on their societies. Each pillar reinforces the effect of the others. By starting to implement these seven pillars, Asian societies have taken off. If the rest of the world implemented them, the whole world might well join the Asian trajectory.

FREE-MARKET ECONOMICS

I visited Beijing in 1980, not long after Deng Xiaoping had launched his "Four Modernizations" program (the modernization of agriculture, industry, science and technology, and the military). However, the shape and texture of Chinese society had yet to change, as two minor experiences I had in Beijing revealed. The first was a haircut. To my surprise, the barber took a very long time to cut my hair (and he did a good job). I had never experienced this before, so I asked him why he took so long. He said that it did not matter whether he did ten or twenty haircuts a day. He would still be paid the same; he had an "iron rice bowl."

The second was a taxi ride I tried to take. Outside my hotel, there were ten taxis and ten taxi drivers waiting. The ten taxi drivers argued over whose turn was next. They were not eager to drive their taxis because whether they drove ten or twenty times, they would get the same amount. They, too, had iron rice bowls.

The Chinese people are clearly among the most industrious people in the world. Just look at the enormous success that overseas Chinese have had in almost every society they have migrated to. Indeed, it was the apparent success of overseas Chinese and the low productivity of Chinese on the mainland that confirmed Deng's suspicion that China had adopted the wrong economic system, the Marxist-Leninist model of production.

China provides the best living laboratory to study the impact of the principles of free-market economics: in the second half of the twentieth century it applied with equal rigor *both* leading models of economic growth, central planning and free-market economics. When Mao Zedong gained total control of China in 1949, he implemented with great vigor the central planning model he had learned from the Soviet Union. It was not a total failure. The political order Mao introduced to China after almost a century of political turmoil led to increases in both agricultural and industrial productivity.

For example, during the First Five-Year Plan (1953–1957), China established more than a hundred large industrial enterprises: some were in basic industries that had remained weak until then, while others were in new industrial sectors such as the manufacturing of aircraft, automobiles, tractors, power generating equipment, metallurgical equipment, mining machinery, and heavy and precision machinery, thus laying a preliminary foundation for subsequent industrialization. Consequently, during the First Five-Year Plan, the average annual increases in the total value of industrial and agricultural output were 19.6 and 4.8 percent respectively.[3]

Mao thought that the Chinese people were capable of doing even more, so he launched the Great Leap Forward in 1958. Despite the exhortations of Mao and the Chinese Communist Party (CCP), the Great Leap Forward was a failure. Indeed, some statistics suggest that China's economy actually declined during the Great Leap Forward. In 1959 and 1960, the gross value of agricultural output fell by 14 percent and 13 percent respectively, and in 1961 it dropped a further 2 percent to reach the lowest point since 1952.[4]

The great irony of China's economic history is that China did actually experience a Great Leap Forward, but only after abandoning Mao's principles of central planning and introducing free-market economics. Many people have heard of China's spectacular economic growth, but few have actually understood the explosive rates at which the Chinese economy has grown.

A brief comparison between Singapore and Shenzhen illustrates the scale of growth China is capable of. Singapore is well-known as one of the world's great economic success stories, one of the four "Economic Tigers" of East Asia. In the first thirty years of Singapore's independence (1965–1995), it experienced rapid economic growth, with an average annual rate of 8.6 percent.[5] Singapore's Gross National Income (GNI) went from US$1 billion to US$86 billion during that same period.

By contrast, Shenzhen was a sleepy little Chinese fishing village when Deng Xiaoping launched his economic reform in 1979. However, it had the good fortune to be near Hong Kong. When Deng declared in 1980 that Shenzhen would be one of the first Special Economic Zones (SEZs), its economy grew quickly. Between 1980 and 2005, Shenzhen's population grew from thirty thousand to eleven million.[6] Its economy increased at an average rate of 28 percent from 1980 to 2004, according to Hong Kong–based consulting firm Enright, Scott & Associates. It ballooned from 270 million RMB (US$32.5 million) in 1980 to 342.2 billion RMB

(US$41 billion) in 2004.[7] Exports from Shenzhen reached US$101.5 billion in 2005—13 percent of China's total.[8] Shenzhen now has the world's fourth-busiest container port and China's fourth-largest airport. Overall, Shenzhen's economy grew 126 times, a much larger growth than Singapore, itself one of the fastest growing economies in the world.

One of the best descriptions of the scale of China's progress since the "Four Modernizations" program was launched is provided by China's leader today, Hu Jintao:

> Since 1949, when the New China was proclaimed—and particularly since the implementation of reform and the opening-up program pioneered by Mr. Deng Xiaoping in 1978—China has undergone a profound transformation never seen in the country before. In a short span of 26 years from 1978 to 2004, China's GDP increased from US$147.3 billion to US$1.6494 trillion with an average annual growth rate of 9.4%. Its foreign trade rose from US$20.6 billion to US$1.1548 trillion, averaging an annual growth rate of over 16%. China's foreign exchange reserve increased from US$167 million in 1978 to US$609.9 billion in 2004. The number of rural poor has dwindled from some 250 million to 26 million. The overall national strength of China has increased remarkably and the quality of life of its people improved steadily. While inheriting and carrying forward their proud past, the 1.3 billion Chinese people are writing a new chapter in history as they march of one mind on the road of building socialism with Chinese characteristics.[9]

What all these statistics fail to capture is the transformation of the human spirit that takes place when people experience this kind of rapid economic growth. Marx was absolutely right when he spoke of the idiocy of rural life. Those who are condemned to the drudgery of toiling on the same patch of soil year after year do not find their spirits uplifted. This is what the Chinese people had been doing for millennia.

The most that many could hope for in their lives was peace and stability so that they could till their lands undisturbed. Indeed, in the Chinese psyche, the condition they fear most is *Bing Huang Ma Luan*, or the turmoil and chaos of war. Most Chinese never dreamed of becoming rich—that prospect did not exist.

So what happened at the end of the twentieth century was almost miraculous. Households used to an annual income of US$467 per annum found themselves earning an annual income of US$4,300 per annum, as young people went from tilling the fields to working in Nike shoe factories. This explains why there is no antiglobalization movement in China. The Nike factories that the antiglobalization protestors condemned at the WTO Seattle Meeting in 1999 were seen as hugely liberating by the young Chinese who worked in them. For the first time in Chinese history, rural Chinese were free to imagine breaking free from endless rural toil. Nothing can be more liberating to the human spirit than the realization that there is finally some hope in one's life.

The explosive impact of the application of free-market economics to China should not have been surprising. Each Asian society that has applied free-market economics has experienced spectacular economic growth. Most discussions on the virtues of free-market economics have focused on efficiency. Clearly, countries that apply the principles of free markets experience huge increases in productivity.

But the real benefits of introducing free market economics is the impact it has on reducing poverty. Hundreds of millions of Asians have benefited as a result. The 2007 World Bank report "Global Economic Prospects: Managing the Next Wave of Globalization" notes that between 1981 and 2001 the number of people living in extreme poverty declined dramatically in East Asia (by over 400 million in China alone). In 2006, half of the poorest tenth of the world population lived in Asia; by 2030 Asia's share in the lowest tenth will be reduced to one-fifth. By contrast, Africa, now home to one-third of the poorest people, is likely to see its share of the lowest tenth double by 2030. Asia's share of world trade more than doubled during 1970–2005 (whereas Latin America's decreased). Within Asia, all regions have captured a rising trade, but the rapid expansion of China's trade over the stands out. In China, 56 million people belonged to the global middle class in 2000. By 2030, there will be 361 million middle-class Chinese, more than the entire population of the United States. The disposable income per urban resident grew from RMB 343 (US $46) in 1978 to RMB 10,493 (US$1,404). in 2005, and the net income per rural resident grew from RMB 134 (US$18) in 1978 to RMB 3,255 (US$436) in 2005. The housing area per capita in urban areas and rural areas have grown from 6.1 square meters and 8.2 square meters to 26 square meters and 29.7 square meters respectively.[10] Many of these dramatic improvements are a result of the introduction of Adam Smith's principles.

Given the dramatic impact the application of Smith's principles has had on the economic productivity of Asian societies, an obvious question that future historians will ask is why it took so long for Asian societies to implement them. We can always try to find complicated answers. But in the case of Asian societies, the answer may actually be very simple. Most Asian societies have a hierarchical view of the human universe; they have a deeply ingrained tendency to believe that all progress in society comes from benevolent and wise rulers. They expect good results to come from top-down decisions. Mao Zedong believed in this.

Over time, we will probably discover that Smith's principles will have a revolutionary impact on Asian thinking. Smith made it clear that the freedom given to every individual to either sell his or her labor or invest his or her capital was the critical driver of economic growth. Thus change would happen not in a top-down fashion but in a bottom-up fashion. Over time, this will corrode the hierarchical worldview of Asians and lead to new perspectives on the human condition.

SCIENCE AND TECHNOLOGY

The same liberation of the human spirit in Asia may also explain why Asians are absorbing and implementing with great gusto the second pillar of Western wisdom: science and technology. Until about the seventeenth and eighteenth centuries, Asian scientific development was almost on par with that of Europe. Then, with enormous bursts of creativity in the field of science and technology, Europe leaped ahead.

Over the past two centuries, a strong conviction developed in the world that the Western mind is uniquely suited to excel in science and technology. We have not fully understood why the West leaped ahead. But we know some of the reasons why Asia slipped behind: a religious mindset that spurned the material world, a lack of belief in the idea of human "progress," a natural deference to authority, and a lack of critical questioning. This gap between the Western and Asian mindsets was seen to be eternal.

So it is stunning to see the degree to which Asians have come to dominate research in science and technology. The Asian mind, which once appeared to be handicapped in this area, has overwhelmingly taken to science and technology research. An October 2006 *Time* magazine cover story, "Asia's Great Science Experiment," cited some impressive statistics. One was a prediction made by Richard Smalley, the late Nobel laureate in chemistry, who said that by 2010, 90 percent of all PhD-holding scientists and engineers will be living in Asia. If this prediction comes true, it will represent a massive shift in the global expertise on science and technology.

Also according to the article, Asian nations have dramatically increased their government spending on science: between 1995 and 2005 China more than doubled the percentage of its GDP invested in research and development, from 0.6 percent to 1.3 percent, while South Korea's funding has risen from US$9.8 billion in 1994 to US$19.4 billion in 2004. Such cash infusions have lured back many seasoned Asian researchers from the West, where science budgets are stagnating or, in some countries, even dwindling. (In the United States, for instance, federal basic-research outlays for physical sciences and engineering as a percentage of GDP have been declining for the past thirty years, to less than 0.05 percent in 2003.) The science push has already yielded results for Asia's developing economies: their share of global high-tech exports rose from 7 percent in 1980 to 25 percent in 2001, while the US share declined from 31 percent to 18 percent, according to the US National Science Foundation. At the same time, the Asian share of all published scientific papers climbed from 16 percent in 1990 to 25 percent in 2004.[11] Charles Leadbeater of Demos, the London-based think tank that organized a major international conference on global science and technology trends in January 2007, said, "The US and European pre-eminence in science-based innovation cannot be taken for granted. It is perhaps too early to say just how and how fast it is shifting, but the center of gravity for innovation is starting to shift from west to east." Further, "the trend is clear—knowledge resources are increasing more rapidly in Asia, particularly in China, than in Europe or the US," said Sylvia Schwaag Serger, science counselor at Sweden's embassy in Beijing.[12]

This explosion of Asian research in science and technology is a result of some wise decisions made several decades ago. The founding prime minister of India, Jawaharlal Nehru, was a brilliant and charismatic leader who helped found the first Indian Institute of Technology (IIT) in Kharagpur near Calcutta in 1951. Six more IITs followed later in Mumbai, Chennai, Kanpur, New Delhi, Guwahati, and Rourkee. Admission into these IITs was based solely on merit. Given the enormous talent pool in India (and one out of fifty applicants were admitted to these IITs),[13] this ensured that the IITs probably ended up collecting the single best pool of talent found anywhere in the world. The IIT Joint Entrance Examination (JEE) is one of the most demanding undergraduate entrance exams in the world. In 2002, while Harvard University and the Massachusetts Institute of Technology (MIT), which are among the most selective institutions in the US, admitted 10.5 percent and 16.2 percent of their undergraduate applicants, only 2.3 percent of applicants won admission to the IIT institutions. CBS featured the IITs in its widely watched news program, *60 Minutes*, as "the most important university you've never heard of." The show's cohost Leslie Stahl suggested, "Put Harvard, MIT, and Princeton together, and you begin to get an idea of the status of this school in India."[14]

Inevitably, some of this talented and trained scientific brainpower was sucked away by the rich institutions in America and Europe. A popular joke of the 1980s suggested that IIT students had one foot in India and another in its national air carrier, Air India. Superficially, this appeared to be a loss to India. Fortunately, some voices like that of the late former prime minister, Rajiv Gandhi, argued, "Better a brain drain than a brain in the drain." The success of IIT and other Indian graduates in America, especially in Silicon Valley, brought two monumental benefits to India. First, it provided a massive boost of cultural self-confidence to a country that had been a British colony for centuries. Second, many successful Indians in the West started a reverse brain drain back to India. When they returned, they were richer in both wealth and experience, making an enormous contribution to India's development. A prominent Indian economist who teaches at Columbia University, Jagdish Bhagwati, said, "The émigrés often work as a Trojan horse, lobbying on your behalf. They use external opportunities to succeed prodigiously in different occupations. And they can bring their skills and funds home to assist the country in its economic takeoff."[15] World Bank statistics reveal that cash remittances from Indians abroad have more than doubled since 1995; in 2005, they totaled US$22 billion. (China, at US$21 billion, was close behind.) Over the past decade India's aggregate remittances totaled US$154 billion. A 2006 J. P. Morgan report says the diaspora is becoming "a powerful catalyst in helping India realize—perhaps even exceed—its aspiration toward 10 percent annual GDP growth."[16] The Indian diaspora is also increasingly focused on helping India to succeed. Apurv Bagri, chair of the Indus Entrepreneurs (TiE), a global network of twelve thousand Indian entrepreneurs, says, "Ten years ago TiE members' main focus was: 'how do we get to Silicon Valley?' Now they're saying: 'How do we engage with India?'"[17]

These stories serve to confirm the Western narrative that only exposure to the Western universe of scientific research has enabled those great Indian minds to blossom. Without this exposure, those minds would have remained competent, but they would not have reached new peaks of excellence in scientific research.

This Western narrative fails to understand that in several Asian countries, including India, Asian scientists have succeeded *without* spending much time in either Western universities or Western research institutes. These homegrown success stories suggest that the "magical" development that propelled Western science and technological research ahead in the past few centuries has now penetrated the Asian cultural fabric. Asians no longer believe that they are inferior to the West in science and technology research. They believe that they can do equally well on their own. And they, like Western countries, must grapple with the sometimes difficult ethical decisions that scientific research presents.

Two remarkable individuals are case studies: Dr. A. P. J. Abdul Kalam, president of India until July 2007 and the undisputed father of India's missile program, and Dr. Raghunath Anant Mashelkar, director-general of the Council of Scientific and Industrial Research (CSIR), India's premier scientific research institute until 2006.

Dr. Kalam had humble beginnings. He studied first in a small-town school in the 1930s—when India was still ruled by the British—and had to sell newspapers to contribute to his school fees. When his father could no longer afford his schooling, his sister had to sell her ornaments to pay for his higher education. The scientific prodigy in Kalam came to the fore during his school days, but it truly stood out when he joined aeronautical engineering at the Madras Institute of Technology. His only stint abroad was a four-month visit to NASA in the US. He joined the Defense Research and Development Organization (DRDO) in 1958 and five years later joined the Indian Space Research Organization (ISRO). Kalam was tasked by Prime Minister Indira Gandhi in the early 1980s to steer the country's indigenous missile development program. Kalam and his team in the DRDO developed five categories of missiles in fourteen years, including the strategic Agni ballistic missile.

Kalam now wants to transform India into a competitive, developed, and prosperous country by 2020. He has charted out a virtual road map to bring about this transformation, identifying five areas in which India has a core competence for integrated action: agriculture and food processing, education and health care, infrastructure development, information and communication technology, and self-reliance in critical technologies. He also proposes taking development to the villages through his developmental model, Providing Urban Amenities in Rural Areas (PURA). Under PURA, he envisions self-sustaining rural clusters connected by roads, transport, and fiber-optic cables for high-bandwidth telecommunication. PURA aims to provide "knowledge connectivity" through education and vocational and entrepreneurial training for farmers, craftspeople, and others. It also plans to improve health and sanitation facilities in these village clusters.

Kalam is Muslim; he is further proof that Muslim minds can be as creative as any others in the field of science and technology research.

The second case study is the story of Mashelkar, who has had an equally remarkable life. His own words tell his story well.

Five years ago, during my presidential address to the Indian Science Congress, I made a prediction: "The next century will belong to India, which will become a unique intellectual and economic power to reckon with, recapturing all its glory, which it had in the millennia gone by," I told the gathering of 5000, among them the country's prime minister.

It must have sounded crazy. How could a country with so many impoverished people, and so many illiterates, rise to have such a central global role? What possibly could have given me the confidence to make such a prediction?

The confidence came from a little boy. In the late 1950s, this boy struggled to have two meals a day while he studied under the streetlights and went barefoot to school. This same boy almost left school in 1960, because his poor widowed mother could not support his education.

My own turn toward science began at a poor school in Mumbai. I remember Principal Bhave, who taught us physics. One day, he took us outside the classroom to demonstrate how to find the focal length of a convex lens. He focused the sun's rays onto a piece of paper and told us that the distance between the paper and the lens was the focal length. Then he held the lens in place until the paper burned. That's when he turned to me and said, "Mashelkar, if you can focus your energies like this and not diffuse them, you can burn anything in the world!" I decided at that moment to become a scientist.

I indeed focused on my goal, invariably placing first in my classes. After earning a bachelor's degree in chemical engineering from Bombay University in 1966, I received fellowship offers for graduate study in the United States and Canada. But I decided to remain in India to pursue my studies toward a Ph.D. I did postdoctoral research in the United Kingdom, held a faculty position there, and then had a brief stint in the United States as a visiting professor. But in the mid-1970s, when attractive offers came my way for faculty positions in top schools in the United States and United Kingdom, I decided to return to India.[18]

When Mashelkar returned to India, he was dismayed to find an unmotivated scientific community. When he was asked to take the helm at the CSIR, he jumped at the chance to help government scientists export their knowledge by selling their research to multinationals. In 2005, the CSIR earned US$1.26 billion from doing contract research for the likes of General Electric, double what it earned ten years earlier. The CSIR received 196 patents in 2005, up from 8 in 1995. Mashelkar also waged a successful campaign against the US patent on the use of turmeric for healing wounds. The turmeric case was pathbreaking: it led to the first revocation by the US Patent and Trademark Office of a US patent based on traditional knowledge in the Third World. As a result, India's first traditional knowledge digital library was established to protect knowledge from bio-piracy. Mashelkar's success also spurred a change in the international patent classification system to give traditional knowledge the place that it deserves.[19]

China's achievements in the field of science and technology are probably greater than those of India. According to "Asia's Great Science Experiment":

China awarded more than 30,000 doctorates in 2004, up from 12,000 in 2001. The nation also graduated 200,000 engineers in 2004. Government incentives, like hefty tax breaks and prized spots at the nation's 100-plus new science parks, have attracted an army of returnees like mouse researcher Wang Zhugang. China has welcomed back 200,000 returnees, who now make up an astonishing 81 percent of members of the Chinese Academy of Sciences. This brain gain has accelerated China's science drive. In the last five years, a coterie of returnee researchers in Beijing has outpaced the competition in the U.S. and Japan by becoming the first to sequence the rice, silkworm, chicken and pig genomes. Meanwhile, Sheng Huizhen, a Chinese biologist who worked for 11 years at the U.S. National Institutes of Health (NIH), returned in 1999 to do stem-cell research in China because ethical considerations were making what she wanted to do nearly impossible in America. The Shanghai government, by contrast, gave her US$875,000 to start a lab, now located in a makeshift space carved out of a converted kindergarten. "This is an open field, and China is willing to allow you to experiment," says Sheng. "Coming back was too good an offer to refuse." Many of the 750 multinational R&D centers based in China—up from 200 in 2002—are also run by returnees. Innovations from these centers include enhancements of Microsoft's Web-search technology and Motorola innovations that allow users to snap pictures of business cards, automatically filing the information in the phone's database. The scientific breakthroughs have been so plentiful that the U.S. National Science Foundation set up a Beijing branch in May to monitor Chinese progress.[20]

Each country's progress in science and technology research will depend on its pool of PhD researchers. Asia is clearly developing a decisive advantage. The World Bank's report "Global Economic Prospects: Managing the Next Wave of Globalization" has shown that the number of Asian students earning US science and engineering (S&E) doctorates has increased significantly. From 1983 to 2003, students from four Asian countries (China, Taiwan, India, and South Korea) earned more than 50 percent of the US S&E doctoral degrees awarded to foreign students—89,700 of 176,000, almost four times more than the students from Europe (23,000). Chinese students received more than 35,300 S&E doctoral degrees from US universities, mainly in biological and physical sciences and engineering. Between 1993 and 2003, students from Taiwan earned more than 19,700 S&E doctoral degrees, mainly in engineering and biological and physical sciences. Over the same period, India students earned more than 17,500 S&E doctoral degrees at US universities, followed by 17,000 S&E doctoral degrees by South Korean students.[21]

Thomas Friedman recently recalled his experience attending the commencement ceremony at Rensselaer Polytechnic Institute, one of America's great science and engineering schools. He says he was struck by one fact as the names of PhD students were read out and each was handed his or her diploma—in biotechnology, computing, physics, and engineering: every one of the newly minted PhDs was foreign-born. "As the foreign names kept coming—'Hong Lu, Xu Xie, Tao Yuan, Fu Tang'—I thought the entire class of doctoral students in physics was going to be Chinese, until 'Paul Shane Morrow' saved the day."[22]

A few days after this column appeared, another *New York Times* columnist, Nicholas Kristof, wrote about his visit to Taishan, a village in southern Guangdong, China, which is his wife's ancestral hometown. He writes,

> Sheryl's grandparents left their villages here because they thought they could find better opportunities for their children in *Meiguo*—"Beautiful Country," as the US is called in Chinese. And they did. At Sheryl's family reunions, you feel rather inadequate without a doctorate. But that education gap between China and America is shrinking rapidly. I visited several elementary and middle schools, accompanied by two of my children. And in general, the level of mathematics taught even in peasant schools is similar to that in my children's own excellent schools in the New York area. My children's school system does not offer foreign languages until the seventh grade. These Chinese peasants begin English studies in either first or third grade, depending on the school.

After his China trip Kristof posted a video of Sheryl's ancestral village on the *New York Times* website. Soon he was astonished to see an excited comment on his blog from a woman who used to live in that village. "Ms. Litao Mai grew up in a house she could see on my video. Her parents had only a third-grade education, but she became the third person in the village to go to college. She now works for Merrill Lynch in New York and describes herself as 'a little peasant girl' transformed into 'a capitalist on Wall Street.' That is the magic of education, and there are 1.3 billion more behind Ms. Mai," Kristof concludes.[23]

MERITOCRACY

The principle of meritocracy is astonishingly simple. It states that since every individual in a society is a potential resource, all should be given an equal opportunity (as much as possible) to develop and to make a contribution to society. No talent should be neglected. Virtually all successful human organizations succeed because they apply the principle of meritocracy rigorously.

The simplest way of understanding the virtues of meritocracy is to ask this question: why is Brazil a soccer superpower and an economic middle power? The answer is that when it looks for soccer talent, it searches for it in all sectors of the population, from the upper classes to the slums. A boy from the slums is not discriminated against if he has soccer talent. But in the economic field, Brazil looks for talent in a far smaller base of the population, primarily the upper and middle classes.

For centuries, Asian societies have avoided implementing meritocracy. Feudal mindsets, which were gradually destroyed in Europe after the Industrial Revolution, have lingered perniciously in Asia. In India, for example, it was inconceivable that a child from the untouchable caste could aspire to modern education and play a leading role in society. Consequently, millions of good quality brains were left underused in the Indian body politic.

The first major Indian figure to break the taboo against the untouchables rising above their caste was Dr. Bhimrao Ambedkar. Born as a Mahar (a group classed as untouchables) in 1891, he bore the brunt of the Hindu caste system in every aspect of his life. At high school he had to sit in the corner of the room on a rough mat, away from the desks of other pupils. At break time, he was not allowed to drink water using the cups other school children used. He had to hold his cupped hands out to have water poured into them by the school caretaker. Nevertheless, his intelligence shone through, and in 1913 he went to Columbia University for his master's degree and later earned his doctorate in economics from the London School of Economics. Back in India, Ambedkar's exemplary educational qualifications meant nothing—his caste was still the main obstacle to his career. He then founded an association called Bahiskrit Hitakarini Sabha to educate and improve the lives of millions of Indian Dalits, a more politically and socially acceptable term for untouchables coined by the British in the 1920s. During World War II, Ambedkar was appointed labor minister by the British viceroy. In 1942 he formed the All-India Scheduled Castes Federation to gather all untouchables into a united political party. After India's independence in 1947, he became the first law minister of independent India and drafted the country's constitution. Ambedkar's social and political revolution had a profound impact: he opened the doors for young children from the untouchable caste who otherwise would not have had the opportunity to receive either education or career advancement.

An article in the *International Herald Tribune* describes one such case:

> Narendra Jadhav, chief economist of India's central bank, grew up in Mumbai, formerly known as Bombay, outside the village caste rigidities, because his father fled them. . . . They settled in Bombay, a teeming port promising anonymity. His father eked out a wage as a municipal worker; his mother sold produce on the street. They lived in a slum, without electricity or private bathrooms. Jadhav's first career goal was to be a gangster, a profession for which he had many local role models. In school, where an affirmative-action program for Dalits paid his tuition, one teacher taunted him publicly as the government's "son-in-law." The Dalit-rights movement altered his course. . . . Jadhav's illiterate father became a devout and early member. Embarrassed by his village accent, Jadhav never spoke in school. But, toiling quietly, he began to top school rankings, even scoring first place in Sanskrit, the divine language of the Brahmins. Egged on by his father, he earned a bachelor's, a master's and doctoral degrees— the last in the United States on a scholarship. At the Reserve Bank of India . . . he rose quickly. His well-wishers now introduce him as "the future president of India." He may or may not become, as politicians have urged, a national political leader, perhaps a finance minister, blending his talents as technocrat and populist.

His is a story of penetrating perhaps the most intricate system of barriers of meritocracy ever conceived. Today, his friends include many of India's most powerful names. Prime Minister Manmohan Singh of India is an old acquaintance. "There are many Narendra Jadhavs, many," [Manmohan Singh] said. "What is happening in India is nothing short of a silent revolution."[24]

Behind the examples of Narendra Jadhav and Bhimrao Ambedkar is another story: that of how a society views its own population. Are the poor a burden or a potentially rich resource waiting to be tapped? The shift to the latter perception explains why India is now on a steadily upward trajectory. Each year India is introducing more gifted people into the global economy than any other society, with the possible exception of China.

A vivid illustration of how India is introducing more untapped brainpower into the global economy is provided by a new school in Bihar, one of India's most backward and feudal states. Today a small group of desperately poor, talented students are entering the IITs, thanks to the Ramanujan School of Mathematics. The school, named after the famous Indian mathematician, trains thirty bright students, meticulously selected from Bihar's least privileged communities, to take the IIT entrance exam. In the first year (2004), sixteen of the group made it into the IITs; the next year, twenty-two made it; in 2006, all thirty (known as the "Super 30") made it into the IITs. Santosh Kumar, one of 2006's Super 30, comes from Dumari, a village whose three thousand residents scratch out meager livings as farmers. "I didn't even know which subjects I was good at, and I'd certainly never heard of IIT. No one had," he says. Then an eighth-grade teacher noticed his mathematical talent and encouraged him to study further. Santosh saw that "education was the only way out of poverty," he explains. After high school, he enrolled in the Patna College of Commerce, and then he heard about the IITs and the Super 30. He applied to and was accepted by the Ramanujan School of

Mathematics and later earned a coveted seat at the IIT in Kharagpur. (He ranked 3,537 out of the 5,000 students chosen.) Santosh now aims to earn a doctorate in chemistry and become an inventor. His hero is Abdul Kalam.[25]

China began using the human resources available at the bottom of its society long before India did. Mao's communist revolution may have failed in many ways, but there was one area in which his revolution succeeded: it destroyed the feudal mindset that had bedeviled Chinese society until early in the twentieth century. He encouraged in China's peasants an enormous sense of pride and equal citizenship. After Mao, they stopped believing that they were naturally inferior. When Deng delivered the economic revolution with the introduction of free-market economics, one reason why China was able to take off so quickly was that the social revolution unleashed by Mao had already broken the class barriers to advancement. The Chinese from all social classes were willing and motivated to move ahead.

The principle of meritocracy is essentially a Western invention, although it could be argued that a Chinese version predated the Western implementation of meritocracy. Inspired by the philosophy of Confucius (551 BCE to 479 BCE), the Chinese emperors had introduced a nationwide system of examinations to select the most intelligent mandarins to serve in the imperial court. But the principle is applied most ruthlessly in Western organizations like Harvard University or McKinsey & Company, Shell or General Electric, where only the best and the brightest are selected to fill key positions. In the area of national governance, however, China applies the principle of meritocracy more ruthlessly than virtually all Western societies today.

The boldest recent reformer in China, after Deng Xiaoping, is probably Zhu Rongji. Despite his Marxist training, which taught him that capitalism was evil, Zhu Rongji noted that it was very good at discovering and using new talent. He praised capitalism for its lack of concern for seniority: "Whoever is qualified will be employed." Zhu therefore challenged the Chinese Communist Party (CCP) to be bold in reforming outdated organizational and personnel systems. "We should resolutely do away with the promotion system under which a person is good when he is said to be good, even though he is not good; and a person is said to be bad when he is said to be bad when he is not, as perceived by the masses. We should bring democracy into play and boldly promote into new leading bodies those people who are publicly recognized by the masses as having persisted in and scored political achievements in carrying out the line of reform and opening."[26] In short, Zhu wanted to apply performance-based meritocracy to the CCP.

China learned many lessons from the collapse of the Soviet Union. One major lesson was that it would be fatal to fill the senior ranks of the party with aging functionaries who stayed on till death. These old men in office would then become obstacles to change and rejuvenation. Leonid Brezhnev, for example, introduced the slogan "Trust in Cadres" in 1965 to win the support of many bureaucrats wary of constant reorganizations of the Khrushchev era and eager for security in established hierarchies. Consequently, the average age of the Soviet politburo members climbed from 55 in 1966 to 70 in 1982.[27] The twenty-sixth Soviet Communist Party Congress in 1981 admitted no fresh faces to the party's fourteen-member ruling politburo. According to "After Brezhnev: Stormy Weather," published on 23 June 1980, "Brezhnev at 73, suffers from several illnesses, including arteriosclerosis. Alexei Kosygin, 76, has had two heart attacks. Dmitri Ustinov, 71, is currently ailing. 'When Brezhnev dies the rest of the Politburo will be gone with the wind,' says one Soviet bureaucrat."[28]

By contrast, the CCP leadership has made systematic attempts to decrease the average age with every Congress. The average age of all politburo members was 72 in the twelfth Congress in 1982; it steadily declined and was 60.6 in the sixteenth Congress in 2002.[29] In fact, during the sixteenth Congress in 1997, all six of the seven-member Politburo Standing Committee, other than Hu, stepped down when they reached or were beyond the mandatory retirement age limit of 70. In the Chinese Central Committee, 180 of its 356 members or 50.6 percent are new entrants. Such a scale of rejuvenation is large by any standards. The average age of the Central Committee member has also steadily decreased from 62 in 1982 to 55.4 in 2002. In terms of education, 98.6 percent of Central Committee members have college education and above, compared with 55 percent in the twelfth Congress.[30]

In short, the CCP is applying the principle of meritocracy as systematically as Harvard or McKinsey. The results of applying this principle are clear. The American private sector is far more dynamic and vibrant than the Chinese private sector both for historical reasons and because it applies meritocracy ruthlessly. By contrast, the Chinese public sector is more dynamic and vibrant than the American civil service because the CCP applies meritocracy more ruthlessly.

I have worked with officials from both the US State Department and the Chinese Foreign Ministry for several decades. The morale of the State Department diplomats has progressively deteriorated over the past few decades, while the morale of their Chinese counterparts has risen. The Americans' morale has declined because the State Department does not apply meritocracy at the highest levels. Few career foreign service officers have the chance, as a previous generation of career officers like Thomas R. Pickering and Lawrence S. Eagleburger did, to become ambassadors. Most ambassadorial positions are reserved for the friends of the administration. While some are chosen on merit, most are chosen because of political connections. This is a form of political corruption and is demoralizing to young diplomats, who see little prospect of rising to the top. Some of the best American diplomats choose to leave. By contrast, in the Chinese Foreign Ministry, ambassadorships are assigned on the basis of merit and ability. Senior ambassadorial positions like the ambassadorships to the UN and the UK are filled by dynamic young diplomats—currently Wang Guangya and Madame Fu Ying respectively.

The importance of the Western pillar of wisdom of meritocracy can be demonstrated by comparing two Asian countries, China and the Philippines. In stark contrast to the meritocratic Chinese political system, political clans still reign in the Philippines, thereby prompting the country's foremost living novelist F. Sionil Jose to comment, "We are poor because our elites have no sense of nation." A 2007 study by the Philippine Centre for Investigative Journalism (PCIJ) shows that two out of three lawmakers in the two-hundred-fifty-member House come from political families, the majority of them second- and third-generation politicians. Nearly 75 percent of provinces and regions and almost 100 percent of major cities are under the control of dynastic families, says Filipino writer Roger Olivares, who compiled an Internet inventory of these dynasties over the mid-term congressional and local elections held in May 2007. Dynasties usually breed mediocrity, which means that middle-class talents have little opportunity to rise to the top of the political ladder. The PCIJ says political families tend to legislate to favor their own rather than national interests. A report in April 2007 by the Makati Business Club showed that only one-third of the eighty-six bills passed by the outgoing thirteenth Congress were of national importance.[31] In short, the Philippines is still crippled by the traditional Asian feudal mindset, while both China and India are progressively shaking it off.

The most meritocratic civil service in the world today is not found in any Western country but in Singapore. The elite civil service ranks are filled by Administrative Service Officers (AOs). To get the best to serve as AOs, the Singapore government tries to pay the most senior AOs almost as much as the private sector. Under the new pay scales announced by the government in April 2007, the head of the civil service can conceivably earn as much as US$1.5 million a year, more than the American president (US$400,000 a year) and the British prime minister (US$350,717 per year) combined. It's a small price to pay if a country wants to progress and succeed in a far more competitive global environment.

PRAGMATISM

Japan was the first Asian country to modernize because having watched Europe colonize most of the world, it realized quickly that it had to change and adapt. The Meiji reformers were remarkably successful in applying Western best practices, and Japan emerged quickly as a major power. In quick succession, it defeated China in 1895 and Russia in 1905, becoming the first Asian country to defeat a European power in centuries.

Why was Japan successful in implementing Western best practices? Here again the simple answer is that the Japanese were completely pragmatic. They approached the challenge of modernizing Japan with no ideological perceptions or blinkers. They were willing to consider Western best practices from any country and were prepared to mix and match policies in an eclectic fashion. Iwakura Tomomi, one of the Meiji reformers, took fifty-four protégés with him during his two-year tour. They patterned their education system after the French centralized system but used American curriculum development; they stressed universal primary education followed by expanding secondary education. They adopted the German system of civil service recruitment through examinations. In the legal arena, they conducted an in-depth study of Western systems of jurisprudence and constitutional law. The reformers also learned Western agricultural techniques to boost the Japanese economy. Dr. Goh Keng Swee, Singapore's deputy prime minister in the early years of Singapore's independence after 1965, observed that, "by studying Western techniques, importing Western experts and introducing new strains through experimental stations, Japanese agriculture made great and continuing advances, so much so that today the number of farmers in Japan is smaller than in the early Meiji period, the increases in the country's population having been absorbed in the 'modern' sector."[32] This spirit of pragmatism was also something Japan had learned from the West, which had made a great leap forward from its Dark Ages by abandoning theological constraints and adopting a modern, liberal, and secular outlook that was willing to learn anything. Japan imbibed that spirit.

The greatest pragmatist in Asia's history is probably Deng Xiaoping. Indeed, his definition of pragmatism is probably the best definition of the term: "It does not matter whether a cat is black or white; if it catches mice, it is a good cat." Deng used this pithy definition of pragmatism to justify the decision to move away from the ideological rigidities of communism.

While Deng's enormous contribution is now well-recognized, it is worth recalling the challenges he faced when he was rehabilitated and put back in office in July 1977. Apart from dealing with the turmoil produced by the Cultural Revolution, he faced a uniquely adverse geopolitical environment. Vietnam was set to invade Cambodia in 1978 after signing a treaty in Moscow on 3 November to secure Soviet protection if China invaded Vietnam in retaliation. Deng went to Washington in January 1979 to explain to President Carter how China would react to the Vietnamese invasion. Zbigniew Brzezinski, President Carter's national security advisor, was present at the meeting, and in his memoirs he described Deng's presentation as "the single most impressive demonstration of raw power politics that I encountered in my four years at the White House."[33] During this visit Deng made the bold decision to expose Chinese society to the remarkable affluence of American society, a huge political risk. It proved the falsehood of the long-standing and oft-repeated claims of the CCP that the American people were poor and oppressed. But Deng's gamble unleashed the enormous energies of the Chinese population.

It would have been excusable for any Chinese leader to focus only on geopolitical challenges in such difficult circumstances (as the Soviet leaders appeared to be doing at the time). Remarkably, Deng also focused his energies on the domestic economic reform that China would have to undertake. As part of his response to the Vietnamese invasion, he decided to visit a few states of the Association of Southeast Asian Nations (ASEAN), including Singapore. These visits opened his eyes to the superior economic conditions in Southeast Asia. In a December 2005 interview with *Time Asia*, Singapore's former Prime Minister Lee Kuan Yew described Deng's likely reaction to his travels:

> I'm convinced that his visit to Bangkok, Kuala Lumpur and Singapore, that journey, in November '78, was a shock to him. He expected three Third-World cities; he saw three Second-World cities better than Shanghai or Beijing. As his aircraft door closed, I turned around to my colleagues; I said, "[His aides] are getting a shellacking. They gave him the wrong brief." Within weeks, the People's Daily switched lines, [writing] that Singapore is no longer a running dog of the Americans; it's a very nice city, a garden city, good public housing, very clean place. They changed their line. And he changed to the "open door" policy. After a lifetime as a communist, at the age of 74, he persuaded his Long March contemporaries to return to a market economy.[34]

Following his visit, Deng worked even harder to promote economic reform. He called on the Chinese people to learn from Singapore: "Singapore enjoys good social order and is well managed. . . . We should tap their experience and learn how to manage things better than they do."[35]

To get his meaning across to a billion people, Deng used brilliantly simple and striking aphorisms. One of his most famous: "To get rich is glorious." It was the ultimate—pragmatic—reversal from state socialism.

In the same pragmatic spirit, Deng declared, "leftism is the greater handicap, as compared to 'rightism.'" He called for an end to name-calling and arguing over socialism and capitalism. Instead, he called for more, greater, faster, and bolder reform:

> Now that the peripheral countries and areas have the lead on us in economic development, if we fail to catch up with them or if

we advance at a slow pace, the public may have grievances when they make comparisons. Therefore, if an idea can help speed up development, we must not stop it but should try to make development still faster. In any case, we must set store on efficiency and quality. We must seize every opportunity to make the country develop quickly. We have a good opportunity now; if we fail to seize it, it will be gone very soon. Slow development simply means to halt. We must strive really hard to upgrade the economy to a new level every few years.[36]

The Chinese government followed this up by inviting Dr. Goh Keng Swee to serve as the economic advisor to the State Council of China on coastal development from 1985 to the mid-1990s. Goh's Meiji-inspired views about development are unequivocal: "If our experience can be used as a general guide to policy in other developing nations, the lesson is that the free enterprise system, correctly nurtured and adroitly handled, can serve as a powerful and versatile instrument of economic growth." He must have shared this idea with his Chinese hosts as well.

Having lived in Asia over the past few decades, I've no doubt that the spirit of pragmatism, first imbibed by Japan in the 1860s, has now spread far and wide in the region. Dr. Mahathir explained his pragmatic economic policies in Malaysia by saying that Malaysia should adopt a "Look East" policy and learn from Japan and South Korea. Similarly, in 1991, when Manmohan Singh, then finance minister of India, was attacked by leftists for allowing foreign investment that would in turn make India subservient to America, he replied that Singapore's ability to defy the wishes of the American government in many areas (despite getting the highest per capita amount of foreign investment) showed that a pragmatic acceptance of foreign investment did not mean a loss of political independence.

One of India's most famous industrialists is Ratan Tata. One of his companies, Tata Steel, received global recognition when it acquired the British steel firm Corus for US$12 billion in March 2007. In late 2005 he told an interesting story. He said that for many years he would travel around India and try to persuade people to learn from Singapore's experience. The inevitable response he got was this: "Singapore is so small. India is so big. What can big India learn from Singapore?" However, when China began to take off in the 1990s and Ratan Tata said that India could learn from China, his fellow Indians could not say that China was too small for India to learn from. The Indian economy began to open up in 1991, mostly because of the balance of payments crisis, but partially also because of the lessons from China as well as the fear of being left behind. Few Indians knew that the Chinese had learned from Singapore, and Singapore from Japan.

CULTURE OF PEACE

The biggest sound coming out of East Asia is the sound that has still not been noticed around the world: the sound of *silenced* guns in the region. By any standard, the silence of the guns is not a normal phenomenon.

The natural expectation over the past two decades has been that with the rise of many new powers, Asia would become dominated by rivalry and conflict, not peace and understanding. Several leading scholars had predicted this almost fifteen years ago. Richard Betts wrote, "one of the reasons for optimism about peace in Europe is the apparent satisfaction of the great powers with the status quo," while in East Asia there is "an ample pool of festering grievances, with more potential for generating conflict than during the Cold War, when bipolarity helped stifle the escalation of parochial disputes."[37] Aaron L. Friedberg wrote, "While civil war and ethnic strife will continue for some time to smolder along Europe's peripheries, in the long run it is Asia that seems far more likely to be the cockpit of great-power conflict. The half-millennium during which Europe was the world's primary generator of war (as well as wealth and knowledge) is coming to a close. But, for better or for worse, Europe's past could be Asia's future."[38]

Not only has East Asia been peaceful for more than two decades, but it has also passed a major stress test that could have triggered conflicts in the region: the Asian Financial Crisis of 1997–1998. It would be difficult to underestimate its severity; there was a major implosion of several Asian economies. Indonesia's economy shrank 15 percent in 1998. More than a half million Indonesian children died from malnutrition, and the country's poverty rate soared to at least 40 percent by 1998. In South Korea in 1998, unemployment rose from a tiny 2.6 percent to more than 8 percent and was still climbing.[39] In the February 1999 *Time* cover story, "Committee to Save the World," Larry Summers said the economic crisis was "spectacular." He had a favorite analogy for the Asian Financial Crisis: "Global capital markets pose the same kinds of problems that jet planes do. They are faster, more comfortable, and they get you where you are going better. But the crashes are much more spectacular."[40]

History teaches us that the combination of a major financial crisis and "an ample pool of festering grievances," in Betts's phrase, should make a lethal cocktail. If indeed East Asia was poised and ready for conflict to grow and spread, this should have broken out in the aftermath of the Asian Financial Crisis. Instead, the opposite happened. Peace consolidated and deepened. Why?

The answers to any question on the causes of war and peace are complex. But some of the key contributing factors are clear. The first is that East Asians have absorbed—almost through the process of osmosis— the fifth pillar of Western wisdom: the culture of peace that has affected relations among the Western states since the end of World War II. Given the hundreds of years of conflicts among some of them, it is truly remarkable that all Western countries have reached the highest peak of human achievement: not just zero wars but zero *prospect* of war between any two Western nations. The world takes this achievement for granted, while rarely acknowledging that this is one of the most impressive accomplishments in human history. If the rest of the world could absorb this Western best practice and achieve a similar level of peace, the world would be a much happier place. Curiously, while the West has been content to preach the virtues of democracy, human rights, and free-market economics to the rest of the world, it rarely mentions the condition of peace it has achieved.

The conventional explanation for this peace is that Western nations explored every other option first, including the mass slaughter of World War I (which may well be remembered as one of the stupidest wars in human history, a stupid war fought by the brightest young minds of Europe) and World War II. The advent of nuclear weapons also made wars between major powers a less attractive option.

This rather negative explanation, while it contains a grain of truth, ignores a significant dimension of the modern condition. The growth of well-educated and affluent middle classes in most Western societies has changed fundamental conceptions of what society should aspire to. In the nineteenth century it was taken for granted—especially in Europe—that the objective of a nation-state was to enhance its power, colonize other nations, and develop large spheres of influence. In the twentieth century—as evidenced by the behavior of Germany and Japan after World War II—national power was enhanced by increasing the size of the economy. Competition in the nineteenth century for political influence and territorial control was a zero-sum game. Competition in the second half of the twentieth century could become a positive sum game. Growing economies could benefit, not harm, each other. They could grow together.

America since 1945 has been involved in many wars. Some were proxy struggles for the wider Cold War contest; some were part of the American tradition of seeking military solutions in Latin America, which it has regarded as its natural sphere of influence since the Monroe Doctrine. The United States has engaged in two costly wars of choice—in Vietnam and Iraq. But the overall American record has been one of remarkable restraint. Given its overwhelming military might (probably the greatest seen in history), the US could have easily invaded and occupied several countries, if not threatened and bullied them into submission. Instead, it has used its military might to guarantee a world order since 1945 that has enabled both America and the rest of the world, especially East Asia, to grow and prosper.

The single most important emerging power in Asia and the world is China. Many strategic thinkers in the West obsess over the menace of China as an emerging military dragon. This is a possibility, but it is also clear by now that this is not the vision of the Chinese leadership and intelligentsia. The overwhelming consensus in China is captured by the words used by one of China's leading thinkers (who is also a close adviser to Hu Jintao), Zheng Bijian, who has said categorically that China believes in a "peaceful rise."

The concept of "peaceful rise" reflects a carefully thought-out consensus within China. The Chinese leaders know how many times China has tried and failed to modernize. The current opportunity to grow and become a developed nation represents the best opportunity China has had. The stupidest thing China could do is to squander it by engaging in any kind of military conflict. China has learned from the positive example of the Western world and the negative example of the Soviet Union, which imploded for several reasons, among them the decision to focus on military development instead of economic development. China has decided to do the exact opposite.

Another major negative lesson from the Soviet Union was that the massive accumulation of nuclear weaponry diminished rather than enhanced its security. Of all the five "legal" nuclear powers, China keeps its nuclear weapons in the *least* operationally ready stage. More than half of its estimated four hundred nuclear warheads are believed to be kept in secure locations. Even the operational warheads in its nuclear triad (land-based missiles, sea-based missiles, and bombers) are not kept at hair-trigger alert like the ones still deployed by the United States and Russia. While its guarded nuclear posture may possibly be linked to its technological predicament, the Chinese leadership seems less enthusiastic in acquiring those capabilities and modernizing the nuclear arsenal. Even the French and the British recently announced plans for upgrading their nuclear forces, while China's nuclear stockpile has remained constant for more than two decades. Modernization, if it happens at all, proceeds at a glacial pace, despite China's growing economic size and capability for building up its nuclear stockpile.

The Chinese leadership may also be conscious of the huge price tag associated with building and maintaining a large and sophisticated nuclear deterrent. According to *Atomic Audit*, a 1998 Brookings Institution study, the United States spent over US$5.5 trillion since 1944 on nuclear weapons systems. The US continues to spend around 7 percent of its US$500 billion annual defense budget on these weapon systems.[41] While the culture of competitive research grants and private contracts helps the American nuclear enterprise to remain vibrant and internally accountable through an elaborate scheme of checks and balances (the government directly employs only a small fraction of those involved in weapons activities), the Soviet nuclear weapons establishment became an albatross for its economy.

The lessons China has learned about war and peace in the modern world are not the only reason why the guns are silent in East Asia. Another critical player has emerged almost unnoticed: ASEAN. Like the EU, it was set up to promote regional cooperation. Both have been equally successful in preventing war between any two member states. The EU is one step ahead of ASEAN, since it has achieved zero prospect of war. The EU is an economic superpower (with a combined GNP of US$13,386 billion), while ASEAN is an economic minipower (with a combined GNI of US$857 billion).[42]

But there is at least one dimension in which ASEAN may be ahead of the EU: diplomacy. In this field, ASEAN is a superpower while EU is a minipower. There are two balkanized regions in the world: the Balkans of Europe and Southeast Asia. Indeed, in terms of diversity in religion, race, language, culture, history, and so forth, Southeast Asia is far more balkanized. This is how the veteran English journalist Dennis Bloodworth described it:

A pack of independent countries today, Southeast Asia can be cut several ways. The fundamental Western colonial influence in Burma, Malaysia, Singapore, and Brunei has been British. In Indonesia, it has been Dutch. In the Indochina states of Cambodia, Laos and Vietnam it has been French. In the Philippines it has been Spanish and American. Ethnically, however, Malaysia, Indonesia, and the Philippines are linked and largely inhabited by brown people of "Malay" stock. Similarly, Thailand (formerly Siam, the one state that was not colonized), Laos, and the Shan States of north Burma are all people, by yellow men of "Thai" origin. But there are many other strains. The dominant race in Burma is related to the Tibetans; in Cambodia it is the darker "Khmers"; and Vietnam is inhabited by "Viets" from South China. Culturally, it is in Vietnam that the "Indo" of "Indochina" ends; people no longer build houses on stilts, and the sarong, which is the costume of Southeast Asia, gives way to Chinese pajamas and the fetching *ao-dai*, itself a variant of the Chinese *cheongsam*. For the Indian culture which in early centuries gave most of Southeast Asia coherence did not impose itself on northern Vietnam, for so long a vassal of China. Religion helps to bring out the two main themes of the subcontinent. The brown Malay world of Malaysia-Indonesia-Philippines is almost entirely Muslim (with the important exception of Christian Luzon). On the other hand, the countries that make up the main blob of the peninsula itself—Burma, Laos, Thailand, Cambodia, Vietnam— are Buddhist. The majority of Singaporeans are immigrant Chinese, who also account (with immigrant Indians) for about half the population of Malaysia and constitute a small but powerful economic minority in other countries of this area, which is backward but not poor in resources.[43]

At the end of the Cold War, if predictions had been made about whether war was more likely in the Balkans or in Asia, there is no doubt that leading Western strategic thinkers would have predicted war in Asia. Yet the exact opposite happened. Why? The EU failed where ASEAN succeeded.

Other equally remarkable diplomatic achievements of ASEAN have also gone unnoticed. For much of the Cold War, Southeast Asia was divided between the noncommunist ASEAN and communist Indochina, dominated by the pro-Soviet Vietnam from 1979 to 1989. As a communist country, Vietnam seemed as strong and as impervious as North Korea and could have remained a force of destabilization. Yet Vietnam has gone from being Southeast Asia's North Korea to becoming its Singapore. It joined ASEAN in July 1995 and has since then fully invested in ASEAN's vision of peace and prosperity in the region. Indeed, in scarcely a decade Vietnam has emerged as a new economic tiger, its economy growing from US$21 billion in 1995 to US$52 billion in 2005. By contrast the EU has still not resolved the obvious problem of Kosovo.

The other remarkable diplomatic achievement of ASEAN is that it has made a major contribution toward enabling the peaceful emergence of new Asian powers. The long history of humanity teaches us that when great powers emerge, there is a tendency for new conflicts to emerge. Against this historical backdrop, the simultaneous emergence of China and India (together with the continued strength of Japan) should present the Asian region with obvious challenges. But instead of growing conflict and rivalries, new patterns of cooperation are emerging. ASEAN has played a key role, being single-handedly responsible for spawning a new alphabet soup of cooperation ventures: ARF, APEC, ASEAN+3, ASEM, and EAS.

Forty years after the creation of the Association of Southeast Asian Nations (ASEAN) in 1967, the three economic giants of Japan, South Korea, and China have failed to create a comparable Association of Northeast Asian Nations. The reasons for this failure are complex. But the consequence has been that the only fora where the three Northeast Asian leaders can meet comfortably and discuss common challenges have been the meetings convened by ASEAN, especially ASEAN+3 (China, Japan, South Korea). Thus ASEAN, still an economic minipower, should be viewed as a diplomatic superpower: it is the region's peacemaker. It has absorbed and is implementing the culture of peace.

RULE OF LAW

The Western notion of the rule of law, in which all human beings are to be treated equally under the law and all citizens subject to the same laws, goes against the grain in Asian minds. Most Asians throughout the ages have assumed that the ruling classes, especially members of royal families and the aristocracy, stand above the law. Indeed, in the minds of the ruling classes, the only function of the law was to enable them to discipline their subjects.

In traditional Chinese legal thought, the law was only a tool through which the government ruled the governed. The emperor (or party leader) was himself above the law, and indeed his every decree or wish was the law itself. Inherent in the Chinese socialist concept of law and *zheng-fa xitong*, there is the idea of *linghouxing* or flexibility, which allows the state, or more specifically the state leader, to interpret the law according to his own or his party's interests.

George Washington University legal scholar Donald Clarke also points out that for millennia the main role of China's courts was to remind citizens of the power of the state. In an essay on China's legal system, he cites a passage written by the seventeenth-century Qing emperor Kangxi: "If people were not afraid of the tribunals, and if they felt confident of always finding in them ready and perfect justice, lawsuits would tend to increase to a frightful amount," the passage reads. "Those who have recourse to the tribunals should be treated without any pity, and in such manner that they shall be disgusted with law, and tremble to appear before a magistrate."[44]

To the Western mind, in contrast, the rule of law is to protect the individual citizen from arbitrary use of the powers of government. It is the concrete implementation of a cherished value: the value of justice. The famous symbol of a blindfolded figure holding the scales of justice captures this deep Western aspiration to create a just society in which the law applies equally to all. Indeed, the pursuit of justice is regarded as one of the highest ethical aspirations any society can have.

Asians are turning to the rule of law not for ethical reasons but for primarily functional reasons. The best example of this is provided by traffic laws. We stop at red lights not for ethical reasons but because it is safer to do so. Traffic lights also create an overall system that enables traffic (as well as commerce and other social activities) to flow smoothly.

For Westerners, it is self-evident why a driver should stop at a stop sign. I have discovered from bitter personal experience why it is not self-evident to Asian minds. In 1973 I was driving home late at night on the main boulevard of Phnom Penh. The city was under siege; it was shelled daily, and there was a curfew. The streets were deserted as I drove home with my diplomatic license plates. Suddenly, out of the blue, a large limousine came out of a side road at sixty miles per hour and ignored the stop sign. It hit my car squarely, but fortunately I survived. When I got out of my car, I understood why the other car hadn't stopped: it was the official vehicle of the chief of police. The driver thought that since he was driving the car of the chief of police, he was above the law and had no obligation to stop at the stop sign.

Most Asians now understand that obeying the rule of law should come as naturally as obeying traffic rules. If they don't, they will fail to set up a modern economy, which can only function if the law provides a basis on which people can make agreements in the confidence that these agreements can be fairly and efficiently enforced. China demonstrates this clearly. The recent push for the establishment of a legal system in China that borrows from Western concepts is driven primarily by economic imperatives. Once China favored a market economy over the previous planned system, laws became increasingly vital to regulate China's economic activities. The central government was forced to devolve financial and fiscal power, property rights, and the material allocation of power to local governments and individuals.[45] The need to attract foreign investment and the confidence of foreign investors led China to embark on the creation of an impartial and consistent legal system. The opening of the economy to the international community is indeed a two-way street, and the established market economies of the West, which China wished to have access to, also exerted external pressure on China to adhere to international norms. A case in point would be the establishment of a judicial review system[46] and the changes in commercial laws and practices to which China committed itself when it joined the World Trade Organization.

Given China's long legal history, the recent progress made in implementing Western-style rule of law since the 1982 Chinese constitution is nothing short of astounding. This is particularly so in terms of laws that curb the abuse of state power over the individual. In 1991, a white paper published by the State Council, "The Situation of Human Rights in China," was the first formal acknowledgment of the concept of human rights by the Chinese government. In the 9,429 laws it passed between 1991 and 1997,[47] the Chinese government paid specific attention to the legal rights of citizens. For example, October 1990 saw the enactment of the Administrative Litigation Act, which gave citizens legal recourse in the event of state abuse of power. In May 1994, China enacted the State Indemnity Law, which stipulates that "where a government agency or its personnel invades the legitimate rights and interests of a citizen, legal person or other organization, resulting in injury while performing its functions, the sufferer shall be entitled to obtain state indemnity."[48] In March 1996, China put in place the Law on Administrative Punishments, which provides mechanisms for investigating and punishing criminal offenses that take place not only in state administrative, economic, and judicial agencies but also within the leadership organs of the CCP itself.[49] Criticisms of the Chinese legal system to the effect that only half of China's laws were enforced have some validity, but nonetheless the enactment of the Administrative Litigation Act produced a sharp increase in lawsuits against the Chinese government (about twenty-seven thousand a year in the early 1990s). The government's decisions were dismissed in an unprecedented number of the cases.[50]

The continuing rapid economic development in China is pressuring the country's legal system to change. The emerging urban elite now see protecting their individual rights as a number one priority. "The rising middle class likes predictability and security, and that's what the law does," says Nicholas Bequelin of Human Rights Watch, adding that the Communist Party recognizes that its future depends on being able to accommodate such demands. "The Party is highly adaptable so long as nothing threatens their basic control."[51] A 2005 report in the *International Herald Tribune* states,

> Today, China's court system is far from an independent entity that can curb government power. Often, the courts remain a pliable tool to reinforce that power. Many judges are poorly educated in the law and corrupt. All judges still must answer to government officials as much as to the law. Political pressure is common, and private trial committees often dictate what ruling a judge must make. But there also are inklings of change. One of the busiest courts in Beijing announced in November 2005 that it should stop punishing judges if a ruling was later deemed politically or legally "wrong." A budding idealism about the law, and its potential ability to transform Chinese society, is evident not only in the number of new lawyers but also in the emerging civic belief that ordinary people have "legal rights." . . . On the campus of the National Judges College on the outskirts of Beijing, the primary educational arm of the People's Supreme Court, roughly 10,000 judges spend a month of every year on professional training. In the past, judges were taught to serve the interests of the Communist Party, but now a different message is emphasized. "We train them with a modern theory of law: that the courts are impartial, on the need for legal justice and of innocence until

proven guilty," said Huai Xiaofeng, the college's president. "We stress that during a trial, you cannot favor the government of the National People's Congress. In the past, they told them to emphasize the political qualities. Now we tell them to emphasize the law and the facts."[52]

Despite these significant advances, China faces an obvious challenge. In theory, members of the CCP are subject to the same rule as ordinary citizens. In practice, most members of the CCP are still treated as though they are above the law. Many may privately believe they are (and this explains the significant cases of corruption involving senior party officials). But the majority of CCP members have high standards of integrity. If they did not, China could not have enjoyed the massive rates of growth it has enjoyed. China's real challenge now is to create a rule of law that applies equally to all, including the CCP members.

In theory, India enjoys an enormous competitive advantage over China because it inherited the British legal system when it gained independence in 1947 and has retained it since then. For over sixty years, the Indians have had a legal system based on Western rule of law. It is unclear, however, whether the Indian legal system functions better than the Chinese legal system. It is well-known that Indian courts are notoriously inefficient and a huge backlog of cases has built up. Former President Kalam said in July 2007 that a total number of 41,000 civil and criminal cases were currently pending in the Supreme Court. He further said that at least 25 million cases were pending in the District Courts and 3.6 million cases in the High Courts of the country.[53] In some civil cases, it has taken several decades to get a decision. Justice delayed is justice denied.

Another problem is that it is unclear whether some members of the Indian elite understand what the rule of law means. The Jessica Lal murder case demonstrates the apparent impunity enjoyed by the well-connected rich in Indian society. Lal, an Indian model, was shot dead in an upscale New Delhi restaurant in April 1999 for refusing to serve drinks to the son

of a former Union minister of the Indian government after closing hours.
More than a hundred people were present when the politician's son
pulled out a gun and fired twice. It should have been an open-and-shut
case, but the accused was acquitted by the Delhi court seven years later, in
February 2006, prompting the influential Indian newspaper the *Times of
India* to run a banner headline: "No One Killed Jessica Lal." The Delhi
police came under fire for their shoddy investigation that led to the
acquittal. The case began to collapse after several prosecution witnesses
retracted their original statements, in which they had identified the
politician's son as the murderer. Fortunately, justice prevailed in the end,
and Manu Sharma, the killer, was finally convicted and sentenced to life
imprisonment by the Delhi High Court in December 2006. Two of his
accomplices were also sentenced to four years in prison. This case vividly
illustrates that the growth of a more educated society in India, in which
people are aware of their rights, has led to greater pressure to apply the
rule of law impartially to all sectors of society.

In Asia, virtually all the elites (with the possible exception of those in
North Korea and Myanmar) recognize that they have to gravitate toward greater respect for the rule of law. They know equally well that it
is impossible to build a modern society and a modern economy without
a modern rule of law. This is the pill that all Asians societies will have to
swallow, bitter though it may be in the early years of application.

EDUCATION

Asians have embraced the virtues of Western education for a long
time, although making education accessible to the masses is a relatively recent phenomenon. Now that the massive populations of Asia
have tasted the sweet fruits of Western education, they have become
addicted to it. This addiction also helps to explain why the rise of Asia
has become unstoppable. According to the 2007 World Bank Report
on globalization, "rising education levels were also important, boost-
ing Asian growth on average by 0.75 to 2 percentage points."[54]

Throughout history, all great civilizations have understood the value of education. Indeed, the peak of each civilization is often associated with the development of great centers of learning. This was true for the ancient Greeks, the Arab Muslims at the height of the Abbasid Caliphates, the Indians at the time of King Akbar, and the Chinese at the time of the Tang dynasty. Not surprisingly, given the dominance of the West over the past few centuries, the greatest universities are now found in the West.

What makes these Western universities truly unique is that they do not see their mission as exclusively directed at the West. Instead, they see themselves as protecting old knowledge and developing new frontiers of learning for all of humankind. American universities—and the great ones should be declared humanity's treasures—have successfully educated elites in the United States and all over the world.

Asia should thank America when its modernization is complete because the US has done more than any other society to train and educate Asian elites. Since World War II, several hundred thousand Asians have studied in American universities and returned home. The total population of Chinese overseas students was about 580,000 between 1978 and 2003, of whom more than 172,800 (about 32 percent) have returned home.[55] In 1998, 7,300 students returned home, nearly five times that of 1990. Up to now, more than 1,000 talented students who have mastered the high-tech world have settled in the Shanghai Pudong area and created more than a hundred fifty companies with a registered capital amounting to US$30 million.[56] In her study of immigrant professionals in Silicon Valley, Anna Lee Saxenian, dean of the School of Information at the University of California, Berkeley, found that 73 percent of Chinese immigrant professionals said they would consider establishing businesses back in their homeland—and a large number had already done so.[57]

India has benefited even more than China from exposure to American education. Indeed, it is the leading nation of origin for international students, with 76,503 students in the US in 2005–2006, followed by China (62,582), Korea (58,847), and Japan (38,712).[58] Today, more and more Indian students are planning to return home after their studies. In a recent informal study carried out among students of Indian origin studying at the University of Chicago's Graduate School of Business, more than 84 percent of the Indian students surveyed were keen to return to India in the near future. About half of them wanted to return within five years of graduation.[59] These returning graduates have provided the yeast for Asia's rise. When these students return home, they bring with them not only the specific technical skills they learned in the US but the entire American ethos—an optimistic view of life and a belief that great societies can be created intentionally. The great American conviction of the 1960s that a generation of the best and brightest could transform society has spread beyond American shores and affected the psychological dynamic of Asia.

Microsoft Chairperson Bill Gates, during a panel discussion at the Microsoft Research Tech Fair held on 27 April 2005 in Washington, DC, talked about this phenomenon in the context of his own company's new research centers in India and China: "[Those R&D centers] are giving us an exposure to the quality of [Indian and Chinese] students—most of whom, historically, would have come to the United States. But more are either not coming at all, or coming here and going back."[60]

Edward Tian is a notable example of the influential role that American-educated Chinese executives play, even in government-supported enterprises. After earning a PhD in ecology at Texas Tech University, Tian started a high-tech venture in Texas. The Chinese national government then recruited him to be the CEO of China Netcom, originally a small start-up telecommunications firm based in Beijing. In 2002, China Netcom merged with a major part of the incumbent China Telecom, at the time the state-owned primary national telephone utility, to form a new, giant-scale China Netcom, with Tian as the president. Tian constructed the backbone of China's modern networks, for both national-level companies and provincial governments. In all, he and his team built more than a hundred major network projects. He was recognized as a "world-class entrepreneur" at the World Economic Forum.

Fu Chengyu is another. He is the president of China National Offshore Oil Corporation (CNOOC), and he led the company's 2005 bid to acquire Unocal. Fu holds a master's degree in petroleum engineering from the University of Southern California. Early in his career at CNOOC, he led the joint management committee, which oversaw joint ventures between CNOOC and global leaders such as BP (later BP Amoco) and Shell.

Several Asian societies are now benefiting enormously from the return of their Western-educated citizens. By 2006, it is estimated that thirty-five thousand expatriate Indians have returned and set up home in Bangalore, one of India's booming high-tech centers.[61] Over thirty-two thousand Britons of Indian origin are also estimated to have returned home.[62] G. Gurucharan, joint secretary in the Ministry of Overseas Indian Affairs, reported that the government had issued more than forty thousand overseas certificates in a six-month period in 2006 alone. The Overseas Citizenship Certificate provides many of the benefits of full citizenship without requiring the surrender of a foreign passport. "In the sixties when people left India the buzz-word was 'brain drain.' We see it now as 'brain-gain,'" he said.[63]

In 2006, forty thousand returnees resettled in China, up from seven thousand in 1999, says David Zweig, a professor at Hong Kong University of Science and Technology. In Vietnam, the government has eased visa requirements and investment restrictions to encourage its émigrés to come home, and since the 1990s thousands of Vietnamese have returned. Take the case of Phuc Than, who in 1975, at age fourteen, fled Vietnam by helicopter when Saigon fell to the communist north. In 1999 Than returned to Vietnam—an avowed capitalist, an electrical engineer, a salesman, and a thirteen-year veteran of Intel. "The US gave me opportunities, but if I leave the US, it won't suffer. If I come back to Vietnam, I have the opportunity to do something great," he says. He has just helped the communist government in

Vietnam win a US$1 billion investment from Intel that will bring forty-five hundred jobs to Vietnam.[64]

Sanatanu Paul is an Indian who spent thirteen years in the US, obtaining a doctorate in computer science, working for IBM in New York, and leading two technology start-up companies. In 2003 he decided to return to India to become the general manager at a software services firm. To him, "right now, India feels like an exciting start-up company, while the West feels like a plodding large company."[65]

The "reverse brain drain" is not limited to information technology alone. In 2002, Arjun Kalyanpur, an assistant professor at the Yale University School of Medicine, returned home to establish India's first company that provides hospitals with tele-radiological services. "There is breathless excitement in India today," he says. "The technology gap between the West and the East has narrowed."[66]

When P. R. Venkatrama Raja's father sent him to the University of Michigan to get his MBA in 1981, Venkat was given a mission: to identify a new business with global potential. Returning to India, an excited Venkat brought back an idea: a software system that integrates all aspects of a company's operations, from manufacturing to accounting to distribution. Only a handful of companies in the world made a similar product—including Germany's SAP and Oracle Corporation of the US. But by relying on cheaper Indian brainpower, Venkat thought he could develop a system for less.

With his father's US$30 million, Venkat hired two hundred MBAs and four hundred computer professionals—the largest private effort of its kind in India. Toiling for seven years, Venkat and his crew finally came up with Marshall 3.0, a Windows-based product, and set up offices in California, Switzerland, Malaysia, and Singapore to market it. Already, Ramco Systems has notched up revenues of US$60 million. Bill Gates launched Marshall on his visit to India in early March 2005.

Asians have benefited enormously from studying in American universities (and universities in Europe, Australia, and New Zealand). The next big challenge for Asian societies is to develop equally great universities on their soil. A promising start has been made. In a 2006 *Times Educational Supplement* ranking of the top hundred universities, fourteen are in Asia, and of the top twenty-five, three are Asian, including Tokyo University, Beijing University, and National University of Singapore. An article in the *New York Times* reported that China is "attracting a growing number of the brightest students, scholars, and professionals from southeast Asian countries" such as Thailand, Singapore, and Indonesia.[67] In the year before the attacks on the World Trade Center, 6,250 Indonesian students received visas to the United States. In 2003, the number was 1,333, a decline of 79 percent. By contrast, 2,563 Indonesians were admitted to Chinese universities that same year, an increase of 51 percent over 2002. Indonesia's post-1945 leadership was dubbed "the Berkeley Mafia" because so many had degrees from the University of California at Berkeley. Will those educated in China dominate a twenty-first-century generation of Asian leaders?

As a result of the success of Asian universities, leading universities in the United States are now soliciting partnerships with their Chinese counterparts. The competition among the top American universities for institutionalized collaboration with Chinese universities is rife. Yale is currently leading the way. Yale emphasizes its ties with China that date back to 1854, when Yung Wing graduated from Yale and became the first Chinese to receive a postsecondary degree in the United States.[68] The school is also proud to claim personal relationships between its faculty members and scholars in Chinese universities such as Fudan University.[69] Yale President Richard Levin has made four visits to China since 2001. Collaborations include the Yale School of Forestry and Environmental Studies and Tsinghua University. The prestigious Yale China Law Center was established in 1999 with the two important missions of assisting the legal reform process within China and increasing understanding of China's legal system outside of China. To date, Yale has in place a total of eighty different exchange programs with Chinese universities.

Stanford University has also claimed close links between its faculty members and Peking University as a strategy to strengthen its relationship with China. Fall 2004 saw the first group of Stanford students arrive at Peking University.[70] Stanford's Institute of International Studies and School of Medicine collaborate with the China Health Economic Institute to develop solutions to the problems of health care delivery in China.

In a first-of-its-kind breakthrough attempt at large-scale collaboration in governance training, Harvard's John F. Kennedy School of Government is currently collaborating with Tsinghua University and the State Council Development Center to train local and central government officials. The deputy director of the center, Sun Siaoyu, along with Joseph Nye, the dean of the Kennedy School, and Chen Qingtai, the president of Tsinghua University's School of Public Management, began this program in 2002.[71]

These remarkably sharp increases in contacts between American universities and their Asian counterparts show the new texture of intellectual life one finds in Asia today. Asians have discovered the value of universities. I have seen firsthand how determined China is to promote and expand higher education. In January 2007 I visited one of China's key cities in southern China, Guangzhou, host of the traditional Canton Fair. It has several good universities, including the well-known Sun Yat-sen University. The Guangzhou government wanted to expand these schools but ran out of space in the city. It then made a bold and rational decision: it built a large campus in the suburbs to allow all seven universities to set up satellite operations. The campus now hosts a hundred fifty thousand students, far larger than any American campus. Nicholas Kristof writes that the boom town of Dongguan, which had no colleges when he first visited it twenty years ago, now devotes 21 percent of its budget to education and has four universities. An astonishing 58 percent of the residents ages eighteen to twenty-two are enrolled in a university.[72]

But education is never about quantity alone but also quality as well as boldness in thinking and imagination. As W. B. Yeats once remarked,

"Education is not filling a bucket, but lighting a fire." In Asia, this fire has been lit, leading to an explosion of cultural confidence. *Business-Week* reports:

> Market research firm Grey Global Group collaborated with the British Council to conduct a detailed study of Chinese aged 16 to 39 and living in 30 big cities. . . . The study was supplemented with data from a Chinese research institute survey of 10,000 university undergraduates. "The main trend that emerged was that the younger generations in China were very confident about their future," said Viveca Chan, an early pioneer in studying Chinese consumers, who was until recently head of Grey's Asia operations. "When I went to school, everyone talked about the American Dream, and everyone in China aspired to go there," Chan said. "Now, the Chinese dream is starting to happen."[73]

Edward Tse, vice president of Booz Allen Hamilton and the firm's managing partner for greater China, said, "One question is in the mind of every fledgling entrepreneur in the high-tech start-ups of Beijing's Zhongguancun neighborhood, the fabrication hubs of Wenzhou, the industrial region of Dalian, and dozens of other Chinese business centers: 'Why not me?'"[74]

The same explosion of cultural confidence has taken place in India. Mouli Raman, cofounder of Bangalore start-up OnMobile said, "For the first time, Indians who have been exposed to the world realize they can do something just as good. They believe they can be world-class."[75] Former Indian President Kalam recalled his meeting with a Class 6 student, who asked him, "Why cannot India become a developed nation before the year 2020?" "It is a question that reflects how the desire to live in a developed India has entered the minds of the youth," he observed.[76]

Mukesh Ambani, managing director of Reliance Industries, who ranked fourteenth on the 2007 *Forbes* list of global billionaires (with a net worth of US$20.1 billion), wants to be the richest man in the world, says Adil Zainulbhai, head of McKinsey's India practice. He likens the India of today to the United States in the wild early days of the dot-com era. He observes that "Indian chief executives have outrageous aspirations. They have no fear. And Mukesh is just the biggest of them all."[77]

The truly remarkable thing about India is that you can get a sense of that ambition and hope even in India's slums. Dharavi, Mumbai's notorious slum and the biggest in Asia, was once a marsh next to the Mithi River, and its first residents would catch fish and sell them to the Portuguese and later to the British. As Bombay grew and industrialized, Dharavi became a "human dumping ground" for dispossessed workers and penniless migrants seeking their fortune. Today Dharavi has a population of between six hundred thousand and a million—and its annual GDP is US$1 billion.[78] Dharavi is home to some of the city's best leatherworkers as well as textile and furniture factories, potteries and bakeries. Most of Dharavi's residents still live in poverty and squalor, but they also have a sense of hope and ambition that has spread throughout India. Niranjan Rajadhyaksha, in his book *The Rise of India*, recalls a conversation he had with an American diplomat: "He told me that he had been to many slums in many countries in Africa and Latin America. What he often saw there was crime and despair, drugs, and urban gangs. A Mumbai slum, he told me, exudes energy and confidence. It was quite unlike what he saw in poor areas of Rio or Lagos or even New York."[79]

In his *Newsweek* article "India Rising," Fareed Zakaria commented on this new phenomenon:

> Indians, at least in urban areas, are bursting with enthusiasm. Indian businessmen are giddy about their prospects. Indian designers and artists speak of extending their influence across the globe. Bollywood movie stars want to grow their audience abroad from their "base" of half a billion fans. It is as if hundreds of millions of people

have suddenly discovered the keys to unlock their potential.
... Jawaharlal Nehru put it eloquently, "A moment comes, which
comes but rarely in history, when we step out from the old to the
new, when an age ends and when the soul of a nation, long sup-
pressed, finds utterance." [80]

3

WHY IS THE WEST NOT CELEBRATING?

WHAT IS "THE WEST"?

In order to explain the current reaction of the Western world to the undeniable rise of Asia, we need to first take a look at the nature and the history of the West.

Territorially defined, it is a collection of states in North America (the United States and Canada) and Europe (the twenty-seven EU member states), Australia and New Zealand that self-consciously define themselves as members of the Western community. The West, like all states, has material interests—economic and military interests, for example—that are of great importance to them. While most Western states enjoy good relations with most Asian states, they are nonetheless (not surprisingly) troubled by the rise of Asia. In the material competition they could experience some real losses (in addition to some gains).

The philosophical dimension of the West is harder to define. Is it, for example, synonymous with its Judeo-Christian identity? In practice, all the Western states are predominately Judeo-Christian (and not Buddhist,

Hindu, or Muslim). However, many Western states are strongly secular, especially in Europe. They prefer to trace their philosophical roots to the great intellectual traditions of ancient Greece and Rome. A study of the classics in the West is therefore focused on those cultures.

The philosophical West has made enormous contributions to humanity. The simple but revolutionary ideals of the equality of man (and woman) and the dignity of the individual are huge Western gifts to humanity. On the basis of these simple ideas, a treasure trove of human rights has developed, leading to vast improvements in the quality of life throughout the West. The philosophical West has also advanced human knowledge to great heights. Modern science and technology is largely a Western gift. Virtually all societies have little difficulty drinking from the deep wells of Western learning and wisdom.

But the material West is different, driven more by a concern for Western interests than for Western values. The tension between Western interests and Western values is vividly shown in the West's attitude to the rise of Asia. At a philosophical level, the West should celebrate. For five hundred years the West has been the only civilization carrying the burden of advancing human knowledge and wealth. Today, it can share this responsibility. It should celebrate the clear presence of Western values in the rise of Asia. The spread of Western modernity into Asia has been a huge gift from the West to Asia. The West should be happy to see the positive results of its gift.

However, the relative lack of celebrations in the West on the rise of Asia shows the West's awareness that while it is gaining in the philosophical dimension, it may suffer some real losses in the material dimensions. There will be no *absolute* losses: most Western states will remain among the most affluent and well-endowed states. However, there will be *relative* losses. The relative material superiority the material West has enjoyed for centuries will gradually diminish.

There will also be relative losses in another key area: power. Western states have accumulated power in a whole range of global institutions. For decades they nurtured these institutions and accumulated this

power. For these global institutions to be effective today, the gre
ers of the twenty-first century must participate in their governanc
decision making. The rise of Asia therefore creates a real dilemma
Western states: Should they be guided by their material interests an
cling on to this power, or should they be guided by their values and
begin to cede and share power?

THE POST-1945 WORLD ORDER

One of the guiding lights in the creation of post–World War II
order was the great American diplomat George Kennan. He provided some sound advice to his fellow citizens. America's influence
abroad, he wrote, was "primarily a question of what we urge upon
ourselves. It is a question of the spirit and purpose of American
national life itself. Any message we may try to bring to others will
be effective only if it is in accord with what we are to ourselves,
and if this is something sufficiently impressive to compel the
respect and confidence of a world which, despite all its material
difficulties, is still more ready to recognize and respect spiritual
distinction than material opulence."[1] Kennan's message to his fellow Americans was a simple one: in your policies toward the rest
of the world, be true to your own values.

However, Western interests will pull Western policies in a different
direction. The 1945 world order, although benign and appropriate for
the era, was not supposed to be rigid and unchanging. It was not
meant to freeze in perpetuity a certain hierarchy of nations in global
decision-making fora. The UN Security Council is a significant body.
It has the ultimate responsibility for meeting threats to international
peace and security. However, the five permanent veto-wielding seats
are reserved for the victors of World War II, namely the United
States, the Soviet Union (now Russia), the United Kingdom, France,
and China. Sixty years later, new powers have emerged. But the UN
Security Council remains the same. All efforts to reform it have failed.

e against change (although China, too, has

he council).

international economic institutions, the

y Fund (IMF) and the World Bank, the cur-

m allows the West to dominate, even though the

of the global GNP has grown by leaps and bounds since creation in 1945. The IMF lost a lot of its prestige and legitimacy in Asia in 1997 when its response to the Asia financial crisis was seen to be dictated by Western interests, not Asian needs. Even more remarkably, even though Asians make up over 55 percent of the world's population and have demonstrated their prowess in economics, in management and in intellectual fields, no Asian has been the leader of either the IMF or the World Bank. An unwritten but firm rule dictates that the head of the IMF should be European and that the head of the World Bank should be American.

This is an obvious anachronism. Common sense dictates that this rule should be scrapped. To remain true to Western values, which proclaim that all ethnic groups and nationalities have equal endowments and equal rights, these two jobs should be open to all citizens of the world. Unfortunately, this is unlikely to happen soon.

The great paradox of the twenty-first century is that this undemocratic world order is sustained by the world's most democratic nation-states, the Western nations. At home they would never allow a minority of the population to make mandatory decisions over the majority. Globally, this is exactly what the West does. The 900 million people who live in Western countries elect governments that in turn control a world order determining the fate of the remaining 5.6 billion people on the planet. Effectively, 12 percent of the world's population control global decision making.

The reason why this reality is not more obvious is because the nature of Western domination of the global order is not fully understood. Many factors contribute, sometimes in combination, to the West's firm control of global institutions and processes. The first pillar is military domination.

Even though America has less than five percent of the world's pop-ulation, it accounts for about 46 percent of all military spending in the world. According to data published by Stockholm International Peace Research Institute, the United States spent US$528.7 billion on defense in 2006, while the total military spending of the world was US$1,158 billion.[2] The US military expenditure was six times greater than the combined military spending of both China (US$49.5 billion) and Russia (US$34.7 billion); its military spending was nearly nine times that of the second largest defense spender, the United Kingdom (US$59.2 billion). In fact, the US spends more on defense than the next twenty-three largest military spending nations combined. Not even the Roman Empire—at the peak of its power—enjoyed such a relative military advantage over its potential competi-tors. Today, no country can afford to declare war on America. It would be suicidal. The entire military capabilities of most nations could not match the firepower that a single carrier battle group of the US Navy could assemble (and the US has twelve aircraft carrier fleets, not one).[3] The extent of US power is evident in its desire to weaponize outer space.

Most of the time American military power is rarely used. There are deep and powerful cultural and institutional restraints on the use of American military power. The American people (despite their liberal gun laws at home) are not trigger-happy, nor do they want their mili-tary to be. Yet even when it is not used, American military power helps to ensure that all nations observe and respect certain fundamental rules. The real reason why most international waterways remain safe and open—and thereby facilitate the huge explosion of global trade we have seen—is that the American Navy acts as the guarantor of last resort to keep them open. Without the global presence of the US Navy, our world order would be less orderly.

Despite this generous American gift to the world, no American politician would want to defend American military expenditures on the grounds that they serve global interests. He or she would have to

declare that they serve American interests, and he or she would be
right in doing so. American ambassadors walk tall in all capitals
because their host governments know the extent of power that backs
them. Most governments in the world pay careful attention to core
American interests; few try to run afoul of them. The small number of
exceptions—Cuba, Iran, North Korea, and Venezuela—only helps to
illustrate how many of the hundred-ninety-odd UN member states
try to stay on the right side of the United States. American military
power buys real influence.

The revival of NATO after 9/11 also illustrates the resilience of military power in Western value systems. For a while, after the end of the
Cold War, NATO was seen as an organization without a mission.
Wags said NATO stood for "No Action; Talk Only." All these skeptics
were silenced after 9/11. When America needed to put together a
strong military coalition to hold Afghanistan together after the
removal of the Taliban, only NATO had the institutional resources
and military capability to do the job. What made this even more
remarkable was the close military cooperation between American
forces and French and German forces while their governments were
squabbling bitterly over the American military intervention in Iraq in
March 2003. The dispute over Iraq was real, not rhetorical. In the sixty
years of trans-Atlantic cooperation after World War II, there has been
no moment as divisive as the Iraq War. Yet these deep divisions did not
prevent or undermine military cooperation in Afghanistan. This was a
vivid demonstration that there is a deep impulse to hold on to Western
military superiority as a key pillar of Western power.

In early 2006, several press reports claimed that despite the deep
differences between America and Germany over the Iraq war, German
intelligence had shared valuable information on Saddam Hussein's
military capabilities with its American counterpart just before the
American military invasion. These reports were denied by the German
government. However, they seemed credible. There is deep and extensive sharing of intelligence information among virtually all Western

countries. From the beginning of history, good militaries have relied on good intelligence. In today's world, Western intelligence organizations are far superior to any of their potential competitors. America, in particular, has created various concentric circles of intelligence cooperation, with the closest circle being the Anglo-Saxon circle involving the British and Australian intelligence agencies.

These strong Western intelligence-gathering capabilities also help to reinforce a second dimension of Western global sovereignty: its political power. Western political domination of the globe is both obvious and difficult to describe. It is difficult to get the nuances just right. Clearly the Western nations no longer dominate the globe as brazenly as they did in the two hundred years before World War II, when European nations felt free to invade or occupy other countries. The British Navy had no qualms about sailing into Canton and demanding that the Chinese allow the free imports of opium to help the British raise revenue to pay for the Chinese tea the British people wanted to drink. As punishment for resisting this "reasonable" British demand, the Chinese were forced to concede Hong Kong for a hundred fifty years. Similarly, Commodore Perry did not hesitate in sailing into Japan with the famous "black hull" American naval vessels to demand that Japan open itself to foreign trade. Those days of crude colonial rule and gunboat diplomacy are long gone.

But it would be a gross distortion of history to suggest that Western political domination of the globe ceased with the end of the colonial era in the immediate aftermath of World War II. The Cold War, especially the intense phase of competition for global influence between the US and the Soviet Union, further distorted the global picture. The Western alliance could legitimately claim that it did not brutally dominate any of its allies in the way the Soviet Union colonized and dominated Eastern Europe. Even at the height of the British Empire, the British rule of India was probably less crude by nineteenth-century standards than the Soviet control of Poland or Czechoslovakia by twentieth-century standards. There was often a touch of finesse in the way the West controlled other nation's destinies, with the British being the deftest of all colonizers. The continuing romanticism about the British Raj, even in previously colonized Indian minds, reveals how carefully the British carried out their colonial rule. The current Western political domination owes a lot to subtlety.

Although America, in both spirit and substance, is the most democratic country in the world, it is often clumsy in exercising political power overseas. A curious mix of moral self-righteousness and a strong desire to exercise control drives American foreign policy. All this makes it even harder to pin down the exact nature of American political domination. It may be best to illustrate this point with a few concrete examples.

Two regions of the world that have experienced continued American political domination in the postcolonial era have been Latin America and the Persian Gulf. The destinies of most Latin American nations have long been influenced by the political preferences of Washington, DC. During the Cold War, when America's primary political interest was excluding Soviet influence, America strongly supported dictatorial regimes from Argentina to Chile, from Brazil to Mexico. At the end of Cold War America decided (for a mixture of self-interested and altruistic reasons) that it preferred democracies: providing vivid confirmation—if any was needed—that Latin America's political destinies had been directed by American preferences.

The explosion of anti-American sentiment that followed some years later only helped to illustrate how acutely aware the Latin American populations were of American political interference. In the immediate aftermath of the end of the Cold War, when American power seemed strong and invincible, governments could get elected by declaring their closeness to Washington. Few went as far as the president of Argentina, Carlos Memen, who said that he wanted "carnal relations" with America. But by the end of the 1990s, such pro-American sentiment had evaporated, to be followed by the election of a series of populist and left-leaning governments in Venezuela, Brazil, Argentina, Ecuador, and Bolivia. One factor that propelled them into power was widespread disillusionment with the effects of American domination of the region. In the Persian Gulf, America exercised a different political strategy. Given American energy dependence on the oil-rich Gulf sheikhdoms, the US made no move to promote democracy in these states. Democracy in Saudi Arabia, for example, would have seen the end of the pro-American rulers and the probable election of political parties with a greater sympathy to the worldview of Osama bin Laden. Hence, throughout the 1990s, when America was busy preaching the virtues of democracy, it simultaneously created a political bubble around the Gulf region to protect the sheikhdoms from the pressure of democratization. This capacity to pick and choose where to promote democratic rule demonstrates how the political dynamic of different regions has been determined by American preferences.

Neither the United States nor Europe can micromanage the internal political evolution of any nation, not even after it has occupied a country like Iraq or Kosovo. However, the West can shelter established rulers, like President Hosni Mubarak of Egypt or President Musharraf of Pakistan, or delegitimize rulers, like President Mugabe of Zimbabwe or President Chavez of Venezuela. Ostensibly the processes of legitimization or delegitimization are based on the domestic record of the rulers. Good leaders are rewarded; bad ones are sanctioned. But look at the British response to two ostensibly bad rulers: President Mugabe of Zimbabwe and President Islam Karimov of Uzbekistan. Mugabe's defiance of Western interests led to constant public exposure of his gross misrule, especially by the globally influential BBC. By contrast, when the British ambassador to Uzbekistan, Craig Murray, reported that Karimov may have carried out one of the worst forms of human torture (boiling prisoners alive), the ambassador was removed. After he was forced out of the British Foreign Service, Murray gave an exclusive interview to the radio program *Democracy Now!*:

When I arrived [in Uzbekistan], one of the things you have to do as a new ambassador is call on your fellow ambassadors, pay courtesy calls. And I kept saying to them, you know, to the French, the German, the Italian: "This is awful. It's terrible what's happening here. There are thousands of people being rounded up in prisons, tortured, killed, disappeared, and it all seems to have the backing of the USA."

And they said to me absolutely straight, they said, "Yes, but we don't mention that. You know, President Karimov is an important ally of George Bush in the war on terror, so there's an unspoken agreement that we keep quiet about the abuses." . . .

How could we pretend that we were going to war to bring democracy to Iraq or to support human rights, when, at the same time, one of our allies, one of the members of the "Coalition of the Willing," was Uzbekistan, which is one of the worst regimes in the world and every bit as bad as Saddam Hussein's regime?

In one classified July 2004 memo, Ambassador Murray wrote, "We receive intelligence obtained under torture from the Uzbek intelligence services via the US. We should stop. . . . This is morally, legally, and practically wrong."

Ambassador Murray also went on to document the close connection between United States and Uzbekistan post–9/11:

The United States has a large military base in Uzbekistan. Uzbekistan is situated immediately north of Afghanistan, and the airbase had been used for operations into Afghanistan, but it was also being made into a permanent facility. It was intended to be a permanent facility. Halliburton were there building all the facilities. And the United States was pumping huge amounts of American taxpayers' money into the Uzbek regime. According to a US embassy press release of December 2002, in 2002 alone, the United States government gave Uzbekistan over US$500 million, of which US$120 million was in military support and US$80 million was in support of the Uzbek security services who were working alongside their CIA colleagues.[4]

If further evidence is needed that Western approbation or sanctions are based on Western interests and not Western values, Muammar Qaddafi of Libya is a case study. Qaddafi has always been a strange and mercurial ruler since the days he seized power through a revolution in 1969. He has also had a checkered record in his relations with the West. He was the subject of a direct assassination attempt by the United States. When President Reagan, who called Gaddafi a "mad dog," ordered the bombing of his home in 1986, Qaddafi survived. But thirty-nine Libyans were killed, including his sixteen-month-old adopted daughter Hanna. This did not restrain him. When he was suspected of being responsible for the terrorist downing of the Pan Am plane over Lockerbie, the UN Security Council imposed sanctions in 1992.

None of this changed Qaddafi's behavior. However, he was truly rattled by the American invasion of Iraq and the subsequent American capture of Saddam Hussein. Fearing that he would be next, Qaddafi completely capitulated. He fully confessed to all his clandestine efforts to secure weapons of mass destruction. Earlier he had also reached a financial settlement with the families of the Lockerbie victims, which led to the removal of UN Security Council sanctions. After he stopped his policies of defying Western interests and concerns, all Western policies of isolating Qaddafi were shelved. Soon after, Qaddafi was officially received in the European Union headquarters at Brussels in 2004. Several Western leaders also visited Libya, including British Prime Minister Tony Blair, French President Jacques Chirac, and German Chancellor Gerhard Schroeder in 2004. As a result, Qaddafi was moved from column B to column A in Western eyes. Yet, throughout all this, the nature of his domestic rule changed not a whit. The determining factor in the decision to reinstate Qaddafi was the degree of his alignment with Western interests.

WESTERN DOMINANCE OF INTERNATIONAL
ORGANIZATIONS

Qaddafi illustrates how Western power uses international organizations, especially powerful organizations like the UN Security Council (UNSC) and the IMF, both of which have the unusual ability to impose sanctions on sovereign states. All UN member states accepted the obligation to respect the mandatory decisions of the UNSC when they ratified the UN Charter. While most international organizations are relatively toothless, the UNSC and IMF are not. Their sanctions have real bite.

The UNSC was, of course, moribund during the Cold War, when the United States and the Soviet Union would cross-veto each other's resolutions. Indeed the council rarely met in the Cold War years. But when the Cold War ended, the UNSC sprang to life and passed resolutions and intervened on issues, with Russia cooperating with America. One man who observed this revival of the UNSC at close hand was Indian Ambassador Chinmaya Gharekhan. He represented India on the UNSC in 1991 and 1992. He describes American attitudes toward the UN in those days: "A US diplomat told a colleague of mine in the Indian mission: We can do what we like with the United Nations."[5]

This was no idle boast. Indeed, throughout the 1990s, with strong trans-Atlantic cooperation and a clear Russian desire to cooperate with the West during Yeltsin's presidency, the UNSC became a powerful tool of Western power. Ambassador Gharekhan cites the specific example of Haiti, which gained the attention of the Clinton administration when the democratically elected President Aristide was removed by a military coup at the end of September 1991. America used its clout to secure sanctions against Haiti. Ambassador Gharekhan makes the following observation:

> Thus, Haitian people would have to continue to be punished because of US domestic compulsions. If there was a secret vote, most members would not support any UN action relating to Haiti since

what was happening there was strictly an internal matter for that country and posed no threat to international peace and security. But decisions are taken in the open and countries are anxious not to jeopardize their relations with powerful countries and end up voting in favour of sanctions.[6]

I represented Singapore on the UNSC in 2001 and 2002, exactly a decade after Ambassador Gharekhan had served. Nothing had changed in the interim. Each time America felt strongly about an issue, it would force the council to accept its point of view.

When American interests were aligned with global interests, there would be no problems. When the United States (together with the United Kingdom) pushed for sanctions to be imposed on the nefarious Charles Taylor of Liberia, the world happily went along with it (although, as the chair of the Liberian Sanctions Committee, I discovered that these sanctions hurt the Liberian people more than they hurt Charles Taylor). However, when American interests diverge from global interests, its dominance of the UNSC could create serious distortions. In 2002, for example, after the launch of the International Criminal Court (ICC), America was afraid that its soldiers participating in international peacekeeping operations might be subject to prosecution by the ICC. To give them immunity from such prosecution, America proposed a resolution in the UNSC providing such immunity. Even though most international lawyers felt strongly that the UNSC had no legal standing to provide immunity from judicial prosecution, and even though most governments (especially those who had ratified the ICC instruments) felt strongly that it was both legally and politically wrong for the council to intervene on such ICC matters, American power prevailed. The US effectively used its power to go against the clear wishes of the international community.

American power is most imposing when it is aligned with other Western interests and opinions. When there is a sharp division between America and Europe, American power does not always prevail. The sharp debate in the UNSC over the American invasion of

Iraq saw strong French and German opposition, together with that of Russia, which scuttled American and British plans to get a council resolution legitimizing the invasion in March 2003. The subsequent decision to proceed with the invasion—despite the refusal of the council to legitimize it—provided an even more powerful indicator of American might. If any other country had tried to do what America did, it would have been subject to all kinds of pressures and sanctions, formal and informal. The US went ahead and faced no adverse consequences (although the effects of the catastrophic decline in American prestige will be felt for some time). Not a single country even contemplated proposing a resolution to criticize the American invasion of Iraq, in the way that many did after the Soviet invasion of Afghanistan in defiance of international norms and opinions. This is a reality of the current international system. Future generations will ask why international organizations were so toothless. American power had made them toothless; they only developed teeth when it served American and Western interests.

All these multilateral organizations, especially those in the UN family, were set up to serve the interests of the 6.5 billion people in the world. This is what the UN Charter declares as its fundamental mission: to serve the interest of humanity. When Western interests coincide with those of humankind, the mission is fulfilled. When they do not coincide, the West prevails. The role and purpose of these multilateral organizations have been distorted by Western power.

The distortions of Western power would be more widely debated, but for the fact that the West controls virtually all media organizations with a global reach. Global newspapers, like the *International Herald Tribune*, which is owned and controlled by the *New York Times*, and the *Financial Times*, or global TV channels like CNN or the BBC would strongly reject the suggestion that they present a distorted view of the world or deliberately hide the distortions caused by the supremacy of Western power. It is true that the individual editors and journalists working in the organizations hold themselves to high ethical and professional standards. Often they are very critical of their own governments, so they reject the idea of their complicity. There are two strange aspects to this rejection. First, the main strength that these Western media organizations claim to have is that they report on the world objectively. To report on the world they have to understand the views and perceptions of humankind. Yet for all their "objective" understanding and portrayal of the world, they are unable to see or understand how the rest of the world sees them: as agents and instruments of Western power. They report on the world, but they cannot see how the world views them. The second aspect is the sheer audacity of this rejection. A visitor from Mars would see clearly that a small group of Western organizations and Western individuals controls and directs global media flows.

There are deep and fundamental causes of this blindness. One powerful cause is the belief that Western interests and values are universal interests and values. One writer who expressed this eloquently was V. S. Naipaul in a famous essay, "Our Universal Civilization." His thesis was simple: Western values are the best human values, and all that the rest of humanity have to do is to absorb them and live by them. The essay was written in 1990, but in the intervening period, especially during the huge outpouring of Western triumphalism at the end of the Cold War, there emerged an even stronger belief that the West spoke for all of humankind. With this assumption deeply buried in the minds of Western journalists, it was not difficult for them to believe that they are serving the universal interests of humankind, not the narrow sectoral interests of the West.

Occasionally, even the leading journals will make a revealing Freudian slip. The most influential newsweekly in the world is probably the *Economist*. In terms of ownership, it remains a British magazine. However, increasingly it portrays itself as speaking for the American point of view. In its editorials the *Economist* often claims to be guided by the highest moral standards, not narrow national interests. However, in an editorial on the human rights situation in Uzbekistan, it let slip that Western interests could occasionally trump Western values in promoting universal standards of human rights:

But doesn't the West ignore equally grisly abuses in Chechnya?
Yes, but there it can at least be argued that friendship with Russia
is in its vital interest. Friendship with Uzbekistan is not. Uzbekistan has gas, but it is not very accessible to westerners. And until
now America has had an airbase, but others in the region will do
just as well. The failure to punish Mr Karimov discredits the
West, and provides ammunition to its enemies. It has gone on for
far too long.[7]

Not long after this editorial appeared, I discussed it with one of the editors of the *Economist*. She admitted that this editorial was a mistake.
On human rights issues, the *Economist* could not be seen to be arguing
that an exception is made for Chechnya on the grounds that Russia was
strategically important to the West. By the logic of this argument,
South Africa should be excused from putting pressure on Mugabe as it
had vital interests in the stability of Zimbabwe. Similarly, India should
be excused from putting pressure on Myanmar because it had a vital
interest in preventing Myanmar from falling completely under
Chinese influence. Yet the Western media has had no hesitation in
criticizing South Africa and India, even though their policies are no
different from Western policies on Russia.

WESTERN DOMINANCE OF THE GLOBAL ECONOMY

The *Economist* is also a weekly witness to the share of global economy
owned by the West. At the end of World War II, the US share of the
global GDP was almost 50 percent. This share shrank in relative (not
absolute) terms as European countries recovered from the ravages of
World War II. The establishment of the European Economic Community also gave a boost to European economic growth. Hence, the
combined shares of the US and Europe have always been over 50
percent, sometimes reaching two-thirds. This happened despite the
fact that all of the West combined has never had more than 20 percent of the world's population. In 2005, the West comprised 13.4

percent of the world's population and controlled 62.6 percent of the world GDP.[8]

Economic power enabled the West to invest significantly in strengthening military capabilities. In 1985, just before Gorbachev came to power, the US and Western Europe had a combined GNP of over US$7,280 billion.[9] The official Soviet GNP figures were always suspect, and one indication of the relative weakness of the Soviet economy was provided when the Cold War ended. By 2000, ten years after the Cold War had ended, Russia had a GNP of US$253 billion,[10] roughly the size of Belgium's. The Soviet Union was outspent rather than outfought.

The economic power of the West is also shown in its share of global multinational corporations, many of which have revenues bigger than the economies of many small states. In the 2006 *Fortune* 500 list, Western countries had 369 of these 500 corporations or 73.8 percent.[11] More importantly, the combined size of Western companies dwarfed that of non-Western corporations.

Western economic dominance is reinforced if you take the view that Japan, in spite of its geographical location, functions not as an Asian but as a Western economy. Japan has aspired to join all the key Western clubs, including OECD (where Japan was for many years the sole Asian member), the Trilateral Commission, and the G-7. Of these groups, Japan was particularly proud of its G-7 membership. The G-7 leaders meet twice a year. Often they accomplish nothing, but because these leaders represent the richest countries, the Western media splashes attention on these non-meetings. Still membership of this group brings inevitable obligations. Even though Japan was reluctant to contribute to the first Gulf War, it ended up paying the largest share. It contributed US$13 billion, compared to the United States, which contributed US$7 billion (less than 12 percent of the total war expenditure, which amounted to US$61 billion).[12] This was powerful evidence, if any was needed, that Japanese economic power was used to advance Western interests.

A large part of Japan's overseas aid furthers major Western (especially American) causes. Japan, for example, has no vital strategic interest in Afghanistan, yet it has provided Afghanistan with US$120 million. It did so to support American objectives in Afghanistan, in solidarity with other Western countries. If Japan's GDP is added to the Western share of the global GDP, the share rises from 62.6 percent to 72.7 percent.

If the Japanese corporations in the list of *Fortune* 500 are listed together with the other Western corporations, the Western share of the list jumps from 369 to 439.[13] This adds another US$3.2 billion in revenue to the share of Western corporations.[14] Since many Japanese corporations also have a vested interest in preserving a good image in the West (and to counter the predatory image that developed in America in the 1980s, seen, for example, in Michael Crichton's novel *Rising Sun*), they make large donations to Western universities, museums, think tanks, and other cultural and educational institutions. At Babson College, one of the top business schools in the United States, for example, the chair of Commerce and Electronic Business is endowed by Toyota. There is a Mitsubishi Heavy Industries Chair in Japanese Studies in the Department of Asian Studies at the University of Texas at Austin and a Toyota Visiting Professorship at the University of Michigan. The Mitsui Chair was established in 1980 at MIT to encourage cultural and technological exchange between the United States and Japan.

This wave of corporate philanthropy began back in September 1972, when Professor Jerome A. Cohen of Harvard Law School announced that Mitsubishi Heavy Industries was donating US$1 million to support a professorship in East Asian legal studies. In June 1973 the Sumitomo Group announced a grant of US$2 million to Yale University. The following month, Japanese Prime Minister Kakuei Tanaka announced during a visit to the White House that the government of Japan would follow the private sector donations to American higher education with significant grants of its own. A Foreign Ministry official later confirmed that ten of the most prominent American centers of Japanese studies had been selected to receive grants of US$1 million each. They were Harvard, Yale, Princeton, Columbia, Berkeley,

Chicago, Hawaii, Michigan, Stanford, and Seattle. The geographic distribution of the grants was hardly accidental.

Koji Asai, former chair of Sumitomo Bank, told the *New York Times* that Sumitomo's gift to Yale was made after the eruption of bilateral trade friction in the 1970s and was intended to promote friendly relations and "to promote Japanese-American cultural understanding."[15] However, the Japanese also realized that to be accepted as a member of the Western community, a community they yearned to belong to, they had to be seen supporting some of the most prestigious and revered Western institutions, especially the great universities. A Japanese Ministry of Education spokesman admitted to a *Times* reporter that Japanese gifts were intended to correct Japan's image as an "economic animal."[16] To join the dominant Western club, Japan was prepared to pay homage to a variety of Western values and to be seen doing so.

Within the West's economic castle is a particular citadel: banking and currency trading. Most of the hundreds of billions of dollars accumulated by the oil-rich Arab countries, for example, have been deposited in and managed by Western banks. In the list of the ten largest banks in the world, there are three American, four European, and three Japanese banks.[17] Similarly, the list of top ten investment banks in the world includes seven American, two European, and one Japanese bank.[18] It could be argued that the ownership of these banks is irrelevant. Their mission is to serve the interests of their customers, not the countries they are registered in. Under normal circumstances, this may be true. In a crisis, however, they are responsive both to their primary regulatory institutions and to their own governments. This is why American banks cooperated with the American government in rescuing Mexico twice in the two debt crises of August 1982 and January 1995. I was present at a small private dinner discussion among New York bankers and accountants in the mid-1980s. The accountants said that by strict accounting standards they should have called on these banks to write off their loans to Mexico. But the New York Federal Reserve leaned on the accounting firms not to impose their normal standards.

The responses of Western banks to the Asian Financial Crisis were no less revealing. When Thailand was in crisis, no pressure was put on Western financial institutions to lend a helping hand. Thailand was not considered strategic in terms of American interests. However, when South Korea began to totter, Washington became really worried. Consequently, all the Western institutions that had made loans to South Korea received phone calls from the US Treasury "advising" them not to pull out. These phone calls saved South Korea. The episode demonstrated how "independent" Western financial institutions could serve US interests.

The enormous power that America wields through its ability to manage and control the world's largest financial institutions was put on full display when *Time* did a cover story entitled "The Committee to Save the World." The magazine cover showed three men standing side by side: Alan Greenspan, the head of the Federal Reserve, Robert Rubin, the treasury secretary, and Larry Summers, the deputy treasury secretary. *Time* accurately described how the three were able to manage and control the global financial system to prevent the effects of the Asian Financial Crisis from reaching American shores:

In late-night phone calls, in marathon meetings and over bagels, orange juice and quiche, these three men—Robert Rubin, Alan Greenspan and Larry Summers—are working to stop what has become a plague of economic panic. Their biggest shield is an astonishingly robust US economy. Growth at year's end was north of 5 percent—double what economists had expected—and unemployment is at a 28-year low. By fighting off one collapse after another—and defending their economic policy from political meddling—the three men have so far protected American growth, making investors deliriously, perhaps delusionally, happy in the process.

It has meant some very difficult decisions. In some of the nations devastated by the crisis, there is a growing anti-US backlash, and politicians such as Mahathir Mohamad complain that Rubin, Greenspan and Summers—and their henchmen at the International Monetary Fund—have turned nations like Malaysia and Russia into leper colonies by isolating them from global capital and making life hellish in order to protect US growth. The three admit they've made hard choices—but they still believe that a strong US economy is the last, best hope for the world.[19]

THE ROLE OF WESTERN UNIVERSITIES

Banks may be the clearest defenders of Western interests— they have a financial obligation to do so—but the corresponding citadel of Western values rests in the West's traditional intellectual institutions and in particular its universities. The especially great American and European universities during the Cold War lived up to their claim of promoting the highest values of Western civilization: a belief in the equality of humankind; a belief in the spirit of free and open inquiry, free from all cultural prejudices; a belief in sharing the virtues of Western education with all segments of humanity and not confining it to Western citizens. No wonder the brightest minds from all over the world chose to go to Western—especially American—universities.

In being true to these core Western values, American universities have served not just the interests of Western society but also the interests of humankind. In doing so, they have played a paradoxical role. On the one hand, by demonstrating that Western institutions can serve the global interests of humanity, they help to bolster the belief that Western values and interests are aligned with universal values and interests. American and other Western universities do more than any other Western institutions to support the belief that Western civilization is indeed a universal ideal.

On the other hand, the Western universities have also done more than any other Western institutions to spark the rise of other civilizations. By opening their doors to hundreds of thousands of non-Western citizens, especially young Asians, they have educated the generation that is leading the renaissance of Asian civilizations. Strictly speaking, if the West wanted to maintain its current domination of the world order, it should have limited access to its universities. The fact that this thought did not even cross Western minds provides vivid proof that Western values, especially the belief that education spreads enlightenment, can trump more partisan Western interests. In real terms, the great Western universities serve as the heritage of humankind.

Western universities also help to legitimize Western power. They add substance to the claim that the West has a "civilizing" mission. There is a deeply held belief in the West that the spread of Western ideas and influence has had a positive influence in the world, even if in the end the acceptance of these ideas leads to a revolt against the West: "Here lies the deepest irony of post-Western history: it is so often in the name of Western values that the West is rejected and it is always with its skills and tools that its grasp is shaken off. Western values and assumptions have been internalized to a remarkable degree in almost every other culture."[20] This "internalization" has meant that many in the rest of the world (with the possible exception of the Islamic world) do not see the acceptance of Western values and assumptions as a threat to them. Indeed, most Asian societies celebrate when their citizens flourish in Western universities. When Professors Amartya Sen of Harvard, Jagdish Bhagwati of Columbia, and Lord Meghanand Desai of the London School of Economics return to New Delhi, they are welcomed as heroes.

WESTERN LEGITIMACY AND THE G-7

This perceived legitimacy of Western power may well be one of its greatest strengths. It is remarkable that even though 12 percent of the world's population dominates global institutions and uses them to further Western interests (sometimes at the expense of global interests), this exercise of Western power continues most of the time to be perceived as "legitimate" in the eyes of the other 88 percent of the world's population. It would be interesting to do an in-depth study of the sources of this legitimacy. This brief chapter can only provide some clues to those sources, not the full answers.

All processes of legitimization ultimately rest on a series of myths. Myths are the stories we use to understand the world. One myth, for example, that the West has perpetuated is that with the end of the Western colonial era, all other nation-states are now independent and free to shape their destiny. The real truth, of course, is that Western colonial domination ended, but Western political, economic, and cultural domination continued.

One global process that illustrates well how the West dominates the world is the G-7 process. In theory, this group only represents a collection of the seven most powerful economies of the world: the US, Germany, the UK, France, Canada, Italy, and Japan. After the Cold War ended, President Bill Clinton, in an effort to engage Russia, included Russia and made it G-8, but Russia is still not treated as a full equal of the original G-7. When these G-7 leaders meet once a year, their meetings should be of interest only to the citizens of their own countries.

Yet, because of the Western domination of global media, each G-7 meeting is treated and reported as a major global event. Often the meetings accomplish nothing; nonetheless there are copious media reports of the statements issued and a tremendous amount of photo coverage. At each meeting the G-7 leaders issue statements that touch on every major global challenge of the day: poverty, AIDS, global warming, terrorism, Africa, etc. These pretentious global statements and massive media coverage create the myth that these seven leaders represent the true leadership of the world. They have also created a secondary myth that when the G-7 leaders meet, they are only interested in meeting global challenges, not promoting their selfish national interests.

Any objective audit of the G-7 process will show that it has effectively done nothing to improve the state of the world. Indeed, the G-7 may have in some instances done some real damage by creating the illusion that they were actually tackling global challenges. Take the case of Africa. For over twenty years, the G-7 leaders have issued countless pronouncements that they are deeply concerned with the state of Africa and have made countless pledges to help Africa. After two decades of such pronouncements, Africa is not much better off. What would it take for the G-7 leaders to admit that their pronouncements on Africa and several other global challenges have had no positive results?

The Western media (which prides itself on being critical and on exposing corruption) has not exposed the failure of the G-7 process to handle global challenges, nor has it admitted its own role in legitimizing the G-7 process by creating the illusion that the G-7 was dedicated to helping the world. Their coverage of the G-7 illustrates the effective role the Western media has played in helping to legitimize the Western domination of global processes.

This perceived legitimacy of Western global domination should have been regarded as a precious asset to be preserved, not demolished, by the West. Unfortunately, in the hubris that enveloped it after the end of the Cold War, the West began to attack some of the very institutions through which the West exercised domination. In the 1990s the US Congress, for example, launched a sustained campaign to cripple the UN by withholding financial payment. But if the UN is destroyed, the UN Security Council dies with it, and the West will have lost one of the most powerful pillars that sustain its dominance.

This hubris also led in the 1990s to the end of long-term strategic thinking in the West. In an earlier chapter I quoted Willy Claes, the former Belgian foreign minister, who said that with the demise of the Soviet Union, there were only two superpowers left in the world: the United States and the European Union. It is therefore hugely ironic that in the almost two decades since the end of the Cold War, both the US and the EU have stumbled geopolitically, with the EU making far more missteps. Both the US and the EU now face a more insecure future, even though they have had two decades to enhance their security without any obvious challenge to them.

Chapter 5 will provide some concrete examples of Western mismanagement in the geopolitical sphere. But its core source is the fundamental assumption in the West that with its triumph at the end of the Cold War, the West would not need to make any major strategic adjustments. The rest of the world had to adjust to the emergence of the two new superpowers, the United States and the European Union. But the new superpowers could proceed on automatic pilot.

The past twenty years have probably seen some of the greatest changes in human history. The biggest shift is that the 88 percent of the world's populations who live outside the West have stopped being objects of world history and have become subjects. They have decided to take control of their own destinies and not have their destinies determined by Western-dominated global processes and institutions. They believe that the time has come for the West to cease its continuing domination of the globe.

Sadly, despite this huge shift in history, Western intellectual life continues to be dominated by those who continue to celebrate the supremacy of the West, not by those who say that the time has come for the West to give up its global domination and share power gracefully. Power is rarely ceded easily. It is perfectly natural to resist any transfer of power. The West will find it difficult. First, there is a near-universal refusal by most Western minds to acknowledge that the West dominates and controls the world in order to serve Western interests. If you deny you are in power, you cannot cede power. Second, there is an even more deeply held belief in Western minds that Western civilization represents the apex of human civilization, and that any alternative would portend a new dark age. Any people who believe this must also believe they have a moral duty to preserve the supremacy of Western civilization. They cannot conceive that a better world could emerge without Western supremacy.

The era of Western domination has run its course, bringing both good as well as harm and destruction to human history. It is futile for the 12 percent of the world's population who live in the West to imagine they can determine the destinies of the remaining 88 percent, many of whom feel newly energized and empowered. For now, the majority is willing to work with the West. However, if the West tries to continue its domination, a backlash is inevitable.

This is why humankind stands at a critical crossroads of history. So far, the West has refused either to admit its domination of the world or to contemplate sharing power in a new world order. This is a prescription for eventual disaster. In the short term—that is to say, now—it will produce a progressive delegitimization of Western power, accompanied by a matching cultural backlash. We have entered the turbulent era of de-Westernization.

4

DE-WESTERNIZATION:
THE RETURN OF HISTORY

Sometimes the hardest things to see are the largest things.

At the height of Western power, when Western influence extended into virtually every corner of the world, the West essentially wrapped the globe with several layers of Western influence. The enormity of Western power made the world believe that there was only one way forward. Yukichi Fukuzawa, one of the Meiji period's most enlightened intellectuals, said to his fellow Japanese, "Our immediate policy, there-fore, should be to lose no time in waiting for the enlightenment of our neighbouring countries in order to join them in developing Asia, but rather to depart from their ranks and cast our lot with the *civilized countries* of the West"[1] (emphasis added).

At the other end of Asia, Kemal Ataturk, the great Turkish leader who ruled Turkey from 1923 to 1938, also believed that Turkey should join the Western world. He expressed this in symbolic terms by calling on his fellow Turks to abandon specifically Muslim head-gear: "The fez sat upon our heads as a sign of ignorance, fanaticism, obstacle to progress and attaining a contemporary level of civilization. It is necessary to abolish the use of the fez and adopt in its place the hat, the headgear used by the *whole civilized world*"[2] (emphasis added).

Both Fukuzawa and Ataturk, together with many of their contemporary Asians, believed that the West represented the ideal they should aspire to. The belief was held as strongly by non-Western minds as by Western ones. Even Sun Yat-sen, the great Chinese reformer in the early twentieth century, said, "We, the modern people of China, are all useless, but if in the future we use Western civilization as a model, we can easily turn weakness into strength, and the old into the new."[3]

Amartya Sen explained how the British taught Indians to devalue their own culture. He cites the 1817 classic *The History of British India*, in which James Mill, an official of the East India Company, disputed and dismissed practically every claim ever made on behalf of Indian culture and its intellectual traditions, concluding that it was totally primitive and rude. This diagnosis reflected Mill's general attitude toward India: he believed that a rather barbaric nation was being uplifted under the benign and reformist administration of the British Empire. Consistent with his beliefs, Mill was an expansionist in dealing with the remaining independent states in the subcontinent. The obvious policy to pursue, he explained, was "to make war on those states and subdue them."[4] Katherine Mayo wrote *Mother India*, which was first published in 1927, to generate support in America for British rule in India. It "added contemporary and lurid detail to the image of Hindu India as irredeemably and hopelessly impoverished, degraded, depraved, and corrupt."[5] Mahatma Gandhi reacted strongly to Katherine Mayo's book, saying, "But the impression it leaves on my mind is that it is the report of a drain inspector sent out with the one purpose of opening and examining the drains of the country to be reported upon, or to give a graphic description of the stench exuded by the opened drains. If Miss Mayo had confessed that she had come to India merely to open out and examine the drains of India, there would perhaps be little to complain about her compilation. But she declared her abominable and patently wrong conclusion with a certain amount of triumph: 'the drains are India.'"[6]

The belief in Western superiority spread effortlessly. In 1835 Lord Macaulay (who, to be fair, did a good job of introducing British education into India) said that English should be the language of instruction for Indians because the historical information found in all the books written in Sanskrit was less valuable than even "the most paltry abridgements used at preparatory schools in England."[7] Almost a century later, in 1923, the great English novelist D. H. Lawrence said, "I become more and more surprised to see how far higher, in reality, our European civilization stands than the East, Indian and Persian, ever dreamed of. . . . This fraud of looking up to them—this wretched worship-of-Tagore attitude—is disgusting."[8] He also added, "It is ridiculous to look to the East for inspiration. . . . One always felt irked by the East coming over us. It is sheer fraud. The East is marvelously interesting—for tracing our steps back. But for going forward, it is nothing. All it can hope for is to be fertilized by Europe, so that it can start on a new phase."[9]

In 2008 the belief in Western moral superiority continues in the West, even though it is usually not expressed explicitly. I encountered a rare expression of honesty when I attended the Seoul Forum and was a panelist with a well-known German political scientist, Karl Kaiser. In his essay "Big Power Relations in the Twenty-First Century" Kaiser wrote, "NATO's action [in Kosovo], though not technically legal, was considered legitimate by all civilized countries and also followed norms contained in other international conventions."[10] The phrase "all civilized countries" was telling. He did not explicitly say that he referred only to Western countries, but in context the meaning and reference were clear.

Such unthinking pro-Western reflexes are shifting on a tectonic scale. Increasingly, the 5.6 billion people who live outside the West no longer believe in the innate or inherent superiority of Western civilization. Instead, many are actually beginning to question whether the West remains the most *civilized* part of the world. What we are witnessing today in effect is the progressive unwrapping of these many layers of Western influences.

The unraveling of Western influence is a complex process. It has many different strands. The West has to understand that this is the major historical trend of our time, that it defines our era. I sometimes feel a little sad when I pick up the leading newspapers and journals of the West and read their analyses of the state of the world. A favorite phrase used by the *New York Times* and *Financial Times*, the *Economist* and *Time* is "the view of the international community." They have this mythical belief that there exists an "international community" that shares the views and perceptions of the West. I once asked the writer and broadcaster William Shawcross whom he was referring to when he spoke of the "international community." After some reflection, he admitted that he was referring to those who lived in the West almost exclusively. It is less a global community of opinion than a self-selecting club.

The rest of the world has moved on. A steady delegitimization of Western power and influence is underway, spurred by a growing perception that while Western societies talk of global needs and interests in their speeches and declarations (read any G-7 declaration), the West will readily sacrifice global needs to satisfy domestic interests. Examine EU policies on foreign aid. Total EU foreign aid in 2005 was €8 billion (US$11.5 billion), but it spent €49 billion (US$70.8 billion) on agricultural subsidies,[11] nullifying virtually all the beneficial effects of its foreign aid. This is hypocrisy, and it is painfully visible. In Turkey, which has long had a tradition of being one of the most pro-Western states and is still trying to join the EU, any politician who argues that the West is best will get into political trouble. I know from personal experience how anti-American Turkey has become. In July 2006 the *Financial Times* reviewed my previous book, *Beyond the Age of Innocence*, and called it "anti-American." A few weeks later, I met with my Turkish publisher to find out when my book would appear in Turkish. She told me, "The mood in Turkey is anti-American. Your book is so pro-American that we dare not publish it in Turkey." A book deemed anti-American by the *Financial Times* was too pro-American to be published in Turkey: that is how sharp the divide has become.

The process of de-Westernization is much deeper than the story of anti-Americanism. The Western media has noticed anti-Americanism; Pew and Zogby surveys have also documented the rising levels of anti-Americanism in the world. But many in the West want to believe that this bout of anti-Americanism is just a passing phase caused by the harsh and insensitive policies of one administration. When the Bush administration leaves, all will change, and the world will go back to loving America. The West will be revered again. All will be well.

This is a mirage. The mindsets of the largest populations within Asia—the Chinese, the Muslims, and the Indians—have been changed irrevocably. Where once they may have happily borrowed Western lenses and Western cultural perspectives to look at the world, now, with growing cultural self-confidence, their perceptions are growing further and further apart.

CHINA

China has traveled the furthest the fastest. Few Chinese intellectuals are prepared to acknowledge openly the degree to which their minds were colonized by the West. Professor Wu Zengding is one exception, and he has written candidly and brutally about the Western colonization of the Chinese mind:

Since the late Qing dynasty, under the growing strength of the West, Chinese intellectuals gradually lost confidence in Chinese civilization. Stemming from a strong sense of humiliation and loss of self-esteem, they endlessly vilified Chinese culture and civilization, regarding it as a hotbed of evils and believing it to be several thousand years of "barbaric history" that several thousands of years of Confucian history was but a form of dark feudal autocracy. In their view, nothing in China qualified as "civilization" in the first place because China did not have freedom, democracy, science, rational thought or "God." These Chinese intellectuals on one hand subverted and de-constructed the myth of Chinese civilization, while on the other, beautified and deified Western civilization, fabricating one myth after another of Western civilization. But in all this, the greatest myth was believing that Western civilization was the authentic universal civilization just because it spent two thousand years in the pursuit of freedom, democracy, science, humanity, truth and God.

The Chinese intellectuals are caught in an embarrassing situation. They have artificially constructed a myth of Western civilization to replace the real truth of Western civilization. But then they do not realize that herein lies the real myth of the West. What the Chinese intellectuals have imagined to be Western civilization is in fact a manufactured product. For centuries, the West has concocted many myths, the biggest myth it concocted being: The West is the true civilization, while non-Westerners are savages. It is not surprising that modern Western political thinkers, in constructing a concept of nation, without exception, juxtapose the two concepts of "state of nature" and "civilized society." In their view, the "state of nature" represents barbarism, ignorance and disorder, while "civilized society" of course means civilization, rationality and order. In historic terms, the "state of nature" has expanded continuously from representing the Native American peoples in the seventeenth century to encompass the African people in the eighteenth century, and ultimately to include Indians, Chinese and other Eastern people in the nineteenth century. Suffice to say that in Western eyes, non-Western people are barbaric in nature, the West being the only true civilization; thus since the barbarians need to be "brought to order" by a rational and civilized society, the domination of the West and the subjugation of the non-West is perfectly justified.[12]

Wu Zengding's views represent the new wave of Chinese thinking. Having met several Chinese intellectuals over the past decade, I could not help noticing their increasing cultural confidence with each passing year. Even if some of them might not agree with Professor Wu's denunciation of Western colonization of the Chinese mind, many would agree with the conclusion Professor Wu reached in his article:

The construction of new China, the great achievements in reform and opening up for over twenty years is a further manifestation of the vitality of Chinese civilization. Thus the success of over twenty years of reform and opening up firstly affirms the great revolution and the construction of China, it then also affirms the strength of the Chinese nation, but mostly it affirms the authenticity of the Chinese civilization and tradition. It is this strength rather than some song and dance in praise of globalization and international practices that has brought China through. This is not a form of narrow-minded xenophobia, but it is the great faith and hope one can place in the ancient Chinese civilization.[13]

This dissolving of the myth of Western superiority represents one dimension of the de-Westernization process in China. But there are other dimensions as well. One other reason for the growing distance between Western and Chinese intellectual discourse on the state of China is the inability of many in the West to understand the new realities of China. A profound revival of China's civilization is occurring. Many in the West cannot even conceive of this because in their view an "unfree" society like China cannot possibly be progressing.

This Western incapacity to see how happy most Chinese are with their current condition reveals how ideologically biased Western observers have become. The Western mind cannot conceive of the possibility that the "unfree" people of China could possibly be happy.

The Western mind has a rigid, one-dimensional, and ideological understanding of the term "freedom."

In the eyes of the West, freedom (a word often written with a capital F) is seen as an absolute virtue. It has to be complete for it to be effective; to speak of any people being "half free" is as ludicrous as saying someone is "half pregnant." The idea that freedom can be relative and can indeed take many forms is alien. But for the Chinese, in real terms—if they compare their lives today with their lives a few decades ago—they have achieved much greater freedom.

Instead of being a simple or unified condition, the notion of "human freedom" can have many layers. In practical terms, most human beings, especially those who live in poor developing societies, can distinguish between these layers. One way of illustrating these layers is to apply them to the people of China, who are perceived in the West as being "unfree."

The fundamental layer of human freedom is freedom from want. A human being who cannot feed himself or his family cannot possibly be free. Famine is more damaging to human freedom than a politically closed society. To tell people who are struggling to stay alive that they are "free" because a distant despotic ruler has been removed will appear meaningless to them. In terms of their daily lives, "freedom" will come with liberation from the fight for survival. In this sense, the Chinese people have never enjoyed greater human freedom. The large populous society of China has suffered famines for centuries. Hundreds of millions have lived under harsh brutish conditions, struggling to find food to feed their families. As a result of China's rapid growth over the last three decades, the number of people living in absolute poverty (under the UN definition) has fallen spectacularly from six hundred million people to slightly more than two hundred million. These four hundred million people who have been rescued from absolute poverty have never felt freer (while still living under the rule of the CCP, whose policies have delivered this freedom to them).

Then follows freedom of security. The only way to enjoy freedom is to stay alive. Dead people enjoy no freedom. Any society that creates higher conditions of security improves the real and practical freedoms that people can enjoy, while a society that diminishes personal security also diminishes human freedom. This is why many people of Iraq find it hard to believe that they are now enjoying greater freedom than they did under the rule of Saddam Hussein, even though it was harsh and oppressive. The chance of a random death from roving trigger-happy militias or roadside bombs was remote under Saddam's rule. Most citizens could walk the street of Baghdad without fear of losing their lives. Remarkably, three and a half years after the American invasion and occupation of Iraq, no one can feel safe flying into the airport or driving from the airport to the city. By contrast, the citizens of Beijing have never enjoyed as much personal security as they do now. The people of Baghdad would love to go to Beijing. The people of Beijing have no desire to go to Baghdad. So where is there greater human freedom?

A third layer of freedom is the freedom to choose one's employment. The spread of this layer of freedom was the critical reason why the Industrial Revolution was so liberating for the masses in Europe. Before the Industrial Revolution the European peasants had no choice but to work as serfs or near-serfs for their feudal landlords. With the arrival of the Industrial Revolution, followed by the modern capitalist economy, all those at the bottom end of the social ladder suddenly discovered opportunities to leave the countryside and find jobs in cities. Millions migrated to the cities in search of a better life. The first wave of liberation felt by European workers came with the ability to choose their own jobs.

Similarly, the rapid economic growth of China has been equally liberating for hundreds of millions of Chinese workers. They no longer feel tied to the harsh working conditions of Chinese agriculture. Millions have migrated to the cities. Between 2000 and 2005, the urban population has increased by over 100 million to 527 million (or 40 percent of the total population), with much of the increase coming from rural-urban migration.[14] Yet when the Western media portrayed these new Chinese workers, they described the working conditions as terrible. The factories that made Nike shoes, in particular, were vilified for employing young girls at extremely low wages to produce their shoes. The age of most employed girls was in the range of sixteen to twenty-two; women older than twenty-five were considered too old and sent back to their home provinces. Most workers earned around US$40 a month, including overtime and bonuses.[15] Yet for these young girls, these miserly low wages were higher than what they could earn in their villages. Working in air-conditioned rooms was also far more comfortable than tilling the soil in the harsh sun. There were also important social freedoms that came from moving out of their tiny peasant homes to urban quarters. This is why millions of Chinese men and women *chose* to move to new occupations. They found the move liberating.

The freedom to choose one's occupation is a freedom that most Westerners now take for granted. Yet in the three thousand years of continuous Chinese civilization, the broad Chinese masses have effectively begun to enjoy this freedom only in the last thirty years, a mere 1 percent of the time line of Chinese civilization. Viewed from this perspective, one can understand why hundreds of millions feel this great sense of liberation with the arrival of free-market economics. Many have begun to leave their provinces for the first time ever and are also enjoying a higher standard of living than any of their ancestors ever had. Many have also begun to travel. Indeed, in numerous Chinese tourist destinations, it is sometimes difficult to find space to walk because millions of Chinese are now visiting places like the Great Wall of China, when once only thousands of Chinese did.

The ability to choose their occupations has been immensely liberating. The Chinese enjoyed none of these freedoms during their three thousand years of dynastic history. Nor did they enjoy it during the brief and chaotic Republican rule of China from 1911 to 1949 or during Mao's rule from 1949 to 1976. It was only when Deng Xiaoping opened the Chinese economy in 1978 that the Chinese people began to enjoy these freedoms.

In January 1979 Deng Xiaoping paid an official visit to the United States. He was received by President Jimmy Carter, who told him that Congress had passed the Jackson-Vanik Amendment in 1974, which allowed normal trade relations only with countries that allowed free emigration. Congress had passed this legislation in an effort to put pressure on the Soviet Union to allow free emigration of Jews. Deng listened impassively as President Carter made his passionate case for the right of free emigration. When President Carter finished, Deng asked him, "How many Chinese would you like me to allow to emigrate to the US? One million? Ten million? A hundred million? You can have as many as you want." His response was enough. President Carter did not push his point any further.

The "hundred million" Chinese Carter could not accept in America were not kept captive. Instead, many experienced a real improvement in their lives. This happened because China adopted the principles of free-market economics that America had preached to the world. America had effectively "liberated" hundreds of millions of Chinese, even though they were still perceived to be technically held captive by the CCP. Over the years, the CCP also loosened the controls on foreign travel. Thus today millions of Chinese travel overseas. Whereas in 1992 only 2.93 million Chinese traveled abroad (most as part of government delegations), a little more than a decade later, in 2006, the number increased to 34.52 million Chinese visiting foreign destinations. From January to March 2007, the number had already reached 9.7 million travelers, a 14.5 percent increase from the same period in 2006.[16] Miraculously, they return freely to their land of "no freedom."

Then comes the freedom from arbitrary arrest and detention, coupled with adherence to the rule of law in a society. This is a relatively new right, even in Western societies. This notion of equal human rights for all human beings was a product of the Enlightenment. In the feudal era, serfs enjoyed no equal rights. Indeed, they had very few rights at all. Many were arbitrarily caught, flogged, and sometimes beheaded for not obeying their feudal masters. This was the norm in European societies until about two centuries ago.

Americans can justifiably take pride in having the longest surviving democracy. The US Declaration of Independence, written in 1776, spoke eloquently of the equal rights of "men." Yet it took America almost a century after it declared independence to free its slaves; it takes time to change social and political norms. This also explains why it took another century for the US to give its black population the full set of civil rights promised in the Constitution. Indeed, almost two hundred years after the great constitution promulgated the notion of equal rights, blacks were not allowed to sit at the front of a bus in the South.

America is a new society, while Chinese society has a continuous history of at least three thousand years. It should not be surprising to see China taking a longer time to implement the same rights that Americans only began to fully enjoy in the twentieth century. This is at least part of the reason why many Chinese still do not enjoy in full the freedom from arbitrary arrest that people in most modern societies enjoy. In theory, China enjoys the same rule of law found in other modern societies. Indeed, the Chinese government has made a concerted effort to understand how the rule of law works in other countries. Thousands of Chinese judges and lawyers have been sent for training overseas. The Chinese government also realizes that no modern economy can function without effective rule of law. If China, for example, cannot provide the same property rights enjoyed by other modern societies, that fact alone will eventually stifle China's economic development.

There is no doubt that in developing greater respect for the rule of law, China will eventually have to resolve a fundamental political contradiction. In most modern nations, the rule of law is sacrosanct. In theory (and often in practice, as President Richard Nixon discovered), no person, not even a president or prime minister, is above the rule of law in Western society. In China, the CCP still remains above the rule of law. Chinese leaders believe that this is necessary to retain political control and stability. But it could also become in due course a check on China's economic development. In this layer of human freedom, China has some distance to travel.

Another expression of human freedom is the freedom to think. Here Chinese society may appear to be at a disadvantage: China remains a politically closed society. But in one of the typical paradoxes of our modern times, China is in social and intellectual terms an increasingly open society. The dictates of modern economics demand that Chinese traders, entrepreneurs, and bankers must have the same access to global information flows that their economic competitors in other modern societies have. At the same time, modern technology, especially the proliferation of access to the Internet, has made it difficult to cut off the flow of information. Indeed, Internet usage is probably growing faster in China than in most other countries. Some estimates suggest that Mandarin may soon replace English as the most widely used language on the Web.

Most Westerners cannot see a distinction between freedom to think and freedom of expression. They see these two freedoms as two sides of one coin. The Chinese can see and feel the distinction. In many areas, their freedom of expression remains limited. However, they are also aware that in the past few centuries they have never enjoyed greater freedom to think. Chinese universities now have the same look and feel as modern American or European campuses.

Two American academics, Yasheng Huang of MIT's Sloan School of Management and Tarun Khanna of Harvard Business School, wrote an essay on the comparative performance of the Chinese and Indian economies. The reactions to their essay in China and India clearly showed the different nature of the intellectual climate that prevailed in these two societies.

The reactions to an earlier article we wrote about the comparative development models (Huang and Khanna 2003) were different in

China and India. These reactions offer clues of likely developments in the two countries. Indian reactions were instantaneous. Groups of Indian entrepreneurs report to us, via e-mail, that they had set up reading groups to discuss the article. Audiences of policy-makers, businesspeople, trade associations, and universities in India and among the Indian diaspora, asked for one or the other of us to present the paper. Clearly, ideas, especially those ideas with an edge, traveled quickly, far and wide in a society with the benefit of a free press.

The initial Chinese reactions were hesitant and even hostile. At least one major Chinese university was exceedingly cautious about allowing a discussion of the argument on campus, pleading reasons of sensitivity. But once Chinese censors decided to publish the piece, on 11 November 2003, on Chinanews.com, an official website run by the Xinhua News Agency, the initially hesitant reactions became a torrent. The university which had objected to the piece immediately dropped its complaint. There were four or five translations of the article appearing in publications ranging from current events journals to serious scholarly outlets. These different reactions are emblematic of the untrammeled flow of information in India and the relatively constrained availability of information in China.

Another reaction to the piece, however, reflects China in a far better light than India. The Chinese reactions, so far, have been more reflective and methodical than those that we have seen in India. A number of Chinese bureaucrats, armed with data and fact sheets of both countries, discussed the paper in scholarly detail with one of us in Boston; clearly they were pre-pared to learn something from the exercise. The Chinese media discussions of the major points raised in our paper are serious in tone and more reflective. It could be a matter of sheer coincidence but the number of official study delegations from China to India, reported in the Chinese press, increased dramatically. Former Chinese ambassadors to India were sought out by the Chinese media for their impressions of the country. Some of the most prominent Chinese intellectuals, while reserving judgment on the conclusion of our article, all pointed out that there is a need to understand more about China's southern neighboring giant.

In contrast, the Indian reactions verged on self-indulgence. The Indian counterparts in government and media, we can only surmise, were far too blasé about the prospect of learning from engagements, or too self-congratulatory to let their rare moment in the sun be possibly eclipsed by academic scrutiny. The stars of the Indian political and bureaucratic firmament did not analyze the article to nearly the same depth as their Chinese counterparts.[17]

A prominent India academic, Pratap Bhanu Mehta, once described the difference between Chinese and Indian societies in simple terms. He said that China was a closed society with open minds while India was an open society with closed minds. In freedom of expression lies one of the greatest strengths of Western societies, if not their greatest competitive advantage. There is a general conviction among Western intellectuals that the capacity of Western thinkers to question dogma has played a critical role in the West's political and economic development.

The leaders of China must be aware that all their efforts to modernize China and bring it into the developed world could fail, if they do not introduce the virtues of freedom of expression into their body politic. Their reasons for hesitation are obvious. If they allow more freedom of expression in the political arena, a lot of questions could be asked about the legality or legitimacy of the rule of the CCP over China. (Curiously, if the leaders of China were to allow such a free debate, it could well result in a consensus that the CCP rule of China was legitimate because it had delivered massive improvements to the standard of living. A robust discussion of the strengths and weaknesses of the current national governance of China would show that no other recent rulers of China have been so benign in intent and impact.)

It may console the leaders of China to learn that despite all the claims to the contrary, the right to freedom of expression is not absolute—either in theory or in practice—in most Western societies. There are many topics that Western politicians do not touch on for fear of political consequences. (Of course, they do not fear imprisonment, only exile to the political wilderness.)

One such topic in the United States is gun control. In April 2007 a student at Virginia Tech, Cho Seung-hui, murdered thirty of his fellow students and two of his professors, and later killed himself; there was a huge outpouring of grief and condemnation, both in America and in the rest of the world. But in the context of the US presidential race none of the nearly two dozen declared or imminent candidates would say openly what virtually everyone outside of America said freely: the episode showed the American folly of allowing free sale of automatic weapons and the degree to which the powerful gun lobby had taken complete political control of the issue in Washington. While many Americans urge politicians in societies with relatively closed political systems to speak "truth to power," American politicians refrain from doing so when it can hurt their political careers. They do not have to fear going to jail; the consequence for them would be relatively minor. Nevertheless, American politicians carefully censor their remarks. Even in America, freedom has its limits.

The most important fact about Western societies is that no leader can stay in office without the explicit consent of the people, even if sometimes the need to listen to popular views—such as the argument in favor of gun ownership—leads to regressive political posturing. This one fact long separated Western societies from non-Western societies and gave Western societies a competitive advantage. The freedom to choose one's ruler is an important layer of freedom, one that all societies should aspire to have. Yet in another cruel paradox of our times, societies that wish to acquire this layer of freedom should aim to achieve it carefully.

Recent history has sadly demonstrated that a hasty and premature rush to democracy without careful preparations can lead to disaster. Slobodan Milosevic, like Adolf Hitler, was elected democratically. He unleashed ruin in the former Yugoslavia, especially for the Muslim populations of Bosnia and Kosovo (where the West is still reluctant to allow democratic self-rule). Most Chinese intellectuals are also acutely aware that China cannot succeed in its goal of becoming a modern developed society until it can take the leap and allow the Chinese people to choose their own rulers. This will be the most painful step that Chinese leaders will have to take. If Chinese leaders are only concerned about their personal welfare and fear losing power in democratic elections (as most communist parties have after the introduction of democracy), it will never happen. But if their main concern is national welfare and not personal welfare, anything is possible. Some of China's recent leaders have demonstrated that they are capable of sacrificing personal interests. When Zhu Rongji became premier of China in 1998, he is reported to have told his assistants to prepare a hundred coffins: ninety-nine for those he would have to slay in the course of introducing painful reforms into the Chinese body politic and the hundredth for him. He would be the victim of his own program. In the end, Zhu Rongji was not slain, but as soon as he left public office, he disappeared from public view. He gave up all of his personal power to avoid becoming a burden on his successors.

China's present leadership is acutely aware that eventually China will have to move to democracy. In October 2006, the president of the Brookings Institution, Strobe Talbott, and its chair, John Thornton, led a fifty-member US delegation to China to meet its leaders. This is what Thornton had to say about the trip:

The key moment of the trip was an unexpectedly in-depth, 75-minute conversation with Premier Wen Jiabao. Half way through the meeting, we asked Premier Wen for his views on the possibility of a democratic future for China. He replied immediately: "This is the most important question in our meeting today. I know you are very much interested in this subject; so am I." He proceeded to devote the remainder of the session to this one issue. Most striking was Wen's desire to engage in depth on the topic. "When we talk about democracy," he said, "we usually refer to three most important components: elections, judicial independence, and supervision based on checks and balances." Although Wen, as with all Chinese leaders, insisted that whatever form of democracy that eventually developed in China would not be a simple copy of western models, his description of the ultimate goals of pluralism still sounded far more familiar than not. He could foresee the direct elections currently held at the village level, if successful, gradually moving up to towns, counties, and even provinces. What happens beyond that was left unsaid. . . . For his part, Premier Wen simultaneously acknowledged the deficiencies of the current system and asked for patience from the West: "We have to move toward democracy. We have many problems, but we know the direction in which we are going." But in order to achieve these goals, Wen concluded, China needed three things above all: "peace, friends, and time."[18]

Overall, it would be wise for the West to stop drawing sharp lines between the "free" and the "unfree" societies. The Chinese people have never been freer. In several of the seven layers discussed above, they are much freer than they have ever been. Relative to their ancestors, they are the freest people China has ever had. As they look ahead to their future, they are confident and optimistic that things will improve. Can the West say the same?

As most Europeans look ahead to the future, they are becoming increasingly pessimistic. They have a genuine fear that some of their freedoms will diminish. Surrounded by a sea of anger in the Islamic world, with several European cities becoming targets of terrorist bombings, their sense of personal security has diminished. With the rise of China and India, most young Europeans fear that they will not be able to compete for jobs against their young Chinese and Indian counterparts. Instead of seeing themselves living on a rich and comfortable plateau, many young Europeans have begun to envy the Chinese and Indians, whose futures seem brighter than theirs.

Against this backdrop of growing Chinese optimism and increasing European pessimism, it is remarkable that some Western commentators say that China has not really achieved anything significant in recent decades. I have met and interacted with many Chinese and European policymakers. The Chinese minds are open, curious, and eager to learn. The European minds contain a paradoxical mix of cultural smugness and insecurity. Of the two, there is no doubt that the Chinese minds are willing to explore bold and innovative solutions. They are happy to think outside the box. Despite this remarkable new vitality in the Chinese mind, the Asia columnist and commentator for the *Financial Times*, Guy de Jonquières, wrote in 2006:

> Asia has no such marketplace for ideas. Stunning though China's growth is, it is impressive as a daring feat of execution, not because it is based on startlingly original development thinking. When "Asian values" were hawked around the region a decade or so ago as some kind of distinctive philosophy, they turned out to be just a self-serving attempt to justify autocracies.
>
> Novel ideas, by contrast, are stimulated by intellectual contention and reasoned dissent. It is no accident that they tend to flow freely in countries such as the US and Britain that not only tolerate but encourage those activities as socially beneficial.[19]

Given the increasing sophistication of Chinese political discourse, it is remarkable how few Western minds understand the scope and significance of the changes China has made. Not many Chinese are willing to speak openly about their frustration with Western pundits, who continue to try to paint China in black and white terms. One Chinese intellectual who is prepared to do so is Lu Yiyi, who writes:

> To unravel the China mystery, Western pundits need first to refine their outdated analytical framework. They have to realize that China has moved beyond the stage where its choices are so simple: either launch further reforms or reverse the course, either more liberalization or more control, either faster growth or more emphasis on stability, either democratize or maintain the authoritarian rule. Now all the contrary tendencies co-exist. If one policy appears to signal a shift in one direction, then there is always another policy which signals an opposite change.
>
> There is a reason behind this. These days specific policies are only intended to address specific issues. They are usually guided by pragmatic considerations rather than any set programme. To try to describe a broad trend from a few policies is misleading. The same goes for specific leaders.
>
> The Communist Party has passed the point of no return and is struggling with the new reality. Nowadays no leader is either a pure reformer or a pure hardliner. None of them thinks and acts in such simplistic terms. The multitude of challenges the country faces does not represent the political leaders with such clear-cut options any more.
>
> Against this background, Western pundits and the public need to start asking some different questions in order to improve their understanding of China. A good example is the issue of political reform. To be sure, no multi-party election has been introduced, nor is it likely to happen in the foreseeable future, but this does not mean political change is not taking place on a daily basis.
>
> Governance reform, if not systemic political reform, has accompanied economic reform since day one and has inevitable political consequences, even if unintended. For example, the organization of public hearings on the price of government-provided

services has encouraged public participation in decision-making, while rules to increase government transparency have contributed to a rise in public scrutiny of the government.

So while asking "if and when political reform will take place in China" gets one nowhere, asking what specific political changes have already occurred will lead to far greater knowledge of the political situation in China, making predictions on China's future political development far easier.

The mystery of China's future not only arises from the uncertainty of the subject matter itself, it is also partly caused by the crude lenses that have been used to view it. Even if we cannot solve the mystery completely, at least we will have a better chance if we sharpen our analytical tools.[20]

Lu Yiyi only discussed the increased complexity of the Chinese political scene, but he could have also spoken of a remarkable development: the rebirth and rejuvenation of one of the world's greatest civilizations. With improved economic performance and the accumulation of wealth, China is now experiencing the same sensation that the West did in its renaissance: connecting once again with its rich past and developing new cultural perspectives.

Museums and galleries are opening in China at an astonishing rate. According to an article in the *Independent*, 100 new museums will open in China before the Olympics in 2008, and in a move that recalls Chairman Mao's five-year plans, the authorities have announced that an incredible 1,000 new museums will be opened by 2015, by which time every significant city in China is expected to have a modern museum. Beijing already has 118 museums and plans to open and build a further 30 in time for the Olympics; Shanghai aims to open 100 new museums over the next four years. Xian, a key point city on the Silk Route and China's capital for more than eleven hundred years, has a world-class and thoroughly modernized museum, the Shaanxi History Museum. Located in a graceful Tang-style building and home to

373,000 cultural relics, the collection ranges from burial items from the early Shang and Zhou dynasties to unicorns from the fourth century BCE and pottery honor guards from the Ming era. The city is also home to China's first underground museum, the Han Yang Ling museum, featuring a world-class collection of relics from the Western Han dynasty.[21]

Ying Zhu, a scholar at the City University of New York, has also argued that trends in television reveal the new waves in Chinese culture. The Chinese people are fascinated by and are reconnecting with their history. Ying writes that

> since the mid-1990s, historical serials have dominated dramatic programming on primetime television in China. The trend climaxed in the late 1990s and the early 2000s with palace dramas, or what the Chinese critics termed "Qing dramas," set in the Qing dynasty (1644–1911). Qing dramas are not a new phenomenon, however. In fact, popular and critically acclaimed TV programs set in the palace of Qing began appearing on Chinese television in the late 1980s. . . . But while the Qing dramas of the 1980s focused on the corruption and cultural decline of the late Qing, those in the 1990s and the early 2000s . . . paid tribute to the prosperity and national unity of the early Qing.

Ying suggests that the famous 1999 TV series *Yongzheng Dynasty* "reminded the Chinese of their former premier, Zhu Rongji, who, by attempting to curb rampant government corruption, earned a reputation as a contemporary graft-buster. Zhu himself was reportedly an ardent follower of the show."[22]

China's efforts to rediscover its past and reconnect with it are likely to be exciting for both China and the world; it will bring about a massive change in international cultural chemistry. China is only just beginning this process of reconnecting with its past. To get a glimpse of what China will behave like when it becomes a rich and successful civilization, we need only to look back and see how China behaved during previous peaks of Chinese civilization. Six decades of communist rule has not changed the Chinese soul, which has developed over thousands of years of history. There is a rich and wondrous well of Chinese culture.

Many Chinese historians will agree that the greatest Chinese dynasty was the Tang dynasty. The period of the Tang dynasty (618–907 CE) is one of the "golden eras" in the history of China. The Chinese empire achieved unprecedented economic and cultural heights, made a number of important inventions, doubled in territory, and consolidated its political influence across the continent of Asia.

The Tang rulers welcomed foreign ideas, making Chang'an, the Tang capital, the most diverse city in the world. Merchants, clerics, and envoys from India, Persia, Arabia, Syria, Korea, and Japan thronged the streets of Chang'an, and foreign tongues were a common part of daily life. Under this period of Pax Sinica, the most important ancient trade route of that time, the Silk Route, reached its golden age, when Persian and Sogdian traders benefited from the exchange between West and East. In the beginning decades of the Tang dynastic rule, especially under the leadership of Emperor Taizong (627–650), China subdued its nomadic neighbors from the north and northwest, securing peace and safety on overland trade routes reaching as far as Syria and Rome. The seventh century was a time of momentous social change; the official examination system enabled educated men without family connections to serve as government officials. This new social elite gradually replaced the old aristocracy, and the recruitment of gentlemen from the south contributed to the cultural amalgamation that had already begun in the sixth century. When the Tang Dynasty was at its peak during the period 710 to 755, China was far ahead of any other contemporary civilization. Indeed, none even came close to matching its level of development.

A rejuvenation of Chinese civilization along the lines of the Tang dynasty would be a blessing for the world. This revived Chinese civilization would be open and cosmopolitan, not closed and insular. Indeed, a confident Chinese civilization may prove even more open and cosmopolitan than the insecure societies of the West. Already, China is doing a remarkable job of introducing the highlights of

Western culture to its population. While many orchestras and opera houses are struggling in Europe and the US, China, with an estimated thirty million piano students and ten million violin students, is on an opposite trajectory. Tests to enter the top conservatories now attract nearly two hundred thousand students a year, compared with a few thousand annually in the 1980s, according to the Chinese Musicians Association.[23] "I honestly think that in some real sense the future of classical music depends on developments in China in the next 20 years," said Robert Sirota, the president of the Manhattan School of Music. "They represent a vast new audience as well as a classical music-performing population that is much larger than anything we've had so far," he continued. "You're looking at a time when, maybe 20 to 40 years from now, Shanghai and Beijing are really going to be considered centers of world art music." According to Paavo Jarvi, music director of the Cincinnati Symphony Orchestra, "Mainland China has a tremendous sense going for it. There is something open. They are reaching out rather than holding back."[24]

The same is true with China and Western ballet. In the *Financial Times*, Clement Crisp writes:

> I make no bones about my admiration for the National Ballet, and my belief that great things in classical ballet have already been achieved, and that greater innovations and artistry will come from China. In its less than 60 years, including those marked by the politicizations of the Cultural Revolution, Chinese ballet has made strides no less amazing than those of the Royal Ballet from its first tender shoots in Ninette de Valois' 1926 Academy of Choreographic Art.[25]

THE ISLAMIC WORLD

If the Western mind finds it *difficult* to conceive of Chinese civilization emerging in an open and cosmopolitan way, it is now actually *impossible* for the Western mind to conceive of Islamic civilization reemerging as an open and cosmopolitan civilization. Indeed, while many Western minds might reluctantly concede that some kind of cultural rejuvenation is taking place in China, none believe that any kind of cultural revival is taking place in the Islamic world. Islam seems to be moving backwards.

Yet a process similar to that in China is likely to be replicated in many Islamic societies. The Islamic world has a diversity of cultures; it contains not one but many rich and ancient civilizations. Most Christians are of European extraction. By contrast, Arab Muslims (who founded Islam) now make up only one-sixth of the world's estimated 1.5 billion Muslims. The seven countries with the world's largest Muslim populations are Indonesia (200 million), India (144 million), Pakistan (140 million), Bangladesh (115 million), Nigeria (94 million), Turkey (66 million), and Iran (65 million).[26] None is an Arab country. Most Muslims live in South Asia and Southeast Asia, where the March to Modernity has already swept through. Indeed, while most Westerners now see the Islamic world as being culturally undifferentiated, this is not how Muslims see themselves. The Turks see themselves as Turks first and Muslims second; the Iranians also tend to prioritize their national identity over their religious one. This does not mean that there is a contradiction between the two identities. It is possible to feel proudly Turkish and proudly Muslim, but there is a question of what percentage of the soul is taken up by each identity.

Cultural identities are not static; they evolve over time, although some roots remain deep. There are obvious reasons for the Islamic soul to be troubled. On the one hand, by any measurement of religiosity, Muslims probably have a deeper commitment to their religion than the majority of contemporary Christians do. They believe that adherence to Islam should inform every aspect of their lives. Muslims are proud of their religion, which gives them cultural confidence. Yet thoughtful Muslims are also aware how poorly most Islamic societies are performing in the new economic era. Many believe that their poor economic performance has in turn led to the humiliation of the Islamic world by the West.

Many leading Islamic statesmen have said that Muslim societies should take responsibility for their own weak economic performances. At an Organization of the Islamic Conference (OIC) Summit in 2003, the former prime minister of Malaysia, Dr. Mahathir Mohammad (who has become infamous in the West for his anti-Western and anti-Israeli rhetoric), gave a speech to the Islamic heads of government that received a standing ovation—even though he was enormously self-critical of the Islamic world. He said,

> We are now 1.3 billion strong. We have the biggest oil reserve in the world. We have great wealth. We are not as ignorant as the Jahilliah who embraced Islam. We are familiar with the workings of the world's economy and finances. We control 57 out of 180 countries in the world. Our votes can make or break international organizations. Yet we seem more helpless than the small number of Jahilliah converts who accepted the Prophet as their leader. Why? Is it because of Allah's will or is it because we have interpreted our religion wrongly, or failed to abide by the correct teachings of our religion, or done the wrong things?[27]

A few years later, when King Abdullah of Saudi Arabia gave a speech to an Arab League meeting in Saudi Arabia in March 2007, he was equally self-critical:

> The question is: what have we done throughout these years to resolve all that [conflicts in Palestine, Iraq, Lebanon, Sudan and Somalia]? I do not want to blame the Arab League because it is an entity that reflects our conditions in detail, so the real blame should fall on us: we the leaders of the Arab nations. Our permanent differences, our refusal to take the path of unity—all of that led the nations to lose their confidence in our credibility and to lose hope in our present and future.[28]

King Abdullah's harsh indictment of Arab leaders "was taken by the Arabs as a breath of fresh air of self-criticism," said Nabil Fahmy, Egypt's ambassador to the United States. This slow change is being propelled mostly by two things: a young population—56 percent are twenty-five or younger—and growing media openness. "Our media is much more open than it ever was in years past," said Fahmy. "So you can't hide the issues. The issues are out there. There is change in the Arab world. Serious change. Is it late? Yes. Is it slow? Yes. But there is change. We need to nurture it more. We need to be wiser." Unfortunately, in the West, particularly in the United States, most of King Abdullah's speech went unnoticed, with the mainstream media focusing on the phrase "illegitimate foreign occupation."[29]

However, even though most thoughtful Muslim intellectuals acknowledge their own responsibilities and failures, they believe that the West has also contributed to their problems. Indeed, by any historical standard, the attitude of the Islamic world toward the West has never been more anti-Western. The global process of de-Westernization is taking place most powerfully in the Islamic world.

All this in turn is having a profound impact on Muslims' sense of cultural identity. The greater the disenchantment with the West, the greater they begin to believe in an Islamic identity as opposed to their own national or regional cultural identity. Malaysia is far from the Arabic lands where Islam originated; Islam arrived there only in the fourteenth century. Until recently Malays identified themselves as Malays first and Muslims second. However, in a 2006 survey conducted by the University of Malaya, it was found that Malaysian Muslims saw themselves as Muslims first, Malaysians second, and Malays third. Among those surveyed, 70 percent identified themselves as Muslims, 97 percent believed that Muslims should not be allowed to leave Islam, and 77 percent wanted stricter sharia laws.[30]

The West has long believed that the fruit of modernity would make societies more secular and less religious. In the Islamic world, modern communications—especially modern media (including Al Jazeera)—

have made Muslims more conscious of the suffering of other Muslims and sharpened their religious identities. Hence when Israel attacked Lebanon in August 2006, in response to the Hezbollah kidnapping of two Israeli soldiers, anti-American and anti-Israeli (and often anti-Western) demonstrations broke out in all corners of the Islamic world, not just in the Arab world. Most Western populations are unaware that the Arabs are a minority within the Muslim world, even though they dominate the Islamic narrative.

There may have been a time when Muslims idealized the West. The last great leader of any Muslim society to believe in the West with great fervor was probably Kemal Ataturk. He created a secular state that tried to emulate the West and strived to join Western civilization. Eighty-three years after he assumed power in 1923, Turkey is still knocking on the doors of Europe in an effort to be admitted as a member of the European Union. In theory Turkey is eligible to enter, but in practice it is not likely to happen. Turkey's exclusion from Europe shows the great civilizational divide between the West and Islam, even though Turkey has tried to demonstrate for several decades that (in J. M. Roberts's memorable phrase) "perhaps they are Westerners now."

Virtually no other society in the Islamic world is trying to demonstrate that "they are Westerners now." Throughout the Islamic world, the Islamist parties are gaining ground. In Pakistan a six-party alliance of militant Islamist groups won nearly seventy seats in the National Assembly in 2002; this was an increase of sixty-six seats since the 1997 parliamentary polls, when they won only four seats. The Islamists in Pakistan campaigned on three major election planks: a visceral anti-American platform, in which they called for the expulsion of all US forces from Pakistan; the acceleration of jihad in the Indian state of Kashmir; and the implementation of the sharia law. (But it must be stressed here that in Pakistan the Islamists will remain a minority.)

In the 2005 municipal elections in Saudi Arabia, one of America's close allies in the Middle East, informal Islamists won six of the seven seats in Riyadh and swept the elections in Jidda and Mecca. Candidates backed by Sunni Islamists also won control of the municipal councils in a number of towns in the Eastern Province. Another close US ally, Kuwait has seen the rise of Islamists in the country's politics: in 2003, Islamists combined to win seventeen of the fifty seats in the Kuwaiti parliament, where they form the dominant ideological bloc.

In Egypt's parliamentary elections in November and December 2005, the Egyptian Muslim Brotherhood won 88 seats, 20 percent of the 444 elected seats despite progressively greater government interference over the three rounds of balloting. That figure understates the significance of the Brotherhood's showing. The group had fielded only about a hundred fifty candidates as part of a tacit agreement with the government that allowed Brotherhood candidates to campaign openly. It won almost 60 percent of the seats it contested.

These signs of growing anti-Western views are further confirmed by several public opinion surveys in the Islamic world about attitudes toward America and the West. Anti-American sentiments in the Muslim world have reached surprisingly high levels, according to the 2006 poll results from Terror Free Tomorrow, a nonpartisan, nonprofit organization whose advisory board includes Senator John McCain and several members of the 9/11 commission. The organization had commissioned the wide-ranging poll on nuclear programs and anti-Western sentiment among Iran's neighbors. When asked how they viewed the United States, 89 percent in Saudi Arabia, 84 percent in the United Arab Emirates, 71 percent in Turkey, and 64 percent in Pakistan answered "unfavorable." Additionally, 66 percent of Pakistanis opposed the US-led war against terrorism. Ken Ballen, president of Terror Free Tomorrow and a former federal prosecutor and counsel to the Iran-Contra committee, said the poll results were "startling" and showed that radical anti-Western views were becoming the consensus in the Muslim world. The data also showed that large numbers of people in several of Iran's neighboring countries—including 70 percent in Pakistan—would favor a nuclear-armed Iran.[31]

According to the 2006 Pew Global Attitudes Project, which was carried out in thirteen Muslim countries, "Muslims in the Middle East and Asia generally see Westerners as selfish, immoral, and greedy—as well as violent and fanatical." With regards to relations between Muslims and Westerners, Turkey was the most negative of the predominantly Muslim nations, with nearly two-thirds opting for "generally bad"—although 77 percent of Nigerian Muslims made the same assessment—followed by Egypt (58 percent), Jordan (54 percent), and Indonesia (53 percent). The Pew analysis concluded that Muslims held "an aggrieved view of the West—they were much more likely than Americans or Western Europeans to blame Western policies for their own lack of prosperity."[32]

So what went wrong? This is where the Western and Islamic narratives diverge completely. In the Western narrative, once the Europeans ended their colonial rule of Islamic territories, from Morocco to Indonesia, they were no longer responsible for their future. The failure of most Islamic countries (with the possible exception of Turkey, Malaysia, and Indonesia) to successfully modernize (like, say, Japan or South Korea) only reflected the internal cultural weaknesses of Islamic societies. Secretly, many Westerners also believed that the inability of Islamic societies to separate religion from the state and embrace secularism was corrosive. They were privately critical of the treatment of women in Islamic societies. The continuation of feudal monarchies and social systems, especially in some Arab societies, was believed to be responsible for the failure of Islamic societies to develop. The Islamic world failed in the absence of the West's guiding influence.

Many Muslim intellectuals are ready to take responsibility for their own failures to develop. In three Arab Human Development Reports produced by the UN Development Program between 2002 and 2004, several Arab intellectuals pointed to their own failures. The 2002 report is openly critical of the performance of Arab regimes in many areas. It faults those regimes for allowing three interrelated deficits to develop: freedom, knowledge, and gender. For example, the report explains, "If development is understood as 'a process of expanding the real freedoms that people enjoy' then the challenge of human development, calculated to include variables associated with various forms of instrumental freedom, remains a real one for over 90 percent of the Arab population."[33] But many Muslim intellectuals would also assert that it would be disingenuous for the West not to take some, if not a lot, of the responsibility for the fate of Islamic societies. Many of the feudal regimes that the Western intellectuals criticize, from Morocco to Saudi Arabia, are kept in office at least in part through Western support. The West has promoted democracy everywhere except in the Islamic world. The West may not exert a direct colonial influence, but its influence is palpable nonetheless. It can raise up or overthrow a regime—it is neocolonial. At least many Muslims believe this to be the case.

The growing conviction among Muslims of the malevolent intentions of the West toward the Islamic world has been strongly reinforced by several Western actions since the end of the Cold War. Many Muslims now believe that the West, for all of its respect for the sanctity of human life (which is reflected in the abolition of the death penalty by the European Union), shows scant concern when innocent Muslim civilians are killed. The United States launched a huge global furor in 1983, when the Soviet Union downed a Korean civilian airliner, yet it showed little remorse when the US Navy guided missile cruiser USS *Vincennes* downed an Iranian civilian airliner in 1988 in the Gulf. Muslims will also mention the initial silence of the West when Muslim citizens were slaughtered in Bosnia (and Dutch soldiers actually handed over young Muslim men to be immediately killed by Serbian warlords). They remember too the launch of cruise missiles into Afghanistan in 1998 in retaliation for the bombings of US embassies in Kenya and Tanzania. The US attack did not kill Osama bin Laden but twenty-one Afghan civilians.

However, it has been the great indifference to the loss of Muslim civilian lives in the Middle East that has now firmly convinced Muslims that in the eyes of the West, Muslim lives do not matter. Since the American invasion of Iraq in March 2003, almost fifty thousand Iraqi civilians have been killed. Many were the victims of fellow

Iraqis, but after the American invasion the US was perceived to be responsible for the fate of Iraq. The 2006 massive Israeli assault against the Lebanese population and infrastructure in response to the kidnapping of two Israeli soldiers—leading to the severe loss of Lebanese civilian lives—served to reinforce the notion that in the Western moral calculus the loss of Muslim lives is unimportant.

This is dangerous. It explains why few Muslims felt any real sympathy for America when it lost three thousand civilian lives on 9/11. Indeed many celebrated the event, believing that it was a just retribution for years of American indifference to the loss of Muslim lives.

As the West continues to believe that Western civilization remains a moral bastion, preserving and enhancing the greatest moral values of humanity, the Islamic world sees the West as a corrupt and decadent force out to preserve its power and dominance under the cloak of moral virtue. An August 2006 article by Marwan Bishara in the *International Herald Tribune* illustrates how even when both sides seem to use the same language and concepts they speak at cross-purposes.

> Behind the fighting in Lebanon, as in Palestine and Iraq, there is a fundamental conflict of views. America sees each as a clash between freedom and terrorism, while the Arabs think in terms of freedom versus military occupation and unjust wars. Unless the two opposing approaches are reconciled politically and diplomatically, the Middle East will sink into perpetual war and chaos.
>
> The Bush administration charges Islamist fundamentalists and their sponsors in Tehran and Damascus with spreading an authoritarian ideology of hate against the will of the Arab majority. Washington believes that there is an American-style freedom-lover inside every Muslim, and that its mission is to drag it out by hook or crook. After all, the cause of liberty in America, according to the new Bush doctrine, is dependent on the cause of freedom abroad. The Arabs, for their part, blame U.S. and Israeli wars and occupations for turning citizens into

freedom fighters and providing terrorist groups such as Al Qaeda with fresh recruits and ideological alibis. They hold America and Israel responsible for death, destruction and surging extremism, in pursuit of narrow geopolitical interests rather than of universal values.

These opposing sets of beliefs come with corresponding myths and images. The United States and its allies invoke 9/11, the Madrid bombings, the London Underground attacks and hundreds of terrorist acts in between, while the Arabs underline the invasions and occupations of 1967, 1982 and 2003; the Abu Ghraib, Kheyam and Guantánamo detention centers, as well as hundreds of massacres, from Der Yassin in 1948 to last month's Qana bombing.[34]

This gap in perception is not just documented by Arab commentators. It is equally well-documented by well-known American commentators. In April 2007 David Brooks, a conservative columnist with the *New York Times*, attended a meeting of Arab and American intellectuals in Amman, Jordan. Afterward he wrote the following:

The problems between America and the Arab world have nothing to do with religious fundamentalism or ideological extremism, several Arab speakers argued. They have to do with American policies toward Israel, and the forces controlling those policies.

As for problems in the Middle East itself, these speakers added, they have a common source, Israel. One elderly statesman noted that the four most pressing issues in the Middle East are the Arab-Israeli dispute, instability in Lebanon, chaos in Iraq and the confrontation with Iran. They are all interconnected, he said, and Israel is at the root of each of them.

We Americans tried to press our Arab friends to talk more about the Sunni-Shiite split, the Iraqi civil war and the rise of Iran, but they seemed uninterested. They mimicked a speech

King Abdullah of Jordan recently delivered before Congress, in which he scarcely mentioned the Iraqi chaos on his border. It was all Israel, all the time.

The Americans, needless to say, had a different narrative. We tended to argue that problems like Muslim fundamentalism, extremism and autocracy could not be blamed on Israel or Paul Wolfowitz but had deeper historical roots. We tended to see the Israeli-Palestinian issue not as the root of all fundamentalism, but as a problem made intractable by fundamentalism. In other words, they had their narrative and we had ours, and the two passed each other without touching.[35]

The most dangerous conflicts in the world are those between any two forces that believe equally strongly that virtue is on their side and the other represents the face of evil. The West sees only its own virtues; it cannot understand the hatred it has generated in the Islamic world. The Muslim world can only feel its own victimization at the hands of Western power; it cannot understand why it is held responsible for creating a more violent and dangerous world.

This gulf in perception is becoming even more acute with each revelation of a terrorist plot supposedly involving Al-Qaeda or its ilk. In August 2006 most Westerners reacted with shock and horror to the discovery of a plot in the United Kingdom in which British Muslims were planning to set off simultaneous explosions on several aircraft, killing hundreds of transatlantic passengers. Most Muslims did not applaud this terrorist plot, but they noticed a sharp distinction between the shock and horror the Western populations felt at the potential loss of life and the relative indifference and acquiescence of the Western populations at the actual loss of life in Lebanon during the previous three weeks.

The West believes that one of the greatest contributions it has made to humanity is to advance the norm that every human life matters. This is why the West is so proud of pushing human rights to the forefront of global concerns. Canada is particularly proud that it has pushed the concept of the "Responsibility to Protect" (that is, international responsibility to protect civilians) and made it a new human rights norm. It did this (together with other leading Western nations) because it had been appalled by the Western inaction in the face of the Rwandan genocide in 1994. "Never again" was a favorite phrase. Yet Canada and the West remained silent and did not mention "Responsibility to Protect" when Lebanese civilians were killed. Ironically, even Israeli civilians are skeptical of this concept of "Responsibility to Protect": the West did nothing to defend them when Hezbollah rockets rained down on the Israeli civilian population.

In a recent significant development, the most powerful critic of Osama bin Laden—blaming him for the loss of innocent Muslim lives—is a powerful Saudi cleric, Salman al-Oadah, a former mentor of bin Laden. In an open letter (described in an article by Fawaz Gerges), al-Oadah asks, "How many innocent children, elderly people, and women were killed in the name of Al Qaeda?" Al-Oadah also holds bin Laden "personally accountable for the occupation of Muslim lands in Afghanistan and Iraq, displacement of millions of Iraqis, killings of thousands of Afghans, internment and torture of promising and deluded young Muslims, and a tarnished image of Islam all over the world."[36] No Western indictment of bin Laden can match the impact of this statement by al-Oadah, a heavyweight Salafi preacher with a large following in Saudi Arabia and abroad.

De-Westernization is happening more rapidly and more deeply in the Islamic world. This, in turn, is freeing up a lot of political and cultural space. The Western assumption is that all this space will inevitably be filled up by radical and fundamentalist forces. In fact, the culturally ascendant forces in the Islamic world are not fundamentalist. Instead, the same forces of modernization that are sweeping through Asia are also sweeping through Muslim societies. There is virtually no way that the March to Modernity could sweep through Asia without affecting the one billion Asians who are Muslims (only about two hundred million live in North Africa and Europe).

The proof that contemporary Muslim societies remain committed to modernization (and not Westernization) is provided by the nature of the governments of the Islamic world. Despite the advance of fundamentalist Islam, only one country in the Islamic world was seized fully. The case of Afghanistan under the Taliban is clearly atypical and, by exception, illustrates the real direction of the Islamic world. The unique circumstances that allowed the Taliban to emerge have not been replicated. Since the images of Al-Qaeda and the Taliban provide the dominant images of Islam in the Western mind, it may be useful to recall that for centuries Islamic societies were among the most tolerant. Amartya Sen challenges the idea of inherent Islamic intolerance: "We are left wondering what could have led Maimonides (a Jewish rabbi, physician and philosopher in Spain and Egypt during the Middle Ages), as he fled the persecution of Jews in Spain in the twelfth century, to seek shelter in Emperor Saladin's Egypt. And why did Maimonides, in fact, get support as well as an honoured position at the court of the Muslim emperor who fought valiantly for Islam in the Crusades?"[37]

In response to Pope Benedict XVI's recent quotation from a fourteenth-century Byzantine emperor, Tariq Ramadan wrote in the *International Herald Tribune*, "The selective memory that so easily forgets the decisive contributions of rationalist Muslim thinkers like al-Farabi (10th century), Avicenna (11th century), al-Ghazali (12th century), Ash-Shatibi (13th century) and Ibn Khaldun (14th century) is reconstructing a Europe that practices self-deception about its own past. If they are to reappropriate their heritage, Muslims must demonstrate, in a manner that is both reasonable and free of emotional reactions, that they share the core values upon which Europe and the West are founded."[38]

The recent democratization of Indonesia also shows the limited impact that the radical and fundamentalist forces of Islam have had on the body and soul of Indonesia, despite the widespread perception that Indonesia is being taken over by extremist Islamic forces.

Michael Vatikiotis, a seasoned observer of Southeast Asia, notes that in Indonesia "it is certainly true that there has been a marked increase in religious observance among Muslims, as there has been among Hindus, Buddhists and Christians across the region."[39] However, he adds, "just like in the US, increased religiosity in Indonesian private life does not translate into making political choices that favor religious rule. In 1999, people who voted for Islamic parties weighed in only at 16 percent, rising just slightly to 22 percent in 2004. That is still only half the number of votes who supported Islamic parties in the 1955 general election." He adds that each time an attempt is made to define Indonesia as an official Islamic state, a healthy majority in the National Assembly have voted in favor of rejecting it.

More recently, the three largest secular parties in Indonesia— Golkar, the Indonesian Democratic Party (PDI-P), and the Democrat Party—have called on the Indonesian government to make all political parties adopt Pancasila as their sole ideology. Pancasila is the state ideology that calls for belief in God, humanity, unity, democracy, and social justice. It does not refer to Islam. This state ideology was a brilliant creation by Indonesia's founding fathers to provide a unifying framework that brings together all the peoples of Indonesia, one of the most diverse countries in the world.

The story of Indonesia also reflects trends in much of the Islamic world. Most governments in the Islamic world want to protect and strengthen their Islamic heritage, but they also want to modernize their societies. This is as true of President Susilo Bambang Yudhoyono of Indonesia as it is of President Musharraf in Pakistan. Indeed, the person President Musharraf appointed as his prime minister fully indicates the direction he wants Pakistan to go in: Shaukat Aziz, a former Citibank executive who used to live in New York. Aziz has a clear focus in his policies. He is trying to attract as much foreign investment as possible to Pakistan; his dream is to turn Pakistan into a modern economic tiger, like South Korea or Singapore.

The best living symbol of a modern Islamic society is provided by Dubai, which looks like Manhattan erected in the middle of the desert. In 2006 I was amazed to discover that Dubai had more construction cranes working than any other city in the world (including Shanghai, which has a much larger population). But the external modernity of Dubai is only half the story. The bigger story is the internal modernity. The senior members of the establishment who run Dubai are among the most modern and sophisticated individuals of any international city. Their goal is to modernize Dubai and other Gulf cities. If Dubai succeeds, it may well provide a new beacon of hope in the Islamic world. Surely the West would support such a development—but perhaps not!

In an effort to promote a dialogue between leading American and Arab intellectuals, President Clinton invited a group of well-established Arab businessmen from Dubai to visit the United States. They traveled with visas and letters certifying that they were going to America to meet with Clinton. But when they arrived in New York, they were humiliated by the American immigration authorities. Fareed Zakaria described what happened to them:

> The first group of participants, mostly CEOs of large companies, were pulled out of the regular immigration lines and made to stand for two to five hours while Department of Homeland Security officials grilled them as to why they were coming to America, whether they had any experience using weapons, what they thought of the Iraq war and other such questions. Half a day into their trip, before they had even left the airport, they were angry and humiliated. So much for improving America's image in the Arab world.[40]

History is full of interesting twists and turns. Future historians will be puzzled that the US tried to derail the very processes of modernization in the Arab world that would serve long-term Western and American interests.

This is precisely the area where India can make a massive contribution to global history. At a time when the world is getting more detached from the West and the West getting more detached from the world, the need for bridge building among different cultures and civilizations—especially between the West and the Rest—has never been greater. In our contemporary world, there are very few natural candidates for this job. India stands out as one of them.

INDIA

India occupies a special place in the Western imagination. Both the Chinese and the Islamic civilizations are seen to be strange and distant civilizations in the Western imagination. By contrast, most Westerners think positively about Indian culture and civilization. This is partly a result of the enormous romanticization of the British Raj in the Western imagination. The British did a brilliant job portraying themselves as benevolent and civilized rulers of the Indian subcontinent. And in some ways British rule was, relatively speaking, benevolent.

This positive view of India has led to the expectation that when India finally emerges as a great power, it will join the Western community of nations. As the world's largest democracy, India is seen as a natural addition to the Western community. That's a presumptuous Western belief. India will be the third great Asian power to emerge after Japan and China. Japan emerged with the conscious aspiration to join the West. China has no such aspirations. India's future directions are not yet set.

India is not immune to the waves of de-Westernization. The mental decolonization of India came much later than its political decolonization. For the first few decades after independence, Indians flocked to study and live in London, which was still seen as the center of their intellectual universe. Today, London has lost its grip on the Indian imagination. Apart from its importance as a financial center, it is seen as just another quaint European city.

Most contemporary Indian intellectuals do not believe that the West is right to place itself on a moral pedestal. The West is no longer seen as the custodian of the highest values of human civilization. Fifteen years ago, if anyone had suggested that Western countries would endorse or allow the use of torture, they would have been dismissed out of hand. But this has happened. In 2005, Irene Khan, the head of Amnesty International, said, "Guantanamo is the gulag of our times." If her statement was untrue, there would have been a huge rush of denials from the West. If her statement was true, there should have been an equally strong chorus of voices to say that this had to stop. Apart from a brief few flutters of regret, nothing really happened. The gulag continued. It was greeted by a loud silence in the West.

The West is not alone in having double standards. All governments, without exception, are guilty of them. However, none of the governments outside the West pretend to be as virtuous as Western ones do. The West does not hesitate to criticize China for its policy on Sudan or India for its policy on Myanmar. Like most Western societies, India too has a robust, free media. If India was drifting toward the West as it emerged, the trend would be reported there. But the Indian media is as critical of Western double standards of morality as any Islamic newspaper. An editorial in the *Tribune* newspaper points out how America has low standards for human rights in its "client" countries while it preaches to India about human rights violations in Kashmir:

> Take the case of the human rights in relation to America's client countries and economies—in some of the Arab monarchies and Sheikhdoms, in the Latin American countries under cruel dictatorships, to mention only these examples—and you see a very different set of attitudes and stances. The human rights violations in those lands are so openly perpetrated as to leave little even to an indulgent imagination. And the heirs of Jefferson and Lincoln in the White House and outside would have to look within themselves for the answer. Clearly, where America's military bases, oil interests, economic hegemony, etc, are affected, a very very benign "Nelson's eye" is to be seen in the scenario. "After such knowledge," what songs and sermons![41]

Another commentary in the same newspaper declares:

> America creates bushfires all over the world. But it expects the world to do the fire-fighting. Terrorism was its creation. But it wants the world to join the war against it. Most nations are ready to oblige. Why? Because their rulers are in some way obliged to America. We are familiar with America's double standards. But not with its Janus face. It champions democracy and human rights, but it also fights for world supremacy. In 1992 Paul Wolfowitz, deputy to the present Defense Secretary, produced a momentous report for the Republicans. It called on America to maintain its military dominance. In 1996 there was a call for the removal of Saddam. Then it was in support of Israel. Today, it is to promote democracy among Arabs. It is wrong to call Bush the villain. I believe Americans have a sense of history. But they do not realize that when American power bows out of the stage (it will not take long before it does so), there will be nothing good to recall it by. In fact, there will be much to loathe it. Like the Greeks, Americans could have aspired for greater things.[42]

India, however, provides encouragement to the West on another front. If the West believes that the progressive disappearance of the Western era in global affairs will imply a moral slippage in the human order, it may be relieved to discover that some of these perceived Western values may actually be Eastern in origin. One of the most thoughtful commentators of our times is the Nobel Laureate Amartya Sen. Long a friend of the West, having spent most of his academic career in the UK and the US, he has tried to demonstrate that Eastern civilizations have also practiced many Western values, sometimes before the emergence of the Western era of world history. He writes:

There have, for example, been frequent declarations that non-Western civilizations typically lack a tradition of analytical and sceptical reasoning and are thus distant from what is sometimes called "Western rationality." Similar comments have been made about "Western liberalism," "Western ideas of right and justice" and generally about "Western values." Indeed, there are many supporters of the claim (articulated by Gertrude Himmelfarb with admirable explicitness) that ideas of "justice," "right," "reason" and "love of humanity" are "predominantly, perhaps even uniquely, Western values."[43]

Sen goes on to point out that this artificial distinction between Eastern and Western values is not historically justified. "A good example is the emperor Ashoka in India, who during the third century BCE covered the country with inscriptions on stone tablets about good behaviour and wise governance, including a demand for basic freedoms for all—indeed, he did not exclude women and slaves as Aristotle did."[44] He concludes his discussion on this subject with a very strong statement: "The claim that the basic ideas underlying freedom and tolerance have been central to Western culture over the millennia and are somehow alien to Asia is, I believe, entirely rejectable."[45]

Jawaharlal Nehru, the first prime minister of India, reminds us that issues of freedom were discussed in India thousands of years ago: "There is a question in the Upanishads to which a very curious and significant answer is given. The question is: 'What is the universe? From what does it arise? Into what does it go?' And the answer is: 'In freedom it rises, in freedom it rests, and into freedom it melts away.' What exactly this means I am unable to understand, except that the authors of the Upanishads were passionately attached to the idea of freedom and wanted to see everything in terms of it."[46]

Sen even suggests that the modern secular state could have been conceived outside the West:

It is worth recalling that in Akbar's pronouncements of four hundred years ago on the need for religious neutrality on the part of the state, we can identify the foundations of a non-denominational, secular state which was yet to be born in India, or for that matter anywhere else. Thus, Akbar's reasoned conclusions, codified during 1591 and 1592, had universal implications. Europe had just as much reason to listen to that message as India had. The Inquisition was still in force, and just when Akbar was writing on religious tolerance in Agra in 1592, Giordana Bruno was arrested for heresy, and ultimately, in 1600, burnt at the stake in the Campo dei Fiori in Rome.[47]

The remarkable thing about Akbar was how far he was prepared to go personally to ensure that his ideas held reign. The following story of how he rescued a Hindu widow speaks volumes about his personal commitment:

> Jaimall, a cousin of Raja Bhagwan Das, who had been sent on duty in the Eastern Provinces, rode hard to comply with urgent orders, and died near Chausa from the effects of the heat and overexertion. His widow, a daughter of Udai Singh, the Mota or Fat Raja, refused to commit suttee, as demanded by the custom of the family. Her son and other relatives insisted that, willing or unwilling, she must burn. Early one morning Akbar heard the news while in the female apartments of the palace, and resolved to prevent the sacrifice. Throughout his reign he insisted on the principle that no widow should be forced to burn against her will. He jumped on a swift horse and rode to the spot, unattended. . . . He was in time, and his unexpected arrival stopped the proceedings.[48]

The examples of Ashoka (who ruled from 272 to 232 BCE) and Akbar (who ruled from 1556 to 1605 CE) show an independent tradition that respects the values of freedom and tolerance, reason, and logic. The West has to stop believing that other cultures are incapable of being as rational as it is.

Against this backdrop, it is clear that the role India will play will be very different from the role played by Japan in the 1970s and China more recently. The natural role for India is to be a bridge between the East and the West. No other society is as qualified.

For centuries, India has acted as a meeting point for several civilizations. When as a consequence of its economic revival India experiences a cultural renaissance, it will not be confined to the Indian subcontinent but will spread far beyond Indian shores. Some of it has already happened, especially through Bollywood. (The geographical footprint of Indian movies stretches from Morocco in the West to Indonesia in the East.)

As Indian writer Shashi Tharoor has written in his column in the *Times of India*:

> Bollywood is Indian culture's secret weapon, producing five times as many films as Hollywood—and taking India to the world, by bringing its brand of glitzy entertainment not just to the Indian diaspora in the US or UK but to the screens of Syrians and Senegalese. A Senegalese friend told me of his illiterate mother who takes a bus to Dakar every month to watch a Bollywood film—she doesn't understand the Hindi dialogue and can't read the French subtitles, but she can still catch the spirit of the films and understand the story, and people like her look at India with stars in their eyes as a result. An Indian diplomat friend in Damascus a few years ago told me that the only publicly-displayed portraits that were as big as those of then-President Hafez al-Assad were those of Amitabh Bachchan (India's Marlon Brando).[49]

This appeal of Indian movies to Islamic populations all over the world is quite remarkable. These movies were made to satisfy the primarily

Hindu population of India. India has also had its fair share of Hindu-Muslim problems, since the partition of the subcontinent into India and Pakistan in 1947. Indian movies have been banned in Pakistan since the 1965 war between the two hostile neighbors. However, when President Musharraf lifted some of these controls by allowing the screenings of two Bollywood movies in 2006, namely, *Taj Mahal* and the 1960 classic *Mughal-e-azam* (that critics refer to as the Indian *Gone with the Wind*), both received an enthusiastic response from the Pakistani population. Interestingly, the First Lady of Pakistan seems to be a Hindi cinema buff. During a state visit to India in April 2005, Begum Musharraf reportedly told Rani Mukherjee, the lead actor in the 2005 film *Veer Zara*, that she "had seen the film" and "liked her role."[50] Mukherjee plays the role of a Pakistani lawyer who fights for the release of an innocent Indian Air Force pilot from a Pakistani prison.

One of Bollywood's strengths is that it has managed to overcome the Hindu-Muslim divide. Leading producers and actors come from both the Hindu and the Muslim populations and have worked well together. They have also produced movies that appeal to both Hindu and Muslim imaginations. *Taj Mahal*, for example, is the story of Mughal Emperor Shah Jehan, the man who built the spectacular Taj Mahal in memory of his wife, Mumtaz Mahal. But it's not just the tragic tale of a mausoleum but also the story of a royal family in which brothers destroyed each other and sons rebelled against fathers in their rivalry for the throne. The leading actress, Sonia Jehan, was delighted to learn that the movie would be shown in Pakistan, particularly because her grandmother Noor Jehan (another famous Bollywood actress) had come from Pakistan. Even during the ban—and despite the bitter rivalry between the neighboring countries—Indian films were hugely popular in Pakistan and illicit copies easy to find. Pakistani producers worked secretly in India for several years, sidestepping the government ban by purportedly going to visit family and friends but getting films edited and music composed in Bombay. Pakistani cultural products are legal in India, where the country's poetry, songs, and television dramas are widely popular. A number of Pakistani poets and singers are superstars in India.

This capacity to bridge the Hindu-Muslim divide is a unique strength of Bollywood. Hollywood, by contrast, is unable to bridge the Christian-Muslim divide and, sadly, reinforces Christian prejudices about Islamic communities rather than diminishes them. The stereotypical Muslim in a Hollywood movie is a dark brooding character who only has evil terrorist designs. Jack Shaheen, a professor emeritus at Southern Illinois University and author of the book *Reel Bad Arabs: How Hollywood Vilifies a People*, writes: "Regrettably, the approximately five to eight million Muslims who live in the United States are confronted with a barrage of stereotypes which unfairly show them as a global menace, producers of biological weapons, zealots who issue fatwas, or burn Uncle Sam in effigy."[51]

It is not only the US Arab and Muslim communities that are affected, writes Shaheen. American television and movies are hugely popular in more than 150 nations of the world. He recalls meeting with a group of Middle Eastern students at Vanderbilt University and asking if they watched American movies. Everyone had. "'When you see Islam being vilified as a faith of violence, when you see yourselves portrayed as terrorists, what do you think?' [he] asked. 'We ask ourselves why Hollywood hates us,'" they said. Show only vilifying images of any group, incessantly, and after a while—a hundred years in the case of the Arab stereotype—it becomes "natural" not to like certain people, Shaheen argues. "It is a sin of omission—we omit the humanity—and of commission—we show only hateful images that make a stereotype that injures the innocent."[52] Over the years, the Council on American Islamic Relations (CAIR) has objected to the negative portrayal of Muslims in several Hollywood films, including *True Lies* (1994), *Executive Decision* (1996), *The Siege* (1998), *Rules of Engagement* (2000), and *Hidalgo* (2004).[53]

Given their different historical experiences, there will be one major difference in the relations that Chinese and Indian civilizations will eventually develop with Western civilization. China has had an essentially insular experience. When Chinese civilization reemerges in pride and strength, it will develop as an alternative civilization, although one that could be as open and tolerant as the Tang dynasty. India, on the other hand, is a meeting place: it has consistently received and absorbed foreign cultural waves.

It is therefore only a matter of time before India resumes its natural role. At a time when many Westerners are convinced that the West cannot coexist in peace with the Islamic world, they should study how India has been able to accommodate so many civilizations—including Hindu, Buddhist, Islamic, and Christian cultures—and how most of them have lived in peace with each other for most of its history.

The record is clear. There is something unique about Indian political and social culture; a spirit of inclusiveness and tolerance pervades the Indian spirit. While the West often tries to discuss the world in black and white terms, distinguishing itself from either the evil empire or the axis of evil, the Indian mind is able to see the world in many different colors.

The Indian capacity for engaging other cultures and civilizations may well define India's role in the relations between the West and the East. It could perform one particular task: to convince the leading minds in the West that they should stop seeing themselves as safe guardians and custodians of one leading civilization, Western civilization, but as guardians and custodians of human civilization. Convincing the West of this will not be easy. A great educational campaign will be needed to make the West see that it is essentially no different from the East.

The end result of the powerful processes of de-Westernization should therefore be the world moving toward a positive destination in which many rich ancient civilizations are reborn, adding to the cultural wealth of the world and unleashing new instincts of cultural tolerance and understanding. The unpeeling of the layers of Western influence from around the globe could well lead us to a happier universe where we will have, for the first time in human history, several different civilizations flourishing at the same time, with simultaneous explosions of knowledge and wisdom. All this could lift the human condition to a much higher level than experienced in any previous century.

5

WESTERN INCOMPETENCE, ASIAN COMPETENCE?

Many leading Western minds are concerned about the state of our world, echoing President Bush's statement that the world is becoming a more dangerous place. In trying to understand the sources of this danger, they assume that the problems are over *there*, not over *here*. Western editorials and commentaries seem to have an almost automatic assumption that the rest of the world is responsible for generating the problems, while the West is struggling to develop and deliver the solutions. The simple goal of this chapter is to lead Western readers to open their minds to the evidence that the West also plays a major part in many global problems. Viewing the recent record, one must ask: Is the West handling key global challenges competently?

To pursue this issue, Western minds must first grasp a paradox. In domestic terms, the West includes the most competently managed nation states in the world. This is natural. They are far more economically developed and have rich material resources and strong institutions, especially strong democratic institutions. Under these circumstances, it would take great skill to become incompetent domestically in a mere twenty or thirty years. Most Western populations receive the domestic governance they deserve. One cannot assume, however, that a government that delivers competent domestic governance is equally good at addressing global challenges.

This chapter will examine the Western experience dealing with four challenges. On the geopolitical front, the Western mind is obsessed with the Islamic terrorist threat. Yet in handling the two immediate and pressing challenges of Iraq and Afghanistan, the West is about to fail. If it does, the jihadists will celebrate. On the economic front we may witness—for the first time since World War II—the demise of a process of global trading negotiations, the Doha Round. Global warming, too, is being mismanaged. Finally, one of the great accomplishments of the world since World War II has been the preservation of the Nuclear Non-proliferation Treaty. At a time when our concern over terrorist access to nuclear technology has never been higher, Western custodians have allowed the nonproliferation regime to weaken significantly.

Since the West sees itself as the source of solutions, not of problems, people there seldom look inward in their search for reasons why these global problems are being mismanaged. Are there domestic structural reasons that explain it? Have Western democracies been hijacked by processes of competitive populism and structural short-termism that prevent their addressing long-term challenges from a broader global perspective? And to go further, are Asian states becoming more competent in handling regional and global challenges?

THE WEST AND THE MIDDLE EAST

The region in which Western policies have been most harmful is the Middle East. It is also the most dangerous region in the world. Trouble in the Middle East affects not just 7 million Israelis and 3.9 million Palestinians. It spreads even beyond 200 million Arabs. It affects 1.2 billion Muslims and the communities they live in. Every time there is a lightning bolt in the Middle East, electricity surges into every Islamic community. This electricity emerges as concern, distress, anger, and rage. It may come as a shock to learn that the West may be responsible for many of these lightning bolts. Many Islamic communities, whether in India or Indonesia, Morocco or Malaysia, who feel the galvanic effects of these lightning bolts, have no doubt about their origins: the West.

The decision by the US and the UK to invade and occupy Iraq in March 2003 will go down as a seismic error, one of the greatest acts of folly of our age. Few recent disasters are as multidimensional.

Among the disasters is the damage done to international law. Until 2003 both the theory and practice of international law was coming to accept that the use of force would be legitimate (or legal) only under two conditions: first, if it is used as an act of self-defense, and second, if it is authorized by the UN Security Council (UNSC). The American-British decision to invade Iraq could not be justified on either count. Just before the invasion in March 2003, the US and the UK presented a draft resolution in the UNSC to seek the council's authorization to invade Iraq. The decision to propose such a resolution confirmed that the US and the UK knew they needed clear legitimization under international law to invade Iraq. Consequently, their decision to invade Iraq after the resolution was explicitly rejected made it clear to the international community that the war was technically illegal.

This created enormous problems. Hitherto, both the US and the UK have been among the main custodians of international law. Indeed, much of the rich fabric of international law that has been woven around the world is a gift from these two countries to the world. American and British minds have developed the conceptual infrastructure underlying international law and provided the political will and drive to have the law accepted in practice. In the case of the Iraq war, neither the US nor the UK will admit that the Iraq war was illegal, nor do they wish to give up their historical roles as chief custodians of international law.

The US and the UK expect to carry on with their previous roles in the international system, including the control and management of the UNSC. Since 2003, both nations have made frequent calls to Iran and North Korea to implement UNSC resolutions. But how can the violators of UNSC decisions also become the enforcers of them?

This problem does not simply involve the war in Iraq. Such behavior also calls into question the legitimacy of our current multilateral order and creates global cynicism and disillusionment. For instance, the more than one hundred fifty million Muslims in India are among the least radical of any Muslim community in the world. Yet they too have become progressively disenchanted with the West because of the Iraq War. One key reason why they have become the political allies of communist parties in some Indian states is because they want to oppose the policies of the US and the UK, even though in every other respect Muslims and communists are uncomfortable ideological bedfellows. Many in the West were shocked that some Indian Muslims were involved in the attempted terrorist attacks in the UK on 7 July 2007. Yet the Islamic world has in its own way become borderless. The anger and anguish of any single Muslim community is now transmitted worldwide instantly.

President Bush went to war with the explicit authority of the US Congress, which legitimized the Iraq War in terms of US domestic law. Many Americans believe that the US Congress is the ultimate legal authority and that its approval resolves all legal objections to the war. Yet the war is inherently illegal under international law, which the US helped create. Something has to give here; these two notions cannot coexist. Paradoxically, the US Congress is treating international rule of law just as the Chinese Communist Party treats domestic rule of law. It is prepared to force others to comply but does not follow the law itself.

Many Britons are aware that the Iraq War is illegal under international law. A few leading British international lawyers, including Phillip Sands, have documented this. Sands has also worked with a

British playwright, Nicolas Kent, to produce a play, *Called to Account*. The theme of the play is that former Prime Minister Tony Blair should be held accountable for going to war illegally in Iraq. A case can be made that the British government has put members of the British cabinet and armed forces in legal jeopardy by going to war illegally. In due course, as the International Criminal Court (ICC) gains strength and courage, some cases concerning Iraq could appear before the ICC.

The illegal dimensions of the Iraq War have created massive political problems all across the globe. But these problems have been enormously aggravated by the remarkably poor execution of the war. Indeed, the execution provides a textbook example of how *not* to invade or occupy a country. The remarkable thing here is that many of the officials involved in the decision-making process were thought to be among the most "competent." Yet these same groups of officials, despite their sterling domestic public service records, have delivered a wretched and flawed military and political operation.

A competent invasion plan should have begun with a study of the history of Iraq, with a view to understanding the lessons of history on how to (and how *not* to) govern the country. A quick study would have exposed the difficulties in managing the varied interests of the Sunni, the Shiites, and the Kurds. Second, the prevailing civil administration and methods of governance in Iraq should have been researched. The decisions on what institutions to retain and what to remove should have been made before the invasion. Third, an attempt should have been made to study the national treasures of Iraq that had to be protected, in order to demonstrate that America was undertaking its occupation with respect for the national concerns of the Iraqi people it was "liberating."

Amazingly, none of this was done. Instead, disastrous decisions were made. America pushed for democracy, without thinking first about how to protect the minority rights of the Kurds and the Sunnis, who would obviously be disadvantaged by the transfer of power to the Iraqi Shiites after centuries. One of the American founding fathers, John Jay, had said at the outset of the American democracy that the one reason why the United States could establish democracy so quickly was because its people were "descended from the same ancestors, speaking the same language, professing the same religion, attached to the same principles of government, very similar in their manners and customs." He added that they were surely "a band of brethren" and "should never be spilt into a number of unsocial, jealous and alien sovereignties."[1] Given the different political fabric of Iraq, somebody should have thought of the obvious difficulties in introducing democracy there. No one did. Instead, an even more disastrous decision was made to dismantle the administration and the military, creating a large army of dissatisfied, angry, and unemployed citizens.

Invasion and occupation are hardly a new developments in history. In Singapore in February 1942, a smaller Japanese army of thirty thousand defeated a larger British army of ninety thousand. Lee Kuan Yew was one of the victims of the Japanese occupation. He describes how smoothly the occupation took place.

> I recalled how when the Japanese captured Singapore in February 1942 and took 90,000 British, Indian, and Australian troops prisoner, they left the police and the civil administration intact and functioning—under the control of Japanese military officers but with British personnel still in charge of the essential services, such as gas and electricity. Except for a small garrison, most of the 30,000 Japanese invasion forces had left Singapore and headed to Java within a fortnight. Had the Japanese disbanded the police and the civil administration when they interned the British forces, there would have been chaos.[2]

In contrast, the American occupation paid little attention to preserving law and order. To make matters worse, Donald Rumsfeld said callously, "Stuff happens," when he learned of the looting of the Baghdad museum. By contrast, the Japanese protected Singapore's national treasures, including the famous Botanic Gardens. The day after the invasion, a Japanese botanist flew in from Tokyo and went straight to the gardens. He told the British curator and the superintendent of the gardens that they should stay in place and carry on their work. His job was to help them, not suppress them. Indeed, this Japanese botanist commissioned some lovely Japanese prints of the flora and fauna in the Botanic Gardens, which are still preserved today.

In Iraq in 2003, ideology trumped common sense. Common sense dictated retention of the military and civil service, even if many members had been tainted by association with the previous regime. The sheer arrogance of the American officials was stunning. None of the neighboring nations were consulted; any of them could have easily predicted the fierce resistance launched by the Sunni minority in Iraq. Indeed, before the war, a senior Egyptian diplomat predicted to me with remarkable accuracy the things that would go wrong. All his predictions came true. Egypt is a key American ally in the Middle East. Why did America not consult Egypt?

The newfound fear of Iran among Sunni Arab countries may be the only positive thing to emerge from the Iraq war. Many Sunni Arab states (including Saudi Arabia, Egypt, and Jordan) believe that this is now the time to make peace with Israel so as not to have to deal with two adversaries at the same time. Hence, it is not surprising that King Abdullah used the opportunity of the special Arab League Summit meeting in March 2007 to relaunch his long-standing proposal of a two-state solution to the Israel-Palestine problem. Opportunities for peace in this area come rarely. An alert American administration would have seized this opportunity. Unfortunately, the United States has only renewed its established track record of incompetence on the Israel-Palestine crisis.

The real tragedy of the Middle East is that peace is finally within reach. Among intelligent observers there is a consensus that the Taba Accords worked out by President Clinton in January 2001 provide a real basis for a lasting settlement. Saudi Arabia is prepared to support them. If America had a balanced policy on the Middle East, it would work to get the Taba Accords back on the table. Initially, the Bush administration appeared ready to support a two-state solution. It was the first American administration to vote in favor of a UNSC resolution calling for a two-state solution. It also announced it would try to achieve a two-state solution by 2005. But in 2008 we are no closer.

Many extremist voices in Tel Aviv and Washington, DC, believe that time will always be on Israel's side. The political stranglehold that the pro-Israeli lobby has in the US Congress, the obvious political cowardice of American politicians on the Middle East issue (while constantly lecturing the rest of the world to speak truth to power), and the sustained track record of American support for Israeli government policies support this view. But history teaches us that no great power forever sacrifices its larger national interests in favor of a small state.

I am a friend of Israel. And it seems evident to me that if it fails to take advantage of this unique window of opportunity to accept the Taba Accords, it will inevitably come to grief. The disastrous Israeli attack on Lebanon only created a new Arab folk hero, Hassan Nasrallah. Cracks are appearing in American support for Israel, as demonstrated by the famous article authored by Steve Walt and John Mearsheimer and the book by former President Jimmy Carter, *Palestine: Peace Not Apartheid*. Michael Massing in his June 2006 article, "The Storm over the Israel Lobby," exposed one very dangerous aspect of the Israeli lobby. It no longer represents the views of the majority of American Jews but of a few extremist businessmen in the United States.

AIPAC [American Israeli Public Affairs Committee] claims to represent most of the Jewish community. Its executive committee has a couple of hundred members representing a wide spectrum of American Jewish opinion, from the dovish Americans for Peace Now to the militantly right-wing Zionist Organization of

America. Four times a year this group meets to decide AIPAC policy. According to several former AIPAC officials I have talked to, however, the executive committee has little real power. Rather, power rests with the fifty-odd-member board of directors, which is selected not according to how well they represent AIPAC's members but according to how much money they give and raise.

Reflecting this, the board is thick with corporate lawyers, Wall Street investors, business executives, and heirs to family fortunes. Within the board itself, power is concentrated in an extremely rich subgroup, known as the "minyan club." And, within that group, four members are dominant: Robert Asher, a retired lighting fixtures dealer in Chicago; Edward Levy, a building supplies executive in Detroit; Mayer "Bubba" Mitchell, a construction materials dealer in Mobile, Alabama; and Larry Weinberg, a real estate developer in Los Angeles (and a former owner of the Portland Trail Blazers). Asher, Levy, and Mitchell are loyal Republicans; Weinberg is a Scoop Jackson Democrat who has moved rightward over the years.

The "Gang of Four," as these men are known, do not share the general interest of a large part of the Jewish community in promoting peace in the Middle East. Rather, they seek to keep Israel strong, the Palestinians weak, and the United States from exerting pressure on Israel. AIPAC's director, Howard Kohr, is a conservative Republican long used to doing the Gang of Four's bidding. For many years Steven Rosen, AIPAC's director of foreign policy issues, was the main power on the staff, helping to shape the Gang of Four's pro-Likud beliefs into practical measures that AIPAC could promote in Congress. (In 2005, Rosen and fellow AIPAC analyst Keith Weissman left the organization and were soon after indicted by federal authorities for receiving classified national security information and passing it on to foreign [Israeli] officials.)[3]

The real tragedy of the current Middle East impasse is that the long-term victims of US failures in this area will be the people of Israel. If they fail to seize this unique moment to achieve a two-state solution with Palestine, supported by Sunni Arabs (who will in turn bring the support of other Muslim nations), Israel will be condemned to a long-term destructive conflict with the entire Islamic world. Deng Xiaoping once used a simple comparison to describe the folly of Vietnam in taking on China. When he was asked how long China could fight Vietnam, he said that we should take a large rock and a small hard stone and continue rubbing them together. Over time, the small stone will disappear. Vietnam soon realized the wisdom of Deng's comments. Despite its obvious hubris following its defeat of America in 1975, it sued for peace with China. Vietnam's population is 84 million; China's is 1.3 billion. The ratio of Israel's population (7 million) to the Islamic world (1.5 billion) is even worse—1:200. Wisdom dictates that Israel should work for peace. Western errors could, however, deprive Israel of this opportunity.

The West has failed to achieve most of its policy objectives in the Middle East. The only one that has been successful has been the securing of oil supplies to the West (and the world). Western policies have been careful and patient in protecting this vital interest. This is why America and the West have made no effort to export democracy to Saudi Arabia or the other Gulf sheikhdoms. Prudence has protected Western interests.

It is therefore amazing that the same prudence is abandoned in dealing with the other Middle Eastern states. In dealing with these nations, America allows ideology to triumph over experience. America has destabilized the Middle East by thoughtlessly pushing its agenda for democracy in a few Arab countries. Those behind the agenda were absolutely convinced that democracy would invariably leave these countries and their people better off, but the record so far shows the opposite. Lebanon experienced a disastrous civil war from 1975 to 1990. Beirut became a living symbol of hell. After the civil war ended, gradually Lebanon began to move back to normalcy (although it clearly remained under Syrian domination). The assassination of Lebanese Prime Minister Rafik Hariri in February 2005 triggered the Cedar Revolution, which the US encouraged and cheered. The Cedar Revolution proved to be a false dawn, upsetting the delicate political balance that had been achieved among the different political parties, and Lebanon is slowly but surely slipping back into the political turmoil from which it had managed to extricate itself before America intervened again.

Democratic elections led to the election of a Hamas government in Palestine and to the election of a Shiite-dominated government in Iraq. These governments represented the wishes of the people. Yet the Palestinian people were subsequently punished for electing the Hamas government. Few Americans noticed the remarkable contradiction between encouraging the people to choose their own representative and then punishing these same people for making their choice. The time has come for America to make a major strategic decision. Will it continue to push for democratic elections in the Middle East? If so, it must learn to live with the consequences of doing so. Even friends of America in the Middle East are encouraging America and Europe to accept the results of these elections.

Saad Eddin Ibrahim, an outspoken sociology professor at the American University in Cairo, was once imprisoned by the Egyptian government. When that happened, the journalist Thomas Friedman and the US government pressed for Ibrahim's release. Ibrahim is a friend of America. In a commentary in the *Washington Post* he wrote:

> More mainstream Islamists with broad support, developed civic dispositions and services to provide are the most likely actors in building a new Middle East. In fact, they are already doing so through the Justice and Development Party in Turkey, the similarly named PJD in Morocco, the Muslim Brotherhood in Egypt, Hamas in Palestine and, yes, Hezbollah in Lebanon.

These groups, parties and movements are not inimical to democracy. They have accepted electoral systems and practiced electoral politics, probably too well for Washington's taste. Whether we like it or not, these are the facts. The rest of the Western world must come to grips with the new reality, even if the U.S. president and his secretary of state continue to reject the new offspring of their own policies.[4]

The fundamental problem is Western strategy toward the Islamic world: there is no strategy. Hence, the persistent incompetence.

THE WEST ON FREE TRADE AND GLOBAL WARMING

Chapter 2 documented recent Western follies in international trade. The West led the push for global trade liberalization. This push for liberalization was driven by several considerations. On the ideological front, there was a strong conviction that low trade barriers and increasing trade interdependence would result in higher standards of living for all.

But now the tables have turned. Indeed, a seismic shift has taken place in Western attitudes. The end of the Cold War made a huge difference. Suddenly, America and Europe had no vested interest in the success of East Asian economies, which were seen not as allies but as competitors. The entry of China into the global marketplace, especially after its admission to the WTO, made a huge difference, in both economic and psychological terms. First, Europeans lost their confidence that they could compete with Asians. Then many Americans also began to lose their confidence in the virtues of economic competition.

This then is the fundamental reason why there is little movement on the global trade talks. Although there are knotty and specific issues, the main reason why global trade talks are stalling is because the "champions" of free trade have begun to lose faith in its virtues. When Americans and Europeans began to perceive themselves as "losers" rather than "winners" in international trade, they also lost their motivation and drive to push for trade liberalization. Neither China nor India (or any other major developing country like Brazil or South Africa) is ready to take on the mantle of becoming the new champion of free trade. China is afraid that it will only contribute to American fears of Chinese global hegemony if it tries to play any kind of leadership role in the world. Hence, China is lying low. So too are America and Europe. Hence, the trade talks are stalled. The end of the Western drive toward global trade liberalization could well mean the end of the most spectacular global economic growth the world has ever seen.

There is now a growing worldwide consensus that global warming represents a real threat. I was present at the World Economic Forum meeting in Davos in January 2007, when this new global consensus was palpable. It was further reinforced by the report "Climate Change 2007: Mitigation of Climate Change," prepared by the Intergovernmental Panel on Climate Change (IPCC), which represents twenty-five hundred international scientists. It states that there is "high agreement," based on "much evidence," that global greenhouse gas emissions have grown since preindustrial times, with an increase of 70 percent between 1970 and 2004. The reports further states that "without additional action by governments the emissions from the basket of six greenhouse gases covered by the Kyoto Protocol will rise by 25 to 90 percent by 2030 compared to 2000." The six gases are carbon dioxide, methane, nitrous oxide, sulphur hexafluoride, PFCs, and HFCs.[5] The main push for developing a global consensus comes from leading voices in the American and European scientific communities, who are the most assertive advocates. Paradoxically, the greatest resistance to any effective action to handle the global warming challenge also comes from the US. This has left the rest of the world confused and puzzled by this manifest Western inconsistency and political failure.

In very simple terms, there is both a "stock" and a "flow" problem. When most people think of greenhouse gas emissions they think of the flow of new emissions. Naturally they believe that this is the cause of the problem. But the greenhouse effect that we are worrying about is not being *caused* by current emissions, even though it is being aggravated by them. The fundamental cause is the stock of emissions we have accumulated, especially in the last two centuries since the Industrial Revolution. Hence, a just and equitable solution to the problem of greenhouse gas emissions must assign responsibility both for the "stock" and for the "flow." Gwynne Dyer has expressed the problem well:

> Put yourself in China's shoes: 500 years ago, average incomes in Europe, India and China were about the same. Then the Europeans got the jump on everybody else technologically, grew unimaginably rich and powerful, and conquered almost the whole world. They also industrialized, and for 200 years it was their industries, their cities, their vehicles that emitted excess greenhouse gases. Now the rich countries are concerned about the consequences, some are even willing to curb their emissions—but they can afford to, because they are already rich and bound to remain so.
>
> But if China imposes the same kind of curbs on its emissions, it will not become a country where most people are prosperous and secure in the generation, or perhaps ever. The same goes for all the other once-poor countries that are now experiencing very rapid economic growth. So the deal must be that they get to keep on growing fast, and the rich countries take the strain. There are two main ways for the developed countries to take the strain. One is to cut their own emissions deeply, leaving some room for the developing countries to expand theirs. The other way is to pay directly for cuts in the emissions of the developing countries: pay them to adopt clean-burning coal technologies, to build renewable energy sources, not to cut the rainforests. Pay them quite a lot because otherwise we all suffer. The developing countries will never get that deal unless they show that they are unwilling to curb their emissions without it. That is

what they are doing, and it is not actually a poker game at all. It is a game of chicken.[6]

When it comes to addressing any problem that arises in the "global commons" (to use a popular phrase in the West), it is natural to expect the wealthier members of the community to take greater responsibility. This is a natural principle of justice. R. K. Pachauri, chair of IPCC, says, "If we have to bring about a global reduction then you know clearly the largest share of reduction has to be brought in by the developed countries. China and India are certainly increasing their share (of greenhouse gas emissions) but they are not increasing their per capita emissions anywhere close to the levels that you have in the developed world."[7] In the case of the greenhouse gas emissions, the wealthier industrial nations of the West have an additional reason to take on greater responsibility: they are primarily responsible for the stock of emission in our atmosphere. Since 1850, China has contributed less than 8 percent of the world's total emissions of carbon dioxide, while the US is responsible for 29 percent and Western Europe 27 percent. Per capita, India's greenhouse emissions are only 4 percent of those of the US and 12 percent of the EU's.[8] Steps toward any solution must include the wealthier Western nations clearly acknowledging their responsibilities, but there are no clear-cut statements to this effect.

Instead, many citizens in Western societies are led to believe that global warming is a result of the recent decisions of China and India (and other newly emerging economies) to industrialize. Their greenhouse gas emissions are pushing our earth to the "tipping point," where potentially disastrous consequences could flow from global warming. This may well be true. We cannot really say for sure. The scientific community is divided on how far we are from this tipping point. But they seem to agree that we should take some action and it should be done soon. Any solution should also include China and India. (See Table 5.1 and Figure 5.1.)

Region/Country	1980	1985	1990	1995	2000	2004
United States	4,754.52	4,585.20	5,013.45	5,292.67	5,815.50	5,912.21
	(26%)	(23.6%)	(23.3%)	(24%)	(24%)	(21.9%)
Europe	4,657.92	4,564.28	4,500.29	4,259.83	4,426.93	4,653.43
	(25.4%)	(23.5%)	(21%)	(19.33%)	(18.5%)	(17.2%)
Japan	937.50	892.96	1,014.85	1,075.84	1,190.06	1,262.10
	(5%)	(4.5%)	(4.7%)	(4.8%)	(4.9%)	(4.7%)
China	1,454.65	1,838.47	2,241.17	2,873.10	3,030.88	4,707.28
	(7.9%)	(9.4%)	(10.4%)	(13%)	(12.7%)	(17.4%)
India	299.76	439.34	588.24	867.08	1,000.69	1,112.84
	(1.6%)	(2.2%)	(2.7%)	(3.9%)	(4.1%)	(4.1%)
World Total	18,333.26	19,412.76	21,426.12	22,033.53	23,851.46	27,043.57

Table 5.1   Data on CO_2 Emissions, 1980–2004, from the International Energy Annual 2004 (in Million Metric Tons of Carbon Dioxide)

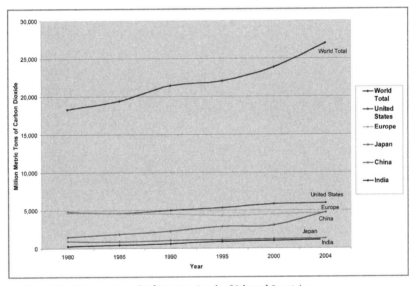

Figure 5.1   A Comparison of CO_2 Emission Levels of Selected Countries

I have spoken to Chinese and Indian officials about this issue, and it is clear to me that both countries are ready to accept their responsibility in this area. Even though China is a major new cause of greenhouse gas emissions, Chinese officials are genuinely worried. The chief economist of the International Energy Agency, Fatih Birol, gave a talk in New York in late 2006. He was asked which country, in his view, had the most environmentally conscious government. Most people expected him to mention one or two Scandinavian countries, or perhaps even the UK. Instead, he named China, to the surprise of everyone in the room.

The new Chinese officials are acutely aware of the challenges that both China and the world face. They are prepared to be "responsible stakeholders" in the management of these global challenges. The question they ask is whether the West is ready to be an equally responsible stakeholder in this exercise and accept its commensurate share of responsibilities. If the West is not prepared to accept this, there can be no solution to the global warming crisis.

Daniel Esty, Hillhouse Professor of Environmental Law and Policy at Yale University, says that although the Chinese government has avoided any commitment to limiting CO_2 emissions, it has set a target of cutting energy use per unit of GDP by 20 percent by 2010—an ambitious goal for a country that gets 70 percent of its power from burning coal. "China has adopted fuel-economy standards that will push average car mileage to nearly 40 miles a gallon over the next five years, and much higher than in the US. And it has promised to reduce water pollution by 10 percent by 2020 and increase industrial solid-waste recycling by 60 percent." He says that these "aren't just empty promises. The State Environmental Protection Agency, which recently acknowledged that air- and water-quality levels are worsening, blocked 163 projects worth US$99 billion in 2006." Furthermore, "startup companies are being launched every day to develop pollution-control technologies, improve energy efficiency, and create alternate sources of power. The US$220 million in clean-tech venture capital China received in 2006 puts it ahead of Europe as a venue for new environmental companies."[9] The good news here is that in this field, China does not need to reinvent the wheel. It can learn a lesson or two from Japan, which weathered the oil crises of the 1970s and from that difficult experience learned to become one of the world's leading countries in energy efficiency. According to an IEA estimate Japan's energy balance—that is, its aggregate energy consumption—is many times lower than that of other industrialized nations. Japan is eager to share its success in energy efficiency with other East Asian countries like China, whose energy demand is rapidly rising.[10]

In his column in the *Financial Times*, Ma Kai, minister in charge of the National Development and Reform Commission, China's chief economic policymaking and planning agency, writes about China's efforts to respond to climate change and global warming. He says that China has worked hard to adjust its economic structure to improve energy saving and cut emissions. "From 1991 to 2005, with national energy consumption rising each year by 5.6 percent, China sustained an annual economic growth rate of 10 percent and lowered its energy consumption per unit of gross domestic product by 47 percent, saving 800m tons of coal and cutting 1.8 billion tonnes of CO_2 emissions." Furthermore, he says, the Chinese central government "had approved 383 projects in wind, hydro and bio-fuel power generation, and the use of methane gas from coal beds. In total, they will cut emissions by 1 billion tonnes. From 1980 to 2005, another 5.1 billion tonnes was absorbed through extensive reforestation and better forest management." Per capita GDP energy intensity will fall by 20 percent between 2005 and 2010, with CO_2 emissions reduced accordingly, Kai reports, adding that "China is committed to addressing climate change in the context of sustainable development, but it should be on the principle of common but differentiated responsibilities."[11]

By contrast, at the IPCC meeting in Bangkok in May 2007, the US delegation attempted to steer the group toward voluntary climate change actions and away from mandatory solutions such as the Kyoto Protocol, adopted by Europe and Japan. "It's especially troubling that the Bush administration was seeking last-minute changes to play down the report's conclusion that quick, affordable action can limit the worst effects of global warming," said Larry Schweiger, president of the National Wildlife Federation. "Rather than embrace the report's window of opportunity message, the Bush administration tried to shut the window and draw the shades."[12] The world will therefore watch very carefully in the coming decades whether Western deeds, especially American deeds, will match Western words on the global warming challenge.

THE WEST AND THE NUCLEAR NON-PROLIFERATION TREATY

The challenge to respond to the threat of proliferating weapons of mass destruction (WMD) is something we should all embrace. A world with more WMD is inherently more dangerous and unstable. There is a very strong consensus that the world should not develop new chemical and biological weapons, and no major power is trying to violate the consensus. Instead, there is strong global cooperation to stop the proliferation of chemical and biological weapons despite the inherent difficulties in preventing them. This is reflected in the global adherence to two major conventions against these weapons: Biological and Toxin Weapons Convention (BTWC) and the Chemical Weapons Convention (CWC). As of June 2005, 171 states had signed the BTWC, and 155 of these countries had ratified it. With regards to CWC, 182 countries have signed and ratified it, so universal adoption is becoming a realistic goal.

Nuclear weapons are a different story. The Nuclear Non-proliferation Treaty (NPT), which was once regarded as a significant step toward international peace and security, is legally alive but spiritually dead. NPT was inherently discriminatory since it divided the world into nuclear haves and have-nots and created a regime of "nuclear apartheid" (a term used by India's former foreign minister Jaswant Singh). The logic of deciding who was legally allowed to keep nuclear weapons was based on an arbitrary cutoff date (January 1967) by which a country should have tested a nuclear device. Despite these problematic foundations, NPT was reasonably effective for two decades in preventing horizontal proliferation (spread of nuclear weapons to more states) but did nothing to prevent vertical proliferation (increase and sophistication of nuclear weapons among the existing weapon states). During the Cold War, despite the many arguments between the United States and the Soviet Union, there was a strong consensus that both should work together to prevent the spread of nuclear weapons. Hence, several countries like Brazil, Argentina, South Africa, Japan, Germany, and South Korea, which could have developed nuclear weapons, backed off. A strong nonproliferation regime held them back. There was no binding law that prevented them. Instead, the leaders of these countries, who could have decided to opt for nuclear weapons, refrained from doing so because they accepted the NPT as legitimate. They believed that a fair bargain had been reached between the five official nuclear weapon states (China, France, Russia, the US, and the UK), which also happened to be the five permanent members of the UN Security Council, and the rest of the world. Both sides agreed that the world would be a safe place if the five nuclear weapon states took steps to reduce their nuclear weapons and work for the eventual goal of universal disarmament, and the rest refrained from acquiring them.

So who killed the nuclear nonproliferation regime? The legitimacy of the NPT is in many ways linked to the legitimacy of the 1945 rules-based order, whose creation was led by America.

Sadly, the first nail in the coffin of the NPT was driven by its principal progenitor, the United States, when it decided to walk away from the 1945 rules-based order it had created. It is impossible to document exactly when this drift began. But when I was Singapore's ambassador to the UN between 1984 and 1989, Jean Kirkpatrick, the US ambassador to the UN, was already treating the UN with contempt. She saw the 1945 order as a set of constraints imposed on the US, not as a set of rules the world followed that the US should help to preserve. One of her deputies, Charles Lichtenstein, made a huge media splash with his remark that the

UN should leave American soil. "We will put no impediment in your way. The members of the U.S. mission to the United Nations will be down at the dockside waving you a fond farewell as you sail off into the sunset," he said. (Not surprisingly, he got his geography wrong. Leaving from New York harbor, one would sail off into the sunrise.)

On the face of it, attacks on the UN system and the 1945 rules-based system wouldn't seem to affect the NPT. But the problem about walking away from the 1945 rules-based order was that the NPT itself had no teeth. It was not self-regulating. The NPT has no mechanism to punish states found cheating. Moreover, signatories could always walk out of the treaty citing the "supreme national interest" clause without inviting any legal action. This is why the United States had to resort to the UN Security Council for dealing with Iraq's violation of NPT, since only the UNSC has the authority and the legitimacy to impose resolutions that all UN member states must observe. However, this legitimacy is deeply interwoven with the fabric of the 1945 rules-based order, especially the UN Charter, which the world has accepted. Once America began tearing holes in this fabric, it opened loopholes for others to walk through. The US and the UK, for example, lost their moral authority to ask Iran to abide by Security Council resolutions when they went to war without the UNSC legitimizing it.

The second nail in the NPT coffin was hammered in by the main custodians of the NPT, the five nuclear weapons states. The NPT was fundamentally a social contract: the five nuclear weapons states agreed to reduce their nuclear weapons while the rest agreed not to develop them. But instead of reducing their arsenals, the five nuclear weapons states have increased them. Since the NPT came into force in January 1970, their total stock of nuclear weapons has been both modernized and increased. If one looks at the evolution of the global nuclear stockpile since 1970, the P-5 countries (especially US and Russia) have enormously increased the accuracy (and hence lethality) of their nuclear weapons. The US stockpile numbers peaked in 1966 (31,700) and the USSR's peaked in 1986 (see Figure 5.2). The

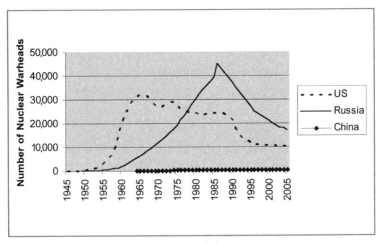

Figure 5.2 Nuclear Stockpile of the US, Russia, and China
Source: Natural Resources Defense Council.

declining numbers are often misleading because even at the currently reduced levels they are sufficient to wreck enormous damage to human civilization. During the Cold War both the US and Soviet Union built their stocks to such an extent that they actually ran out of sufficient number of militarily/economically significant targets and began assigning more weapons for each targets. More weapons were assigned to destroy a given target, even though additional weapons did not enhance their security. Instead, they helped kill the NPT.

The U.S. has been among the chief violators of the letter and spirit of the NPT. James Carroll points this out in his March 2007 commentary in the *International Herald Tribune*:

> When the United States announces plans to station elements of its missile defense system in Poland and the Czech Republic, why are Russian complaints dismissed as evidence of Vladimir Putin's megalomania? On March 12, 1999, Poland, Hungary, and the Czech Republic were admitted to NATO, in violation of American assurances to Moscow that NATO would not move east from the

unified Germany. Now NATO looks further east still, towards Georgia and Ukraine. And Putin is paranoid?

Last week, the Bush administration announced plans for the first nuclear weapon in more than 20 years, a program of ultimately replacing all American warheads. So much for the nuclear elimination toward which the United States is legally bound to work by the Nuclear Nonproliferation Treaty. Washington simultaneously assured Russia and China that this renewal of the nuclear arsenal was no cause for them to feel threatened. Hello? Russia and China have no choice but to follow the US lead, inevitably gearing up another arms race. It is 1947 all over again. A precious opportunity to turn the world away from nuclear weapons, and away from war, is once more being squandered—by America. And what candidate running for president makes anything of this?[13]

From time to time, common sense has tried to enter the discussions on nuclear weapons. Ronald Reagan, a Cold War hawk, said more categorically than any American president that the world would be better off without nuclear weapons:

One of the first statistics I saw as president was one of the most sobering and startling I'd ever heard. I'll never forget it: The Pentagon said at least 150 million American lives would be lost in a nuclear war with the Soviet Union—even if we "won." For Americans who survived such a war, I couldn't imagine what life would be like. The planet would be so poisoned the "survivors" would have no place to live. Even if a nuclear war did not mean the extinction of mankind, it would certainly mean the end of civilization as we knew it. No one could "win" a nuclear war. Yet as long as nuclear weapons were in existence, there would always be risks they would be used, and once the first nuclear weapon was unleashed, who knew where it would end? My dream, then,

became a world free of nuclear weapons and for the eight years I
was president I never let my dream of a nuclear-free world fade
from my mind.

He also added: "I call upon the scientific community in our country,
those who gave us nuclear weapons, to turn their great talents now to the
cause of mankind and world peace: to give us the means of rendering
these nuclear weapons impotent and obsolete."[14] In short, Ronald Reagan
called for the abolition of "all nuclear weapons," which he considered to
be "totally irrational, totally inhumane, good for nothing but killing, possibly destructive of life on earth and civilization."[15]

In his memoirs George Shultz, Reagan's secretary of state,
describes the unfortunate failure to eliminate nuclear weapons during Reagan's presidency. He comments on how the disappointing
Reykjavik negotiations between Reagan and Gorbachev hinged on
the single word "laboratory." He writes that Reagan was convinced
that any research, testing, and development of SDI (Strategic Defense Initiative) technology should continue while strictly observing
all provisions of the Anti-Ballistic Missile (ABM) treaty. Gorbachev,
on the other hand, was adamant that research and testing of missiles
must be prohibited in space and instead be restricted to the laboratory, finally declaring, "it's 'laboratory' or good-bye."[16]

Most serious strategic thinkers dismissed Reagan's comments about
eliminating nuclear weapons, thinking that he had gone soft in the head.
But now that the NPT is undergoing a near death experience, other
leading voices are coming out to repeat the common sense that Reagan
expressed. In an article in the *Wall Street Journal* on 4 January 2007, four
leading Americans, namely, former Secretary of State George Shultz,
former Defense Secretary William Perry, former Secretary of State
Henry Kissinger, and former Senator Sam Nunn of Georgia warned
that the world was now on the "precipice of a new and dangerous nuclear era" and "unless urgent new actions are taken, the U.S. soon will
be compelled to enter a new nuclear era that will be more precarious,

psychologically disorienting, and economically even more costly than the Cold War deterrence." Former Defense Secretary Robert McNamara conveyed the same message even more forcefully in the 2003 documentary *Fog of War*. These efforts may be too late. The world has essentially lost its trust and confidence in the five nuclear weapon states. Instead of seeing them as fair and competent custodians of the NPT, they are widely perceived to be among its primary violators. In private, the five nuclear weapon states have always been cynical about their obligations to the NPT. Now the cynicism has become public knowledge.

The decision by the five states to ignore the Israeli exception was especially damaging. It was hard to tell when exactly the world began to be aware that Israel was developing nuclear weapons. Avner Cohen's "Israel and the Bomb" mentions that Israel began its nuclear program in earnest in 1958, when it constructed the core of its nuclear infrastructure in Dimona. In 1966–1967 Israel completed the development stage of its first nuclear weapon, and it already had a rudimentary, but operational, nuclear weapons capability during the 1967 Arab-Israeli conflict. By 1970 Israel's status as a nuclear weapon state became an accepted convention, although its nuclear policy remains opaque to this day. It was more or less confirmed when Mordechai Vanunu, a technician and dissenter from Israel's nuclear establishment, gave a sensational interview to the *Sunday Times* in 1986 detailing Israel's nuclear weapons program and plutonium production facilities, some of which were built below ground to avoid detection. While the French contributed the most to Israel's nuclear program, it would be difficult to believe that the Americans came to know about it only after the *Sunday Times* reported it. Given the extreme level of insecurity that Israel lives under, it is not surprising that it strove to acquire these weapons. What is surprising is the total silence of the five nuclear weapon states on Israel's acquisition of nuclear weapons. To the best of my knowledge, not a single nuclear weapon state has made a public comment on this Israeli move.

Their silence therefore allowed Israel to create a loophole in the nonproliferation regime through which others could walk. Even more dangerously, it delegitimized the NPT in the eyes of Muslim nations. For the NPT to have any prospect of surviving in perpetuity, it had to be perceived to be fair. There is no doubt that the NPT would die if the Islamic world believed it to be illegitimate. Sadly, this has happened, and the consequences are profound. When the West sermonizes that the world will become a more dangerous place when Iran acquires nuclear weapons, the Muslim world shrugs its shoulders. Their standard response is, "If Israel can have nuclear weapons, why not an Islamic country?"

This also explains why, when the International Atomic Energy Agency (IAEA) debated the Iran nuclear weapon issue in June 2006, Malaysia—a moderate Muslim country—was one of the key defenders of Iran. Even moderate Muslims no longer believe in the legitimacy or fairness of NPT (although, to be fair, what Malaysia had argued in the IAEA was that Iran should have a right to acquire nuclear technology for peaceful use).

The NPT was virtually dead by the time India and Pakistan exploded their nuclear weapons in 1998. Because of the legacy of Mahatma Gandhi, who advocated nonviolence, and Jawaharlal Nehru, India had always taken pride in being one of the most law-abiding members of the international community. In fact, India was one of the early proponents of the nuclear test ban, although it was also the main reason for the failure of Comprehensive Test Ban Treaty talks in 1996 because of its insistence on a time-bound commitment to complete elimination of nuclear weapons (which was part of the "grand bargain" between the P-5 and the rest but to date has never been honored). When the international community condemned and applied sanctions on India for its 1998 nuclear tests, it should have made a dent in the Indian psyche. Instead, it had no impact at all. Virtually all Indians saw through the hypocrisy and double standards of those who were condemning them. The five nuclear weapon states had not respected their own obligations under NPT: hence, in Indian eyes, their sanctions had no moral legitimacy. Others, like Canada and

Australia, which criticized India, had remained silent about the Israeli exception. The near unanimous rejection of the NPT by the Indian establishment (which is otherwise very conscious of international opinion) showed how "dead" it had become.

A big mistake that the nuclear weapon states had made was to ignore the real security concerns that India and other large states have. Once China had the bomb, India knew that it had no choice but to have one. India could have actually tested nuclear weapons long before China if it had consciously pursued a weapons program from the beginning. The Indian nuclear program was driven more by grandiose aspirations of doing "big science" and using nuclear energy for long-term energy security. In contrast China was far more pragmatic and had a focused nuclear weapons program from the beginning. It is only more recently that China has turned to civilian uses of nuclear energy. Effectively, we now have five nuclear weapon states, three semi-legitimate nuclear weapon states (Israel, India, and Pakistan), and two developing nuclear weapon states (North Korea and Iran). When North Korea and Iran walk across the nuclear threshold, they will bring across with them many others: Japan (which can go nuclear in weeks), South Korea, and perhaps Brazil, Argentina, Turkey, and so on. Iran's acquisition can potentially create a domino effect in Saudi Arabia and Egypt. Pandora's box will have then completely opened.

Contrary to what the West wants the rest to believe, the biggest source of nuclear proliferation are the nuclear weapon states themselves, especially the US and Russia, which still stock and continue to develop thousands of nuclear weapons. This fact was bluntly pointed out by none other than Mohammed El Baradei, the director general of the IAEA, in an article that appeared in the *Economist*: "The very existence of nuclear weapons gives rise to the pursuit of them. They are seen as a source of global influence, and are valued for their perceived deterrent effect. And as long as some countries possess them (or are protected by them in alliances) and others do not, this asymmetry breeds chronic global insecurity."[17]

The reliance on nuclear weapons for national security by countries
that also possess the most powerful conventional military forces sends
the wrong signal to states without nuclear weapons. It must also be
mentioned that the NPT is still surviving because of the silent majority—the hundred-sixty-odd countries that signed the NPT in good
faith and in the process gave up their sovereign right to develop these
weapons. While these countries may feel they lack the clout to remind
the P-5 countries about their NPT obligations, they alone have the
moral credibility to put pressure on the world to address the larger
goal of universal nuclear disarmament. This needs to be addressed
with a sense of urgency because global warming concerns have raised
the prospects of a burgeoning civilian nuclear industry. Nuclear power
will play a significant role in generating electricity in many countries in
the coming decades. Addressing the long-pending issue of nondiscrim-
inatory disarmament and global management of nuclear weapons and
materials will be crucial to win the support and confidence of a skeptical public worldwide. And to accomplish this the NPT must acquire
teeth and credibility in the eyes of many.

There is still a small window of opportunity available to turn the
clock back on nuclear proliferation. Most intelligent people worldwide
see the utter stupidity of moving toward a world with more nuclear
weapons. It is one of the most tragically stupid things we could do as
common humanity to create such a world. In the second half of the
twentieth century, despite the problems we found in the Cold War,
there was a general sense that we were moving toward a more civilized
order. Now, as the twenty-first century opens, we seem to be sliding
backwards.

The four examples of Western incompetence discussed in this
chapter could create huge problems for our world if they continue to
be mismanaged. But the world could face an even bigger problem if
these few examples prove to be not four isolated challenges but a
reflection of a deeper structural problem. Western leaders, who used
to be careful and prudent in international affairs during the Cold War

(because of their huge fear of the Soviet Union), may have developed this tendency toward international incompetence because they now pay attention only to short-term electoral considerations, not the long-term dangers faced by their societies. The new rise of protectionism in the West is fueled by politicians out to win votes to get elected, even though many are aware that protectionism could lead to serious long-term damage to their societies.

Similarly, an obvious solution for America to consider in meeting the global warming challenge is to impose higher taxes on gas consumption. This would increase fuel efficiency and reduce carbon dioxide emissions, American dependence on the Middle East region, and American budget deficits. In short, all good will flow from this simple solution. This is why the Princeton Project on National Security, a bipartisan report written by Anne-Marie Slaughter and John Ikenberry, argued, "Massive U.S. consumption of oil threatens American security by transferring an enormous amount of wealth from Americans to autocratic regimes and by contributing to climate change and degradation of the environment. The only solution to these problems is to decrease our dependence on oil and provide incentives for investments in energy alternatives. Toward this end the United States should adopt a national gasoline tax that would start at fifty cents per gallon and increase by twenty cents per year for each of the next ten years."[18] Yet not a single American politician is prepared to sacrifice his or her political career by advocating an obvious and common-sensical solution. This indicates both the nature and the scale of the structural problem the world faces in getting American leaders to focus on global challenges.

Another deficit of the Western mind is the increasing tendency to see problems from a black and white perspective. President George W. Bush carried it to an extreme when he said, "Either you are with us, or you are with the terrorists."[19] Most of the 5.6 billion people who live outside the West do not want to be either with or against the West. Instead, they want to focus their energies on improving their livelihood, and where they can

work with the West to achieve these goals, they will. They are not programmed to support or oppose the West. Indeed, in most parts of the
world, each for its own complex historical reasons, there are subtle and
nuanced views of the West and its impact on the rest.

One big step the West needs to take to improve its understanding
of the world is to drop its black and white perspective and begin to
understand that since the majority of the world's population are
transforming themselves from objects of history to subjects, the
world will almost by necessity become more complex.

THE WEST AND IRAN

Iran is one of the world's most complex societies. In many Western
minds, the only images of Iran are negative ones: a country oppressed
by a harsh theocratic regime, a country dedicated to destabilizing its
neighborhood, a country determined to become a rogue nuclear
weapon state like North Korea. Many believe that there is no hope of
reforming Iran. Hence, at the time of the writing of this book, there
were constant whispers and hints that the only solution to the Iran
problem was a military one.

Iran could be invaded. However, a military invasion would be disastrous. If the invasion of Iraq has severely debilitated both the military
capability and the soul of America, a military invasion of Iran would be
even more of a disaster for America. Iran has a stronger capability to
retaliate and a deeper capacity for absorbing pain and suffering. It has
the stomach for a protracted struggle. The United States does not (as
demonstrated by its impulse to leave both Iraq and Afghanistan despite
the unfinished business in these two theaters).

The alternative way of invading Iran has already begun. The March
to Modernity—the greatest moving force in Asia—has started to pene-
trate Iran. Unbelievable? Here is an excerpt from a report on a visit to
Iran by Zuraidah Ibrahim, a female (and a Muslim) correspondent
from Singapore's *Straits Times*:

One night in the Islamic Republic of Iran, we went in search of a "happening" café off Tehran's main thoroughfare of Valiasr Street that friends had texted me about. . . .

It was an upmarket food court. There were standalone counters, selling American-style fast food in McDonald's colors but declaring Iranian authenticity with the name "Boof," two coffee joints and an Italian restaurant, Roma.

But it was the people who provided food for thought that night. This was a place to hang out, to see and be seen, and make friends with members of the opposite sex. There were young women garbed in fitted leather jackets, drain-pipe slacks and stylish knee-high boots of foreign makes, Louis Vuitton among them.

Their faces were a canvas of deftly blended colors with lashings of eye-liner. Their hair was either poufed up by spray to stand high or flattened into bangs, with scarves strategically draped to hide and yet flaunt tinted tresses.

The men were just as slick, hair heavy with gel and just like the women, streaked with highlights. One had a T-shirt advertising US-AID, a plea for fashion assistance, perhaps, from that other evil empire, the United States? The scene at the café was nothing out of place in today's world of consumerism and cultural experimentation. But one struggled to fit it into the box that political rhetoric and news headlines have placed Iran.[20]

Ibrahim has hit the nail on the head: the main problem is that the Western world has a one-dimensional view of an immensely complex and rich society. The many dimensions of Iran are rarely understood, even by leading Western minds.

Iran is first and foremost the descendant of a rich and proud civilization, the Persian civilization. Treasure troves of wisdom from the Persian civilization are still waiting to be rediscovered. Even though most Iranians wear their Islamic identity proudly, they are even prouder of their unique Persian culture, which they believe (in private) to be superior to the relatively primitive culture of the Arab lands (where Islam was born). Most Iranians have a deep knowledge of their own history and civilization.

The Iranians I have met are among the most sophisticated people I have ever encountered. During a 1996 trip to Iran I visited a city on the Caspian Sea. We had dinner with the governor of the province, a representative of the government run by the ayatollahs in Tehran. Over dinner he and I discussed Western philosophy, which we had both studied in college. After only a few minutes, I quickly realized that I was way out of my depth. His knowledge of Western philosophy was far greater than mine, and he had an especially deep understanding of ancient Greek philosophy. Coverage of Iran in the Western media had led me to expect that I would encounter the closed mind of a mullah; instead, I met a subtle and complex mind.

Given the sophistication of Persian culture, it would be unnatural for Iranian society not to be affected by the great March to Modernity that has been undertaken by China, India, and much of Asia. The Iranians consider their civilization a peer of China's (and in private they believe that they are culturally superior to South Asian cultures since the Mughal Empire inherited its best elements from Persian culture). The Iranians thus assume they can match what China and India are doing; they have a perfectly natural longing to walk down the same path as China and India.

It would serve the interest of the whole world, including the West, to see Iran join the March to Modernity. If Iran were to embark on this road, its society would be profoundly changed. Iranian politicians would become like the politicians of Tamil Nadu, and not like the Tamil Tigers. They would begin to promise their constituents free TVs, instead of speaking of the glories of martyrdom. India, China, and other Asian societies would welcome Iran on the March to Modernity. Ironically, the West is holding Iran back from taking this road. A variety of sanctions and other pressures continue to push Iran away from entering the modern world.

The main obstacle is America. No leading American politician would dare advocate the establishment of diplomatic relations between the US and Iran. He or she would be crucified for making the suggestion. Very few Americans are even aware that the absence of diplomatic relations is highly abnormal. Diplomacy was invented over two thousand years ago, as kingdoms or tribes encountered each other to help societies talk to their enemies. Diplomacy has deep roots and well-established practices. Nevertheless, modern America is not able to contemplate or implement what our ancestors were able to do two thousand years ago: establish diplomatic relations with an adversary state.

The standard American response to this argument is that Iran moved itself out of the community of civilized nations when it held fifty-two American diplomats and embassy staff in Tehran hostage for 444 days. There is no doubt that this act of hostage taking was deplorable. But even more deplorable things have happened between other nations. A senior Indian diplomat told me that American diplomats would always encourage the Indian government to have more diplomatic dialogues with Pakistan to help prevent a nuclear war between the two neighbors. This senior Indian diplomat agreed to do so. But he then asked the Americans why they didn't talk to Iranian diplomats. If Iran had harmed America by holding its diplomats hostage, India believed that Pakistan had done it greater harm by carrying out a sneak military attack at Kargil and other terrorist attacks on India, including an attempted attack on the Indian parliament. Would America talk to Iran if Iranian agents had tried to storm Capitol Hill with guns and bombs? Yet this is what America advised India to do with Pakistan. Could America practice what it preaches to others?

The violent rhetoric of Iranian leaders, especially President Ahmadinejad, has undoubtedly made it difficult for all Western diplomats to talk to Iran. Undoubtedly, there is much that is deplorable in his rhetoric. But Fareed Zakaria has reminded Americans that Mao Zedong made even more violent statements. Mao said in 1957, "If the worst came to worst and half of mankind died, the other half would remain while imperialism would be razed to the ground."[21] Despite this rhetoric, America managed to achieve a grand bargain with China. One of the biggest breakthroughs of twentieth-century diplomatic history was President Nixon's visit to China in February 1972. As the guest at a banquet in Beijing, Nixon lavishly praised his hosts and declared:

As you said in your toast, the Chinese people are a great people, the American people are a great people. If our two peoples are enemies the future of this world we share together is dark indeed. But if we can find common ground to work together, the chance for world peace is immeasurably increased.

In the spirit of frankness which I hope will characterize our talks this week, let us recognize at the outset these points: We have at times in the past been enemies. We have great differences today. What brings us together is that we have common interests which transcend those differences. As we discuss our differences, neither of us will compromise our principles. But while we cannot close the gulf between us, we can try to bridge it so that we may be able to talk across it.

So, let us, in these next 5 days, start a long march together, not in lockstep, but on different roads leading to the same goal, the goal of building a world structure of peace and justice in which all may stand together with equal dignity and in which each nation, large or small, has a right to determine its own form of government, free of outside interference or domination. The world watches. The world listens. The world waits to see what we will do. What is the world? In a personal sense, I think of my eldest daughter whose birthday is today. As I think of her, I think of all the children in the world, in Asia, in Africa, in Europe, in the Americas, most of whom were born since the date of the foundation of the People's Republic of China.

What legacy shall we leave our children? Are they destined to die for the hatreds which have plagued the old world, or are they destined to live because we had the vision to build a new world?

There is no reason for us to be enemies. Neither of us seeks the territory of the other; neither of us seeks domination over the other; neither of us seeks to stretch out our hands and rule the world.

Chairman Mao has written, "So many deeds cry out to be done, and always urgently. The world rolls on. Time passes. Ten thousand years are too long. Seize the day, seize the hour."

This is the hour, this is the day for our two peoples to rise to the heights of greatness which can build a new and a better world.

In that spirit, I ask all of you present to join me in raising your glasses to Chairman Mao, to Prime Minister Chou, and to the friendship of the Chinese and American people which can lead to friendship and peace for all people in the world.[22]

What Nixon achieved with Mao America can now also try to achieve with Iran. America can take the first step toward a more civilized discourse by not calling Iran names. It was a huge mistake for President Bush to lump Iran into the "axis of evil." This remark achieved nothing (apart from gaining notoriety for the speechwriter who coined the phrase). Most Americans were also not aware that such a callous remark poured salt into Iranian wounds.

Most Americans have seen themselves as victims vis-à-vis Iran ever since American diplomats were held hostage by Iran. Few Americans are aware that the Iranians have even greater reason to feel victimized by the US. Twice in the twentieth century America intervened decisively in Iran to thwart the democratic process there. It is not just the mullahs in Iran who remember this. Almost all Iranians, no matter where they live, remember what America has done. The economics correspondent of the *Financial Times*, Scheherazade Daneshkhu, who is of Iranian origin, explains how America had damaged Iran:

> Almost 30 years after Pahlavi crowned himself shah in 1925, the Iranian people had another go at establishing democracy. From 1951–53 they backed Mohammad Mossadeq, the elderly, independent-minded prime minister who nationalized the Iranian oil industry. Once again, this action pre-dated similar movements in the region, notably the nationalization of the Suez Canal by Egypt's Gamal Abdel Nasser, the 50th anniversary of which has fallen due this year [2006].

But this democratic experiment was again thwarted, this time after Kermit Roosevelt, grandson of President Theodore Roosevelt and head of the Central Intelligence Agency's Middle East division, backed by the British, engineered a coup to overthrow Mossadeq and put Mohammad Reza Pahlavi, Reza Pahlavi's son, on the Peacock throne.[23]

Virtually every Iranian today knows that when Iran elected Mohammad Mossadeq as its prime minister in 1951, the CIA engineered a coup to remove him in 1953. This event is also common knowledge around the world and has deeply penetrated the Iranian psyche and conditioned the Iranian attitude toward the West. Indeed, it may have affected the modern Iranian psyche as much as 9/11 has affected the modern American psyche. American intellectuals would be shocked to meet any thoughtful international leaders who did not know about 9/11. Similarly, Iranian intellectuals would be shocked to encounter a senior global personality who had never heard of Mossadeq. In the buildup to the Iraq War, Tony Blair was given a briefing on the Gulf region. An analyst referred to the Mossadeq chapter, and Blair apparently asked, "Who is Mossadeq?"

A similar level of ignorance affects the American-Iranian relationship. The first lesson that the US should have learned from its disastrous invasion of Iraq is that it must try to understand the history and culture of the country it is dealing with. In her brilliant article comparing US knowledge of Iraqi culture today with the deep understanding of Japanese culture that American occupation forces brought with them when they occupied Japan in 1945, Nassrine Azimi writes,

> Shoichi Koseki, a professor of constitutional law in Tokyo, has described some of the American preparations for the occupation of Japan, which started while the United States was still at war. Already in 1944 for example, more than 1,500 American military and civilian administrators were being put through intensive six-month courses at America's best academic institutions—Harvard, Yale, Stanford, Michigan, Northwestern.
>
> They studied with teachers educated in Japanese universities, learning not just about politics and economy, but also the language, and the workings of local government and the educational system of Japan. Ruth Benedict's "The Chrysanthemum and the Sword" was mandatory reading.
>
> The U.S. Department of War, for its part, closely studied Japan's prewar cinema. Weeks after the occupation began, American officials were consulting with local filmmakers and writers about the use of film in the country's post-war reconstruction.
>
> Certainly those were different times, and Japan was a different country. But the Japanese were probably just as alien to the Americans as Iraqis and Afghans are to Western nation-builders today.[24]

By contrast, when America invaded Iraq, no such preparations were made. As Azimi asks, "How, for example, did it inform the dispatch of some 120,000 mostly Christian soldiers to Iraq—a Muslim country and one of the most ancient civilizations on earth?" American ignorance of history and culture is truly astonishing at a time when the rest of the world is increasingly both affected by America and well-educated about America.

America and Iran are not the first two nations to feel victimized by each other. History is replete with many examples. Most of them have gone on to establish diplomatic relations with each other. America stands as the exception in refusing to contemplate such a move or even to contemplate a direct dialogue with Iran. In May 2006 President Ahmadinejad made the surprising gesture of writing an eighteen-page letter to President Bush in which he offered to begin a dialogue with America. He wrote, "For some time now I have been thinking, how can one justify the undeniable contradictions that exist in the international arena—which are being constantly debated, especially in political forums and amongst university students. Many questions remain unanswered. These have prompted me to discuss some of the contradictions and questions, in the hope that it might bring about an opportunity to redress them."[25] President Bush refused to reply. The American media mocked the letter. Virtually all American pundits dropped heavy doses of sarcasm in their comments on Ahmadinejad's letter. No one said that writing personal letters is one of the most civilized forms of discourse and a good first step to resolve misunderstandings. Iran took the first step, but America decided not to reciprocate.

The key point to emphasize here is that the West is losing the ability to communicate effectively with the Islamic world. In his *New York Times* article "The Politics of God," Mark Lilla quoted President Ahmadinejad's letter at length:

In May of last year, President Mahmoud Ahmadinejad of Iran sent an open letter to President George W. Bush that was translated and published in newspapers around the world. Its theme was contemporary politics and its language that of divine revelation. After rehearsing a litany of grievances against American foreign policies, real and imagined, Ahmadinejad wrote, "If Prophet Abraham, Isaac, Jacob, Ishmael, Joseph or Jesus Christ (peace be upon him) were with us today, how would they have judged such behavior?" This was not a rhetorical question. "I have been told that Your Excellency follows the teachings of Jesus (peace be upon him) and believes in the divine promise of the rule of the righteous on Earth," Ahmadinejad continued, reminding his fellow believer that "according to divine verses, we have all been called upon to worship one God and follow the teachings of divine Prophets." There follows a kind of altar call, in which the American president is invited to bring his actions into line with these verses.[26]

He added that when Westerners read a letter "like Ahmadinejad's, we fall mute, like explorers coming upon an ancient inscription written in hieroglyphics." He then says:

The problem is ours, not his. A little more than two centuries ago we began to believe that the West was on a one-way track toward modern secular democracy and that other societies, once placed on that track, would inevitably follow. Though this has not happened, we still maintain our implicit faith in a modernizing process and blame delays on extenuating circumstances like poverty or colonialism. This assumption shapes the way we see political theology, especially in its Islamic form—as an atavism requiring psychological or sociological analysis but not serious intellectual engagement. Islamists, even if they are learned professionals, appear to us primarily as frustrated, irrational representatives of frustrated, irrational societies, nothing more. We live, so to speak, on the other shore. When we observe those on the opposite bank, we are puzzled, since we have only a distant memory of what it was like to think as they do. We all face the same questions of political existence, yet their way of answering them has become alien to us. On one shore, political institutions are conceived in terms of divine authority and spiritual redemption; on the other they are not. And that, as Robert Frost might have put it, makes all the difference.[27]

In short, the West needs to make an urgent effort to understand the Muslim mind better.

It would have been both brave and wise for President Bush to respond to President Ahmadinejad along the lines of Nixon's toast to Chairman Mao in Beijing: "We have at times in the past been enemies. We have great differences today. As we discuss our differences, neither of us will compromise our principles. But while we cannot close the gulf between us, we can try to bridge it so that we may be able to talk across it." It is actually quite remarkable that Nixon was able to say these words when America still had no diplomatic relations with China. Talking through differences is another civilized thing to do. Most Americans are unaware that Ahmadinejad's predecessor, the moderate President Mohammad Khatami, tried several times to start a dialogue with America. It would have been reasonable for America to respond positively. In private, many American diplomats, including President Clinton, wanted to respond positively. However, they were afraid of being crucified domestically. This may well be the biggest handicap for American foreign policy. Sensible foreign policy options are killed by the hugely divisive and often dysfunctional domestic political process.

The paradox here is that while America would like Iran to be a stable and predictable actor in the world, the US itself remains one of the most unpredictable actors on the world stage. An example was given by Nicholas Kristof, who documents at length how the Iranian government made a breathtaking proposal to normalize relations with America. Iran offered an olive branch, but America spurned it. In Kristof's words,

> In the master document, Iran talks about ensuring "full transparency" and other measures to assure the U.S. that it will not develop nuclear weapons. Iran offers "active Iranian support for Iraqi stabilization." Iran also contemplates an end to "any material support to Palestinian opposition groups" while pressuring Hamas "to stop violent actions against civilians within" Israel (though not the occupied territories). Iran would support the

transition of Hezbollah to be a "mere political organization within Lebanon" and endorse the Saudi initiative calling for a two-state solution to the Israeli-Palestinian conflict.

Iran also demanded a lot, including "mutual respect," abolition of sanctions, access to peaceful nuclear technology and a U.S. statement that Iran did not belong in the "axis of evil." Many crucial issues, including verification of Iran's nuclear program, needed to be hammered out. It's not clear to me that a grand bargain was reachable, but it was definitely worth pursuing—and still is today.

Instead, Bush administration hard-liners aborted the process. Another round of talks had been scheduled for Geneva, and Ambassador (Javed) Zarif (Iranian Ambassador to the UN) showed up—but not the U.S. side. That undermined Iranian moderates.

A U.S.-Iranian rapprochement could have saved lives in Iraq, isolated Palestinian terrorists and encouraged civil society groups in Iran. But instead the U.S. hard-liners chose to hammer plowshares into swords.[28]

Today, any suggestion that America should talk to Iran is dismissed with the retort that Ahmadinejad is beyond the pale. With his extreme statements on Israel and with his organization of the holocaust-denial conference in Tehran in December 2006, Ahmadinejad has proven that he is uncivilized. If this is the real reason why America will not talk to Iran, why then did it reject the overtures made by Khatami, a modern political figure by any standards? The simple point I am trying to make here is that the political obstacles preventing a dialogue between America and Iran exist in both Washington, DC, and Tehran.

Both America and Iran are complex societies. In both political systems there exists a spectrum of voices. In America the spectrum ranges from right-wing Republicans to left-wing Democrats. In Iran it ranges from extremely conservative religious mullahs to moderate modernizers. In both countries there are constant tussles to grab the key decision-making posts, and in both cases the people will ultimately decide which end of the spectrum ends up in political office.

Both the US and Europe claim that they would like to see the moderate modernizers gain ascendancy in Teheran over the wildly radical voice of Ahmadinejad. If so, it is curious that America is leading the charge toward containment rather than engagement with Iran. Containment inevitably helps the extremist voices who want to keep Iran closed. Engagement helps those voices who want to open up and reform Iranian society.

LEARNING FROM ASIAN COMPETENCE

The case of Iran clearly demonstrates how ideological considerations distort the decision-making processes in the West. This is one additional factor that contributes to an emerging pattern of Western foreign policy failures. By contrast, there is a growing tendency outside of the West to adopt pragmatic approaches to global and regional challenges. This may explain, in part, the rising tide of Asian competence.

The time has come for the West to consider the possibility that other nations and communities are as competent, if not more competent, in managing global and regional challenges. The recent record of some Asian countries and regional organizations serve as evidence of growing Asian competence, which also explains why the guns are virtually silent throughout East Asia today. The EU, in achieving zero prospect of war, which represents the peak of human civilization in this dimension, seems to have been a far more successful regional organization than any of its Asian counterparts, including ASEAN. The EU has been enormously successful in delivering both peace and prosperity to its own member states. This success is formidable, but it is remarkable how the EU has failed in delivering peace and prosperity to its neighbors.

It is inevitable that the economic and political situation in North Africa will eventually affect the EU. If North Africa became peaceful and prosperous, the EU would benefit. If North Africa becomes more troubled, the EU will suffer. This has indeed happened. Thousands of boat people try to enter the EU illegally. New terrorist groups in North Africa are threatening the EU. In July 2006 French President Jacques Chirac warned what would happen without economic development in Africa in the coming decades: "One cannot solve a problem outside of its context, and the context here is obviously North-South. Today, there are 950 million Africans in Africa, 450 million under 17. In 2040, there will be two billion. If we do not develop this Africa, they will flood the world," he said.[29] Although Chirac was warning the world, the real danger is faced by Europe because it is the only developed region contiguous to Africa. (See Figure 5.3, which shows the scale of the shifting demographics of Europe and Africa.)

The shrinking demographics of the EU states and the exploding demographics of Africa clearly mean that the EU has a vested interest in sharing its peace and prosperity with its neighbors. But this has not happened. Remarkably, there is little honesty in the European analysis of this catastrophic strategic failure.

Similarly, the little Western analysis I have seen on the EU's failures in the Balkans seems to suggest that these were only errors of *omission* made by the EU. The general Western understanding of what happened in the Balkans is that the EU tried to prevent war in the Balkans and failed. But this is only one part of the story. There were far more serious errors of *commission*.

Another region where the EU has tried and failed to provide diplomatic leadership has been the Middle East. It is a founding member of "the Quartet" (which also includes the US, Russia, and the UN), which has been working hard for years to bring peace to the Middle East. It would be fair to say that the Quartet has failed. It may not have just failed to bring progress; as in the Balkans, there may have been some serious reversals.

It was actually on a European initiative that the Quartet started to meet in April 2002. Based on previous contacts at the Sharm al-Sheikh

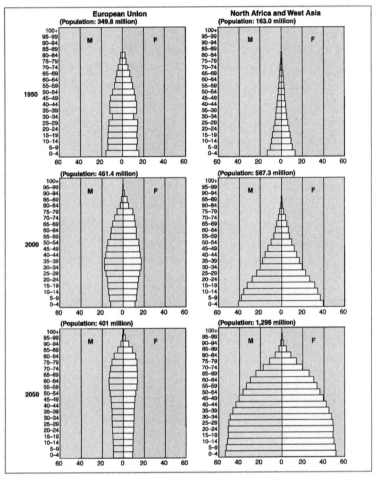

Figure 5.3 Population Size and Age Distribution for 1950, 2000, and 2050 in an Anticipated Enlarged European Union of Twenty-Five Countries and in Twenty-Five Countries in North Africa and West Asia

Source: Joel E. Cohen, "Human Population: The Next Half Century," Science 302, 14 November 2003, 172.

summit in 2000 and the United Nations General Assembly in 2001, the Spanish EU presidency together with the high representative of the EU's Common Foreign and Security Policy, Javier Solana, invited the UN secretary general and the US and Russian ministers of foreign affairs to a high-level meeting on the Middle East peace process in Madrid. In the following years the Quartet members convened, albeit erratically, about a dozen times, but with little outcome. The so-called road map to peace that was negotiated in September 2002 by the Quartet, legitimized by UN Security Council Resolution 1515, and accepted by Israel as well as the Palestinian Authority has not been implemented. It was only in early 2007 that the Quartet experienced a revival, following a renewed European and US commitment. In February alone the Quartet met twice, and its meetings were surrounded by a number of missions by its members across the Middle East region. Despite all this diplomatic activity, the Quartet has achieved little. To make matters worse, Egypt, a moderate Muslim nation, has accused it of being politically unbalanced. On 30 May 2007 Egypt blasted the Quartet for blaming the Palestinians for the recent upsurge in fighting and sparing Israel any criticism. Alaa el-Hadidy, a spokesman for Egypt's foreign ministry, described the Quartet's statement as "unbalanced." "This is tantamount to giving a green light to Israel to continue its operations in the Palestinian territories," el-Hadidy said. "The credibility of the Quartet, as a neutral side, is now at stake."[30]

A European reader at this stage may wish to interject that North Africa, the Balkans of Europe, and the Middle East are unusually difficult regions. True. But they are no less politically difficult than either the Balkans of Asia (Southeast Asia) or East Asia in general. In contrast to the EU, China has shown restraint and remarkable diplomatic skill in managing its geopolitical environment. If there was a scale of geopolitical competence, with ten being the highest score, the former Soviet Union would get a two, the EU a four, the US a six, and China an eight or nine.[31]

Deng Xiaoping's pragmatic wisdom has outlived him, becoming firmly embedded in Chinese political culture. It explains why China's relations with virtually all of its neighbors have actually improved since he died. The same is true of China's relations with other major powers and regions. This may be purely an accident of history, but more probably it reflects the tremendous geopolitical acumen of Beijing in managing China's relations with the world. This is another huge feature of the Asian political landscape that Western commentators have not taken note of: the global impact of Beijing's geopolitical acumen.

A few case studies illustrate the depth and breadth of China's skillfulness. The most difficult relationship between China and any of its neighbors is clearly the one with Japan. The wounds have not fully healed from the period of Japanese occupation of China from 1931 to 1945. From time to time, the Chinese perceive the Japanese to be behaving insensitively by carrying out actions that demonstrate a clear lack of remorse for Japanese atrocities committed during the occupation. The decision of former Prime Minister Junichiro Koizumi to visit the Yasukuni shrine, which honors Japan's 2.5 million war dead, including 14 convicted war criminals, every year during his six-year term in office between 2001 and 2007 clearly angered the Chinese. One of the lowest points in the Sino-Japanese relationship occurred in April 2005, when there were widespread demonstrations against Japan in China following the publication of a Japanese history textbook *Atarashii Rekishi Kyokasho* (New History Textbook), which downplayed the nature of Japan's military aggression in the First Sino-Japanese War, Japan's annexation of Korea in 1910, the Second Sino-Japanese War, and World War II.

Against this backdrop, it would be perfectly reasonable to expect a continuing downturn in Sino-Japanese relations. The mistakes in this relationship have not been made by the Japanese alone. In November 1998, for example, Chinese President Jiang Zemin had a six-day state visit to Japan that was nearly a disaster. For reasons that are still not yet clear, Jiang decided to use his visit to lecture every senior Japanese official he met on Japan's poor record of atoning for its sins in World War II. In his public speeches in Japan, Jiang expressed his unhappiness with Japan's reluctance to apologize unequivocally for its aggression during its occupation in China. At a meeting with Japanese legislators, Jiang, referring to Japan's invasion of China, said that history was a mirror. "By making history a lesson for both China and Japan, and by preventing tragedy from

being repeated, the two countries can develop long-lasting relationship for the first time," the Chinese president said.[32]

Several news articles suggest that China had expected the Japanese
government to tender an unqualified written apology during Jiang's
official visit. China had even taken it for granted that such an apology
would be of the kind that the Japanese prime minister and the Japanese
emperor tendered during the visit by South Korean President Kim
Dae Jung in October. However, nothing of the sort happened. What
Jiang got on arrival in Tokyo was the usual statement of "deep
remorse" by Prime Minister Keizo Obuchi, echoing a statement made
by another Japanese prime minister, Tomiuchi Murayama, in 1995.
Obuchi, despite belonging to the progressive Japanese Socialist Party,
which then headed a coalition government, had refused to incorporate
the statement into the official joint statement. During Jiang's visit,
Japan's Chief Cabinet Secretary Hiromu Nonaka said that Japan had
apologized enough for the war in China, which he said was undertaken
by a "small group of militarists."[33] It was, therefore, unsurprising that
there was no signed joint communiqué issued at the end of the
Chinese president's visit.

Despite these enormous difficulties and tensions built into the Sino-
Japanese relationship, the Beijing leadership has succeeded in ensuring
that this relationship never completely went off the rails. In April 2007
China even managed to put the relationship back on a positive track
during Chinese Premier Wen Jiabao's three-day official visit to Tokyo.
Wen was able to deliver a speech to the Japanese parliament (the Diet)
that was both politically acceptable to Japan's detractors in China and
politically palatable to a skeptical Japanese public. He displayed enormous political skill, taking personal charge of this challenge. As he told
Chinese residents in Japan, "I did a lot of preparation. Every sentence
is written by me, and I did all the research work myself. Why? Because
I feel our nation's development has reached a critical moment. We
need to have a peaceful and conducive international environment."[34]
In his speech at the Japanese Diet, Wen said,

We, the Chinese Government and people, have all along taken a forward-looking approach. We believe that we need to take history as a mirror to guide the growth of our ties in the future. By stressing the importance of drawing the lessons from history, we do not mean to perpetuate hatred. Rather, we want to secure a better future for our relations. Since the normalization of diplomatic ties between China and Japan, the Japanese Government and leaders have on many occasions stated their position on the historical issue, admitted that Japan had committed aggression and expressed deep remorse and apology to the victimized countries. The Chinese Government and people appreciate the position they have taken. We sincerely hope that the Japanese side will act as it has stated and honor its commitment. Peace will bring benefit to China and Japan, while confrontation can only do harm to them. We should carry forward the friendship between the two peoples from generation to generation. This is in keeping with the historical trend and meets the desire of the two peoples, and it is also what Asia and the international community hopes to see.[35]

The political difficulties inherent in the China-Japan relationship are probably as difficult and intractable as those in the Israel-Palestine, Greece-Turkey, India-Pakistan, or even America-Iran relationship. In some ways, the political wounds in the Sino-Japanese relationship (when you consider thirty-five million Chinese were killed in the Japanese occupation) may be greater than any of the others. Nevertheless, since China has a deep national interest in preserving good ties with all of its neighbors, it is prepared to accept Deng's advice to "swallow bitter humiliation."

The Chinese leadership also takes the "long view" in a way that few Western leaders seem capable of doing now. Few major nations have been as painfully humiliated as China has been in the past two hundred years. If the Chinese wanted to focus on their previous wounds and humiliation, they would have plenty to work with. The decision not to do so reflects a very carefully thought-out strategy. Eventually, as China becomes strong and powerful, its neighbors will have to adapt to its rise and acknowledge Chinese power. China need not impose its views or perspectives on others. Others will eventually adjust if China succeeds in its single-minded goal of promoting economic development. This policy was spelled out in an editorial by Yang Baibing, secretary of the CCP Central Committee's Secretariat, secretary general of the Military Commission, and director of the military's General Political Department in the CCP's mass-circulation general newspaper, *People's Daily*. Echoing Deng's thinking, he said in 1991,

> This is a golden opportunity for China's reform and construction. If we do not meet the time, we may otherwise be punished. We must make full use of the current favorable conditions both at home and abroad to push our economic construction onto a new stage and lay a foundation for rapid development in the next century. If we say that from mid-1800s to the mid-1900s, the Chinese nation finally stood up through more than 100 years of heroic struggles, in which one stepped into the breach as another fell, then from the mid-1900s to the mid-2000s, through another 100 years of struggle, our country will completely shake off poverty and truly stride along toward becoming a developed and prosperous country as a giant in the East.[36]

China has made a major effort to learn from the mistakes of other major powers. In 2006, China Central Television broadcast an engaging twelve-part documentary, *Rise of the Great Powers*, which analyzed the emergence of nine great powers, including Spain, England, and America, and endorsed the idea that China should study the experiences of nations and empires it once condemned as aggressors bent on exploitation. The series did not try to project any kind of ideological worldview but attempted to be as objective as possible in its analysis. The message conveyed to the Chinese public was a subtle one: China has the potential to become a great power, but it also has to understand why great powers had succeeded and failed in the past. "Our China, the Chinese people, the Chinese race has become revitalized and is again stepping onto the world stage," said Qian Chengdan, a professor at Beijing University and the intellectual father of the series. "It is extremely important for today's China to be able to draw some lessons from the experiences of others."

Having failed in the great power game in the nineteenth and the first half of the twentieth centuries as well as having wasted the first eight decades of the twentieth century in its efforts to modernize, China was not expected to emerge as the most astute and effective geopolitical player of the twenty-first century. But it certainly has. Deng Xiaoping left behind a lot of political wisdom for his successors in Beijing to follow. Much of it is captured in the famous twenty-eight characters that Deng used: (1) *lengjing guancha*—observe and analyze [developments] calmly; (2) *chenzhuo yingfu*—deal [with changes] patiently and confidently; (3) *wenzhu zhenjiao*—secure [our own] position; (4) *taoguang yanghui*—conceal [our] capabilities and avoid the limelight; (5) *shanyu shouzhuo*—be good at keeping a low profile; (6) *juebu dangtou*—never become a leader; (7) *yousuo zuowei*—strive to make achievements. Point number five (*shanyu shouzhuo*) is especially significant. It explains a lot of Chinese behavior in international fora. When WTO talks break down, the American, European, Brazilian, and Indian ministers rush to provide their "spin" to the international media, but no Chinese face ever appears. This reflects a carefully considered decision to continue to have a low profile while China gradually emerges as a great power.

The geopolitical chessboard of the twenty-first century will be far more complex than the chessboards of the nineteenth and twentieth centuries, marked for the first time by the entry of several non-Western major powers. The decisions that affect the world can no longer be made in a few Western capitals whose cultural parameters in analyzing problems and solutions are essentially similar. Now new cultural and political perspectives have entered the scene. On this complex chessboard, most Western commentators expected (with good reason) that the Western powers would continue to be the most shrewd and adept geopolitical actors. Instead, they have floundered.

Their incompetence has also provided significant opportunities that China has been able to cleverly and carefully exploit without paying any serious political price in many quarters. China has accumulated more credits on its ledger than any other major power. After a shaky beginning with the shooting and death of a PLA pilot in the Hainan China-US air collision in April 2001, China has succeeded in establishing an extremely close relationship with the Bush administration, despite its domination by neocons suspicious of China. The geopolitical accidents of 9/11 and the invasion of Iraq helped. But China was able to strengthen its relationship with America without damaging its ties with the Islamic world. In the same period, it also significantly improved its relationships with all of its neighbors. Even more important, China is emerging slowly but carefully as a global geopolitical player by making careful inroads into Latin America and Africa.

In the Western Hemisphere, China is taking advantage of failures of half-hearted market reforms and Washington's unwillingness to pursue "good neighbor" relations in Latin America with much enthusiasm. National Defense University Professor Cynthia A. Watson notes, "The 1990s turned into a period of severe disappointment as free markets led to rampant corruption and unfulfilled expectations in Latin America while Washington became the world's superpower rather than a partner for the region."[37] Moreover, China's flexibility counters more rigid US approaches, postulates Stephen Johnson.

Obtaining any kind of assistance from the United States requires compliance on a battery of restrictions, including observing human rights, protecting the environment, promising not to send U.S. military personnel to the International Criminal Court (ICC), not assisting current or former terrorists, and not using U.S.-provided equipment for any other than its stated purpose.

American commitments also depend on legislative approval and can be reversed if the mood in the U.S. Congress shifts. China, on the other hand, can bargain on the spot without a lot of caveats.[38]

In Africa, besides the quest for natural resources, China is increasingly making its presence felt in many ways, and not all of them are controversial. Under the auspices of the UN, the China-Africa Business Council opened in March 2005; headquartered in China, it was created to boost trade and development in the region. It has peacekeepers in Liberia and has contributed to construction projects in Ethiopia, Tanzania, and Zambia.[39] China is the only country to host a massive summit attended by a large number of African leaders (in November 2006).

There are about nine hundred investment projects on the African continent estimated to be financed with Chinese money. As Chinese Premier Wen Jiabao's eight-day tour to Africa began in June 2006, the political tagline of noninterference was highlighted in the official English-language *China Daily*. "China has been offering no-strings-attached financial and technical aid to the most needy in Africa," said an editorial in the paper. "It has been encouraging the African countries to develop their economy through trade and investment in infrastructure and social institutions, without dictating terms for political and economic reforms." A Western diplomat based in Beijing commented, "It reads like a direct rebuke of US and Western powers' foreign policy on the continent. . . . It is one of the first times they [Chinese] have so openly articulated their diplomatic priorities in Africa, and it is meant to present them as a more attractive world power than the US."[40]

In this same period (2001–2006), both the United States and Europe saw their global standing and influence diminish. Anti-Americanism reached new heights all around the world. In most parts of the world, it did not pay to be identified as pro-American. Some of this rancor toward America may disappear when the Bush administration leaves office in 2008. But unless America becomes as adept as China in managing geopolitical relationships across the globe, it could find that its global standing will continue to slip.

The European states have also had a bad beginning in the twenty-first century. Almost all their energies have been consumed by efforts to keep the EU integration process on track. This internal focus on short-term challenges has prevented EU leaders from taking the long view to see how Europe's standing could be enhanced in different parts of the world. This has inevitably led to a decrease in the EU's global influence. Many in the rest of the world are astonished that EU leaders and officials spend so much of their time on their *internal* arrangements when most of their emerging challenges are coming from *external* sources. A deep structural flaw has developed in the EU decision-making processes. Virtually no EU leader dares to suggest that the EU should spend more time looking outside rather than inside the EU. Europe's relations with the Islamic world could soon reach crisis proportions; no European politician seems able to lead Europe into a constructive long-term relationship with the Muslim world.

Another major geopolitical failure by Europe has been its inability to recognize that its continued domination of certain global processes have gone from being a symbol of its great power status to becoming a symbol of its growing irrelevance. Four of the G-7 members are EU nations. The G-7 is meant to represent the most powerful countries of the world. In theory, this gives the EU a firm hand on the steering wheel of a key global vehicle. In practice, *because* the Europeans continue to dominate the G-7, it has become progressively less relevant to the rest of the world.

This sharp observation by the *Economist* underscores the point: "The G7 once held great sway over exchange rates. When it met, in a previous incarnation, in New York in September 1985, it engineered a near 30% decline in the dollar. When it reconvened a year and a half later in Paris, it promptly halted that decline. By breaking bread with the Chinese on Friday, the current G7 is tacitly admitting that it can no longer achieve very much without them."[41]

The EU shows little ability to recognize its own shortcomings, preferring instead to believe it is destined to succeed, no matter what it does. But the decision-making processes of the EU are almost programmed to make the EU fail, especially in addressing long-term challenges. When the EU leaders meet to discuss common European responses to global challenges, they are guided not by an overall strategic assessment of the long-term interest of Europe but only by the short-term interests of each leader's domestic constituency. The long-term interests of the continent are sacrificed. The decisions are not always made based on the interests of five hundred million EU citizens but sometimes made in the interest of eight million citizens of one country. One recent episode demonstrates how this happens.

A few years ago, Austria elected a far-right government. In its election campaign, it declared its opposition to Turkey's entry into the EU. When Austria participated in the EU's discussion on Turkey, it proceeded to block progress in the discussions, taking advantage of the consensus rule in EU decision making and vetoing any positive decisions on Turkey. In practice, the bigger EU member states could have used their considerable influence on the Austrian government to give way, but none was prepared to pay the short-term price of alienating Austria for the long-term gain of protecting Europe's interests vis-à-vis Turkey. In this way eight million Austrians can determine the fate of seventy-one million Turks and then damage the long-term interests of five hundred million Europeans.

The EU's failure in developing a constructive long-term relationship with a key neighbor, Turkey, stands in sharp contrast with China's success in developing a constructive, long-term relationship with ASEAN. Objectively, if one were determining betting odds on whether the EU-Turkey relationship or the China-ASEAN relationship would do better, the odds should have favored the EU-Turkey relationship. The EU is rich and powerful, and Turkey has been keen to join the EU. There could well have been a happy outcome. China started its modernization program only in 1979. Before that, it had developed a hostile relationship with ASEAN, a pro-American noncommunist entity seen as anti-Chinese in its approach. Yet in less than three decades the relationship has gone from hostility to a close partnership. Relations between ASEAN and China first improved after the Sino-Soviet split, when China and America drifted closer together in the 1970s following the famous visits by Kissinger and Nixon to Beijing. They became even closer when ASEAN and China worked together in the 1980s to reverse the Vietnamese occupation of Cambodia.

At the end of the Cold War, when America lost interest in ASEAN and began to drift away, China continued to court ASEAN. Even more significantly, it made an enormous contribution to helping ASEAN weather the Asian Financial Crisis of 1997–1998. At considerable economic cost to itself, Beijing refused to devalue its currency, maintaining a rate of 8.3 renminbi to US$1. Had China devalued, as it had done by 33 percent in 1994, that would have made its exports less costly and also undermined efforts by the affected ASEAN countries to restore their economies. In addition, China gave economic assistance of more than US$1 billion to Indonesia and another US$1 billion to Thailand, the two economies most affected by the crisis. Many ASEAN countries still remember that America dithered before reaching out to help during this crisis. Japan, which also had the resources to stimulate recovery, helped less than China. The US and Asian nations had called on Japan to draw in more imports from its Asian neighbors to help their earnings, but Prime Minister Hashimoto said, "Japan needs to worry about its own self-interest. We are certainly not arrogant enough to think that we can take the role of locomotive for Asia."[42]

China's decision to help ASEAN was based not merely on altruism but on real politik. China's vice minister of foreign trade and economic cooperation, Long Young-tu, said, "We have evaluated the pros and cons and decided that it is in the best interest of China not to devalue. This might affect China's competitive position but we have more important things to do." According to Richard Halloran, former *New York Times* correspondent in Asia and Washington, "the Chinese leadership apparently saw the economic crisis as an opportunity to enhance

China's standing. Beijing sought to revive the Middle Kingdom's dominance over Asia and gradually build political pressure that would force the US to withdraw its military forces."[43] Halloran's words reiterate the Chinese wisdom in seeing an opportunity in every crisis. China used the 1997 crisis to secure long-term political gains. By contrast, America was motivated only by short-term political calculations.

China further changed the chemistry with ASEAN by making a remarkably generous offer. At the ASEAN-China Summit in November 2001, Chinese Premier Zhu Rongji stunned the ASEAN leaders by offering a free trade agreement (FTA). To demonstrate concretely that its offer was serious, China even offered unilateral concessions to the ASEAN countries. It offered an "early harvest" to the ASEAN countries by offering duty-free access to the Chinese market on six hundred agricultural products, including live animals, meat, fish, dairy products, other animal products, live trees, vegetables, fruits, and nuts. The Chinese leaders then confirmed their seriousness by completing the negotiations for the ASEAN-China FTA in record time. A year after the proposal, the final FTA was signed by the Chinese and ASEAN leaders at the eighth ASEAN Summit in Phnom Penh, Cambodia. According to the agreement, the two sides will establish an FTA within ten years, first with the six original ASEAN states—Brunei, Indonesia, Malaysia, the Philippines, Singapore, and Thailand, followed by the less developed ASEAN members of Vietnam, Laos, Cambodia, and Myanmar by 2015. China also accorded the three non-WTO ASEAN members, Vietnam, Laos and Cambodia, most-favored-nation status. The China-ASEAN FTA, when implemented in totality, will constitute a common market of 1.7 billion people, with a combined gross domestic product (GDP) of US$1.5 to 2 trillion.

Even without the remarkable generosity of the Chinese unilateral concessions, the offer of an FTA was a remarkable act in itself. ASEAN has had much longer "dialogue" relationships with fellow-capitalist countries like the US, Japan, and the EU. Until recently, ASEAN trade with these countries was far greater than its trade with

China. In economic terms, there were far more synergies between ASEAN and these developed economies than between ASEAN and China. Few would have predicted even ten years ago that China would make such an offer.

In theory, an FTA is a trade agreement. In practice, it represents a strategic calculation that the two parties have long-term interests in forging a closer partnership or that one party has an interest in strengthening the other party. The US decision to offer Mexico trade access through the North American Free Trade Agreement (NAFTA) was driven by a cold calculation that if America did not help to strengthen the Mexican economy (even at the cost of exporting jobs to Mexico), Mexico would end up sending more illegal immigrants to America. Hence, when Mexico joined NAFTA, it appeared to be the big short-term beneficiary in economic terms. In reality, the US became the bigger beneficiary because it did not have to worry about political and economic instability at its own doorstep.

The same cold geopolitical calculations that drove America to offer Mexico an FTA led China to offer an FTA to ASEAN. China was helping to preserve political and economic stability at its borders by strengthening the ASEAN economies. But other geopolitical calculations also influenced its decision. China is acutely aware that its steady rise could one day alarm America, the prevailing great power of the day. If America one day "woke up" and decided to contain a rising China just as it contained the Soviet Union, it could have used ASEAN countries (many of whom were American allies or friends in the Cold War) to encircle China. Hence, in a preemptive strike against any possible American encirclement, China shared its prosperity with its ASEAN neighbors. According to US analyst Joshua Kurlantzick, Chinese "soft power" in Southeast Asia is now so potent that, for the first time since 1945, the US is "facing a situation in which another country's appeal outstrips its own in an important region." China's aid to the Philippines is now four times as generous as that offered by America; twice as many Indonesians are now studying in China as are studying in the US.[44] With strong economic ties to China, the ASEAN countries would not be disposed to join any containment policy against China. Remarking on China's remarkable ASEAN policy, the National University of Singapore scholar Sheng Lijun writes, "China is no longer using the simplistic either black-or-white, either friend-or-enemy attitude, as in the Cold War to look at the complex world now. This has fundamentally changed its ASEAN policy and added a lot of flexibility to its diplomacy, which accounts heavily for its initiatives in the China-ASEAN FTA."[45]

If the EU were as capable as China in calculating its long-term geopolitical interests, it would have tried to match China in proposing an FTA to its neighbors in North Africa, the Middle East, or the Balkans. Instead of trying to deepen cooperation among its member states (with questionable long-term gains in terms of protecting the external interests of the EU), the EU should have tried to widen the impact of its prosperity by sharing it with its neighbors. Despite the size and strength of its economy, little of the EU's prosperity has spilled over into its immediate neighbors to the south. This is a result of the absence of any long-term strategic thinking guiding EU's policies.

Many EU officials will vehemently deny this analysis. They will point to the enormous amount of aid the EU has given to its neighbors, the various partnership agreements signed between EU and its neighbors, and the numerous summit meetings it has organized, including with its Mediterranean neighbors. It is true that the EU has not been inactive. But an audit of the *impact* of the EU on its neighbors may actually show that the EU has effectively shared little of its prosperity and, in some cases, may have done real damage with its huge agricultural subsidies. Take, for instance, the European-Mediterranean Partnership (EMP), also known as the Barcelona Process. The EMP was started in November 1995 with the aim of building the foundations for a new regional relationship between the EU and the ten North African and Middle Eastern Mediterranean signatory states (Algeria, Egypt, Israel, Jordan, Lebanon, Morocco, Palestinian Authority, Syria, Tunisia, and Turkey). Its most ambitious goal is the creation of a free trade zone between the two banks of the Mediterranean by 2010. However, according to the 2005 EU Commission–sponsored study "The Impact of EU Enlargement on the Euro-Med Partnership," a huge economic gap between the EU and the ten partner countries remains and continues to grow. Indeed, the sum of the GDP of the partner countries is only as high as the Spanish GDP alone. The study noted that "economic inequality between Europe and the rest of the Mediterranean has created a structure of asymmetrical interdependence, giving the EU the upper hand in all negotiations in the Euro-Mediterranean process."

During the same period, the EU also began devoting the vast majority of its technical and financial aid to prospective members. The EU enlargement has turned Cyprus and Malta, which until May 2004 were partner countries, into full members of the Union. It has also added eight more members: the Czech Republic, Estonia, Hungary, Latvia, Lithuania, Poland, Slovakia, and Slovenia. By 2003, the EU was allocating €545 (US$788) per capita per year to the accession counties, compared to a miniscule €14 (US$20) per capita per year to the Southern Mediterranean countries. Consequently, in contrast to the EMP Mediterranean partner countries, the new member states of the EU have grown much faster: the combined income of the partner countries remains at only one-tenth of the combined income of the new EU members.[46]

According to the nongovernmental organizations Friends of the Earth Middle East and Oxfam International, most agricultural products from the Southern Mediterranean countries with an advantage over EU products are subjected to the Community's Common Agricultural Policy (CAP) restrictions. Trade tariffs on fruit and vegetables vary by product and season, with the highest tariffs being imposed during periods when imports compete with homegrown products. Olive oil is an example where Southern Mediterranean countries could compete against EU products were it not for the €2.3 billion (US$3.3 billion) that EU olive oil producers receive from the CAP every year.[47] Jean Yves Moisseron of the Institute of Research for Development in Egypt says the financial assistance to Mediterranean countries is divided between that presented by the European Commission and that presented on a bilateral basis. The latter is five times higher than that presented by the EC. However, he also showed that across the ten years of the Barcelona Process, there has been a drop in bilateral assistance, which has not been compensated by increases in EC aid. Moreover, he showed that the actual assistance disbursed was only 40 percent of the pledged amounts, compared to US assistance, which was 100 percent disbursed during the year for which it was earmarked.[48]

The best way of measuring the quality of geopolitical performance is to look at the actual impact of policies, not debate their theoretical merits. In the case of China, the record will show that it has effectively shared its prosperity. Its neighbors are benefiting from rather than enduring China's rise. By contrast, after expanding its membership from fifteen to twenty-seven (and the new members have benefited a great deal from the EU, not least from some of the generous handouts the EU gives to its new members), the EU has had little positive impact on its periphery. The economic gap between North Africa and the EU has grown over the years, not shrunk. These results demonstrate a failure in geopolitical performance.

When the Cold War ended in 1989 and Europe looked confidently into the future while China remained deeply traumatized by Tiananmen, few would have dared to predict that in the following two decades, the EU would underperform in defending its long-term geopolitical interests while China would outperform every other country in the world. This is why any lingering Western assumption that the developed Western countries will naturally do a better job in managing global challenges than any of their Asian counterparts will have to be rethought. An objective assessment would show that Asians are proving to be capable of delivering a more stable world order.

6

PREREQUISITES FOR GLOBAL LEADERSHIP: PRINCIPLES, PARTNERSHIPS, AND PRAGMATISM

The time to restructure the world order has come. We should do it now. The clearest explanation for why the world has to change has been provided by the prime minister of India, Manmohan Singh. In December 2006 he said,

> Just as the world accommodated the rejuvenation of Europe in the post-War world, it must now accommodate the rise of new Asian economies in the years that lie ahead. What this means is that we need global institutions and new global "rules of the game" that can facilitate the peaceful rise of new nations in Asia. It also means that existing global institutions and frameworks of cooperation must evolve and change to accommodate this new reality. This is as true for the reform and revitalization of the United Nations and the re-structuring of the United Nations Security Council, as it is true for the management of multilateral trading system, or for the protection of global environment or for the security of world energy supplies.[1]

Restructuring will prove to be both difficult and easy. It will be difficult, because there are no natural leaders to do this job, since the West has become part of the problem while Asian countries are not yet ready to step in. It will be easy because the path we need to take is clear. We don't have to invent new principles to improve global governance—the principles of good governance in domestic societies can and should be applied to global society. "Best practice" at home can be applied to global governance. I therefore remain optimistic that we can create a better world.

In the absence of a natural global leader, we will have to resort to time-tested principles to produce social and political order. Three of the best principles are Western principles: democracy, rule of law, and social justice. Asia took off by imbibing the seven pillars of Western wisdom; the world can become a better place by implementing these three Western principles. We can also complement them with the ancient virtues of partnership and pragmatism. In short, there is hope. But first we have to understand why we have no natural leader to take us there.

Effectively, there are only four real candidates to provide global leadership today: the United States, the European Union, China, and India. No other entity has the capability or historical authority to attempt it.

America is obviously the strongest candidate to provide global leadership, as it has been since 1945. It has done more good for the world than any other country has, as my last book, *Beyond the Age of Innocence: Rebuilding Trust between America and the World*, documents. The 1945 rules-based order that America principally authored is a very special gift to the world. And America, more than any other country, launched the March to Modernity that most of humanity is moving toward. The US has also developed an elite who feels comfortable thinking in global terms. When the administration in power fails to meet its global responsibilities, American civil society can mobilize to change government policies.

But the America of 2008 is a very different country from the America of 1945. It is far less self-confident. John Foster Dulles, secretary of state in the early years of the Cold War, had no hesitation in offering free trade access to Japan. He was absolutely convinced of America's superior competitive abilities. If Dulles were alive today, he wouldn't understand what Lou Dobbs was ranting about. But Dobbs and his closed mind represent the new face of America. The election of Nancy Pelosi as Speaker of the House of Representatives further confirmed this; she has a protectionist tendency. In the field of security, the neocons have done enormous damage to America's global stature with their belief that America can act alone and stand alone. This is simply wrong. The events of 9/11 should have taught a lesson that America the great is not America the invulnerable. Yet instead of America reengaging the world, the gap between it and the world has never been wider.

Europe should also be, like America, a natural candidate to lead the world. For over two centuries, Europe has dominated world history. Decisions made in London or Paris, Berlin or Madrid have had global repercussions. Now completely peaceful, Europe today is also a model of a rules-based society. It has woven an intricate set of regulations to govern behavior among its members. A law-abiding region can help to create a law-abiding world.

But Europe has not been able to extend its benign influence outside its territory. Neither the Balkans nor North Africa has benefited from its proximity with the European Union. Most of the EU's economic policies toward the rest of the world have been distorted by the differing domestic dictates of the member states. The interests of rich French farmers trump the interests of poor African farmers. These poor African farmers are then forced to migrate illegally to Europe. An enlightened European policy would work toward creating jobs in Africa to prevent illegal immigration—but there are few enlightened external European policies.

History teaches us that leadership in any era is provided by emerging powers. For example, when America replaced the UK as the world's leading power, it moved naturally to providing global leadership. By the same logic, China should eventually take over the mantle of global leadership from America. In its own way, it is providing global inspiration, if not leadership. There is a sense of despair about the prospect of development in parts of Africa, Latin America, and the Islamic world. Their contacts with the West have only damaged their self-confidence. By contrast, the rise of China from abject poverty to successful modernization has been inspirational for them. When Hu Jintao visits Africa and Latin America, the Western media portray him as a rapacious resource-hungry new colonialist. China is certainly interested in resources, especially as a latecomer to the game. But it is also interested in long-term partnerships. Many African and Latin American states feel burned by their contacts with the West; China provides them an alternative partner for development. In many Muslim countries today, it would be politically suicidal for political leaders to say (as Kemal Ataturk said a century earlier), "Let us emulate the West." But the same politicians would gain political dividends for saying, "Let us emulate China." China is also developing the most robustly self-confident society of any major power today.

However, to provide global leadership, it will have to overcome one of its natural tendencies to remain insular. For much of its history, Chinese civilization saw no reason to engage the world. The response of Emperor Qian Long to the emissary of British monarch George III in 1793 revealed as much:

> The Celestial Court has pacified and possessed the territory within the four seas. . . . The virtue and prestige of the Celestial Dynasty having spread far and wide, the kings of the myriad nations come by land and sea with all sorts of precious things. Consequently there is nothing we lack. . . . We have never set much store on strange or ingenious objects. Nor do we need any more of your country's manufactures.[2]

The last century and a half of brutal contacts with the West have awakened China from its slumber. It now demonstrates greater civilizational strength. But China lacks a vision for the world. The Chinese mind has always focused on developing Chinese civilization, not developing global civilization. China today is willing to be a responsible stakeholder in the global order, but it shows little interest in leading the creation of a new global order. The Chinese leaders are also acutely aware that it will take China several more decades before it eliminates its rural poverty. Holding China together as a country and as a political entity will be a big enough challenge in this period of rapid change and development. Given these overwhelming domestic concerns, the Chinese leaders have little appetite to lead the world. For sound geopolitical reasons, they would also like to avoid making Americans fear that they are about to lose global leadership. Deng Xiaoping, in his famous twenty-eight characters, had said, "Be good at keeping a low profile."

Unlike Chinese leadership, Indian leadership is more cosmopolitan. The Indian elite who attend the annual Davos meetings feel very much at home. Most of the leading Indian elites have been trained in the best Western universities, especially in America. They speak English with ease, and they have developed strong personal networks with Western elites in the media, academic, business and financial communities.

At a time when many in the West are convinced that the West cannot coexist in peace with the Islamic world, India's example—though imperfect—is better than almost any other. With the growing cultural distance between the West and the East, India is likely to once again resume its natural role as the meeting point for the great civilizations.

However, India, in terms of national strength, is by far the weakest of the four. The size of its GNP is merely US$800 billion compared to US$12,448 billion for the United States, US$13,386 billion for the EU, and US$2,245 billion for China.[3] It also has a typical profile of a developing country, with huge pools of poverty (with more people living on less than $1 a day than all of Africa), huge developmental challenges, and many other pressing domestic and regional concerns.

It has the advantage of a well-established democracy, although recent elections have resulted in weak and fractured coalition governments. This inevitably leads to some inconsistencies in external policies. India is poised to become a major beneficiary of open global trade. Yet it has to reflect the view of some protectionist domestic constituencies in its trade policies. Some of the political parties in the coalition practice contradictory policies; for example, the Communist Party of India (Marxist) welcomes foreign investment in the state it rules, West Bengal, but opposes it nationally. Indian leaders, like Chinese leaders, have a lot to preoccupy them at home.

If neither America nor Europe nor China nor India can provide global leadership, are we lost? Since pessimism is very much in vogue in many learned circles in the West, it is vital to emphasize one important optimistic truth: by any standards, the world is a much better place in 2008 than it was in 1945. Far more people in the world wake up feeling optimistic about the future than ever before in human history. The main reason why history is moving in this positive trajectory is because many people all over the world have both the motivation and the capacity to learn and implement best practices from other societies. We have also discovered that in many areas we do not need to reinvent the wheel. If we have found the right principles to develop social order domestically, why not try to apply them globally?

New Principles of the Global Order

Most modern societies apply, directly or indirectly, the key Western principles of domestic governance (democracy, rule of law, and social justice). The challenge in the twenty-first century is to apply them globally in a careful and prudent fashion.

The principle that is the foundation of government in Western society is the principle of democracy. And the fundamental premise on which democracy is based is that each human being in that society is an equal stakeholder in the domestic order. This is why the government is selected on the principle of "one person, one vote." This has produced long-term stability and order in Western societies. If we want to produce similar long-term stability and order in global society, democracy is a cornerstone of the global order. This means that all 6.5 billion inhabitants of our planet should become equal stakeholders in the global order. The big question is how we apply the principles of "one person, one vote" to the global order.

Many Western minds, even the most sophisticated Western minds, may react with horror to such a suggestion. But they should pause and reflect on their reaction: they will come to understand better the subconscious assumptions about the world underlying their reaction. They will begin to realize that their assumptions remain rooted in the nineteenth and twentieth centuries even though the world has sailed into the twenty-first century.

The first assumption is the belief that the only real social unit that matters in our lives is the nation-state. But the world has changed irrevocably. When a SARS epidemic broke out in a small Chinese village, it did not stop at national borders; it crossed over into Hong Kong and then spread simultaneously to two cities on the opposite sides of the globe, Singapore and Toronto. There are many other examples that illustrate global interdependence—in finance and security, in the social and political fields (look at the new borderless cyber communities and the instant spread of new political viruses, like anti-Americanism). In short, the world has shrunk. All 6.5 billion inhabitants of Planet Earth sail on the same boat.

Nevertheless, we do not have a captain or a crew for the boat as a whole. We only have captains and crews to protect each cabin. None of us would sail into an ocean on a boat without a captain or crew to sail the boat, but that is exactly how we expect our globe to sail through the twenty-first century. And we actually get surprised when global crisis after crisis breaks out. We avoid thinking about how global issues should be managed, and then we get surprised that problems surface.

Global *government* is not the answer. Global *governance* is needed urgently. We need to develop both institutions and rules to manage the world as a whole, institutions and rules that reflect the wishes and interests of 6.5 billion inhabitants.

The West knows that the amount of political and economic space it occupies in the world is shrinking. The logical consequence is that the Western domination of several global institutions will also have to diminish—not a prospect that many Western countries relish. Many Western minds are searching for new ways to sustain Western domination or to strengthen those institutions that remain dominated by the West. One such new process that has been proposed is the creation of a "community of democracies." The Princeton Project on National Security has suggested that such a community would legitimize new global approaches. This idea is deeply flawed. The efforts to use Western-dominated institutions like the UN Security Council or the IMF and the World Bank will also not work. We truly need fresh thinking, and to get there, we first have to demolish some of the old thinking.

The notion that a community of democracies might lead the management of the globe rests on the idea that democracies inherently enjoy greater moral legitimacy because their governments have been elected. Since governments in the nondemocracies like China have not been elected by their own populations, they enjoy less political legitimacy. It is never said so explicitly, but one underlying reason for calling for the world to be run by a community of democracies is to justify the exclusion of China from global governance. A deeper assumption buried in this call is the belief that Western democracies (which will naturally lead such a community) are the most "civilized."

The paradox here is that to have the world run by a community of democracies is essentially an *un*democratic idea, if the population within that community represents less than half of the world's population. This idea is flawed both in theory and in practice: in theory because it is based on the assumption that a human community is better off when only a minority have a say in its governance and in practice because a community of democracies will be no more capable of factoring in the greater good of humanity than the community of nations as a whole. The leaders of any democracy are elected on the promise of serving their own domestic constituencies, not the global constituency. Indeed, it can often be fatal for a politician in any modern democracy to be accused of putting "global" interests ahead of "domestic" interests. A community of democracies is just as likely to create pools of selfishness that take care of their selective interests, not global needs.

If we are to inject the spirit of democracy into global governance and global decision making, we must look for institutions in which all countries of the world (and consequently all peoples of the world) are represented. Such institutions can only be found in the UN family. One of the key reasons why UN institutions like the World Health Organization (WHO) and World Meteorological Organization (WMO) enjoy widespread global legitimacy is because they have universal membership. When they meet and adopt decisions, these decisions enjoy legitimacy because they are seen to be adopted by all countries of the world.

One great irony here is that while many in the West are willing to work with specialized agencies like WHO and WMO, they are reluctant to strengthen the core UN institution from which all these specialized agencies come. I am referring to the UN General Assembly (UNGA). No other institution in the world can match the UNGA in meriting the title "the Parliament of Man" (as Paul Kennedy called his book on the UN). It is the most representative body on our planet. If we are looking for one body that represents the spirit of democracy across the globe, there can be no better institution than the UNGA.

However, having spoken to Western audiences over the past two decades, I am acutely aware that many Western countries are deeply skeptical of the UNGA. Indeed, the mere mention of the UNGA is likely to elicit guffaws. The Western critics are right to point out the imperfections of the UNGA. But in its imperfection, it actually serves as a useful symbol of the imperfect world we live in. Any decision adopted by this imperfect assembly will enjoy legitimacy in the eyes of the 6.5 billion people who live in this imperfect world.

For all its imperfections, the UNGA has at times shown more common sense and prudence than some of the sophisticated Western democracies. Any recourse to the UN General Assembly will result in more time taken to secure a decision or agreement. It cannot be surprising that the messiness of decision making in domestic democracies is amplified in decision making in the global arena. It takes time to persuade all people to march in the same direction, but this is precisely what gives legitimacy to the result. It is supposed to ultimately reflect the wishes of the people. Most countries in the world respect and abide by UN decisions because they believe in the legitimacy of the UN. The legitimacy the UN enjoys in the eyes of the majority of the world's population is a huge asset. If well used, it can provide a powerful vehicle to secure critical decisions on global governance.

There would be a revolt in America if anyone proposed that the US Senate should be ignored and instead be replaced by a selective council comprised of the representatives from only the five most populous states in America: California, Texas, New York, Florida, and Illinois.[4] Such an undemocratic suggestion would be rejected out of hand because it would be both unjust and unviable. The population of the other forty-five states would deem any such proposal as absurd. Yet such a proposal accurately describes how the world is run today: instead of turning to the UNGA (where there is universal representation of the 192 nation-states), America and Europe prefer to turn to the UNSC, which is effectively run by the 5 permanent member states.

Having served as an ambassador to the UN for over ten years, I have had many opportunities to study in depth American policies toward the UN. I have been struck by the almost total lack of awareness in the West of the fundamental contradiction in American policies toward the UN. A medical analogy may explain this contradiction best. No surgeon would try to rescue a limb of any human body while simultaneously weakening the heart. The heart is central; if it stops, all limbs die. Ironically, this is exactly what America is trying to do with the UN: it is constantly trying to weaken the effectiveness and legitimacy of the UNGA while trying hard to control and strengthen the decisions of the UNSC. But the UNGA is the heart of the UN, while the UNSC is only a limb. If the UNGA dies, the UNSC will die too.

Where does the UNSC get its legitimacy? What causes the world to accept and comply with its decisions? The simple legal answer is that all UN member states agreed to abide by the decisions of the UN Security Council when they joined the UN and ratified the UN Charter. However, there is also a big difference between "legality" and "legitimacy." Legal decisions can be illegitimate. Before the United States came into being, Americans lived under the rule of King George III, who had the legal right to pass laws that were binding on the inhabitants of the colonies. It was the perceived lack of legitimacy of King George's edicts that led eventually to the declaration of independence.

The decisions of the current UN Security Council have begun to feel like the edicts of King George III. They will remain legal for a while, but their legitimacy will gradually erode over time. It is an obvious but unpleasant truth that the five permanent members of the UNSC serve as dictators of the world. They make decisions that are binding and mandatory on 6.5 billion people without allowing them to have any say in choosing the permanent members. Only monarchies and dictators enjoy perpetual rule, without seeking reelection and without being held accountable. Most modern societies abhor permanent unelected rule. This explains why some leading European voices recognize that the UNSC is facing a crisis of legitimacy. In a brave essay entitled "Towards World Democracy," Pascal Lamy, a leading European intellectual, writes, "The real power of the UN lies in the Security Council, and more, specifically, in the right of veto. That is the exclusive privilege of its five members, whose legitimacy (based on who won the last World War) is, to say the least, 50 years out of date."[5]

The UNSC's refusal to bend to the American will in March 2003 on the Iraq War was a rare exception. Most of the time, the UNSC simply agrees with the American agenda. There are two simple structural reasons why the council normally bends in favor of the American agenda. First, most of UNSC decisions are effectively a result of negotiations among the five permanent members. The fundamental principle that guides their negotiations is very simple: "You scratch my back, and I scratch your back; you claw my back, and I claw your back." America's overwhelming power enables it to reach bilateral deals with the other permanent members—bilateral deals that sacrifice global interests.

The second reason why the Security Council bows to the American agenda is that the nonpermanent members, who serve on the council for rotating two-year terms, rarely find it in their interest to stand up to America, even if it is pushing in the wrong direction. In 1999, when Brazil was serving on the UNSC, it had an unusually able and effective ambassador to the UN, Celso Amorim. He noticed that the UNSC discussions on Iraq were not going anywhere. After intense negotiations, he proposed that three panels should be set up to investigate different dimensions of the Iraq problem. Most Security Council members agreed with his approach. When Brazil held the presidency of the Security Council in January 1999, a UNSC resolution was adopted to establish these three panels.

Then something surprising happened. Out of the blue, in the very middle of Brazil's term on the council, Ambassador Amorim was transferred to Geneva. It was an obvious demotion. Everyone was puzzled since he had been an effective ambassador. President Chirac asked the president of Brazil what happened. He was told that Washington had called Brazil and said, in effect: "If you want America to support you in areas that matter to you (like the IMF), then you should support America in areas that are important to America (like Iraq)." Brazil would have to pay a price in its bilateral relations if it ignored the wishes and interests of America. The call came not from the Bush administration but the

Clinton administration. Regardless of which American administration is in power, American behavior is consistent: it will make countries pay a heavy price if they go against American interests on the council. If this behavior continues, it is only a matter of time before the UNSC is generally perceived to be an instrument of American foreign policy.

America abused the Security Council again after the creation of the International Criminal Court (ICC). The mandate of the council is clear: it has the primary responsibility to respond to threats to international peace and security. It has no mandate to pass judgment on legal issues. When in 2002 the ICC came into existence, the US decided not to join it. However, even though the US did not ratify the ICC statutes, its citizens were *not* exempt from its provisions. American soldiers who committed war crimes could, for example, be hauled before the ICC (even though this was very unlikely, as the ICC provisions made it clear that primary jurisdiction rested with national authorities). However, America wanted to obtain absolute immunity for its soldiers. Taking advantage of the mandatory nature of UNSC resolutions, America proposed a draft resolution stating that the Security Council authorized immunity for American peacekeepers from ICC provisions.

Virtually, all international lawyers agreed that the Security Council would be exceeding as well as abusing its authority to pass judgment on the legal scope of the ICC. Nothing in the UN Charter allowed for this. That was also the reaction of most of the UNSC members when the American draft resolution was introduced. All the European members of the council had ratified the ICC treaty or convention. The British delegate made an eloquent statement stating that under British law, treaty obligations were mandatory. Hence, the UK could not vote for any resolution that was inconsistent with its treaty obligations. Despite these fine words and the clear understanding by international law experts that the UNSC had no authority to pass judgment in such areas, the council did eventually adopt a resolution providing American soldiers with immunity from ICC provisions. In the end, American power trumped international law.

Within a year or two, America recognized the folly of using the Security Council to circumscribe the ICC; in 2004 America withdrew the resolutions. But this episode brought out a very important lesson: the standing and legitimacy of the UN Security Council cannot be taken for granted. For the council to remain an effective institution, it must be perceived to have legitimacy.

The UNSC clearly faces the loss of its legitimacy in the eyes of the world. The time has come to make some radical changes in its structure and working methods. A former Pakistani foreign secretary said:

> The Security Council is left with no role in preventing conflicts or resolving disputes. Its deliberations are conducted in a theatrical manner through stage-managed debates and choreographed scenarios. There is no transparency in its proceedings. The open meetings of the Security Council are merely a talk-show in which member states are heard not listened to. Its decisions on critical issues are made either in Washington or reached behind closed doors among the Big Five in the ante-rooms of the Council's chamber.[6]

A Turkish columnist wrote, "The United Nations served a very important purpose by bringing together nations to heal the wounds of two world wars. However, the structure of the organization was formed by the winners of the war, providing privileged veto status in the UN Security Council. Since the establishment of the UN up until the present, the privileged members did not see any harm in using the UN to legitimize their own policy priorities."[7] Gyorgy Fodor was even more blunt in the liberal Hungarian newspaper *Magyar Hirlap*, writing, "What kind of institution is one of which the reorganization and the reorientation to the new world is hindered by built-in brakes? The Security Council cannot be reformed, expanded, narrowed, terminated since the present members of the Security Council do not want this and would veto it. Is this clear? It is 21st century surrealism. . . . This UN cannot be reformed: it should be destroyed and a new one should be built."[8]

There are at least three changes we will have to introduce to preserve the legitimacy of the UNSC. The first is to end perpetual rule. Applying this common-sensical principle to the Security Council is not easy. If the privileged positions of the great powers in the UN system were abolished, there is a clear danger that the UN could go the way of the League of Nations. If America were to walk away from the UN, both America and the UN would suffer. Hence, some way must be found to anchor the great powers of the day in the UN. The best way would be to retain the veto. This would ensure that the UN would not commit an act of folly by making a decision against the express wishes of any great power. Conferring veto powers on some countries and denying them to others would create inequality. But these inequalities would reflect the inequality of power in the world.

To serve as a true reflection of the world, the veto-bearing members of the UNSC should preferably reflect the great powers of 2045, not of 1945. This is in many ways the nub of the problem with the UNSC. The current permanent members have taken advantage of the veto to preserve great power status in the UN and to entrench themselves in perpetuity in the Security Council. For the UNSC to remain alive and relevant, it must create a system to allow new great powers to obtain the veto and for old great powers to cede their position graciously. New Asian powers like Japan and India should be given veto rights to reflect their new weight in the international system.

The biggest obstacle to change comes from Europe. There is a strong developing consensus that with the development of a Common European Foreign Policy by the European Union, it would be more logical to have Europe represented with a single European seat, in place of the UK and France. Any other formula, including the proposed addition of Germany, would only lead to Europe being overrepresented in the Security Council. Since Europe has less than 10 percent of the world's population, it is hard to justify three European vetoes on the Council. Hence, the only logical and viable solution is to have a single European seat, together with newly emerging powers. Implementing this in practice will not be easy. However, it is vital for the UN to reach a clear consensus that the veto-bearing members must be composed of the great powers of our time, not the great powers of the past.

The second change that needs to be introduced into the Security Council is the principle of accountability. It has now become a fundamental principle that all modern organizations should be held accountable for their actions. The Security Council is probably the last major organization in the world that still refuses to be held accountable in any way. When I was on the UN Security Council, I said—as strongly as I could—that if Bill Clinton and Kofi Annan could apologize for their failures to prevent genocide in Rwanda, the Security Council should also do the same. In some ways, the UNSC should be held even more accountable for the genocide in Rwanda: it has a constitutional mandate to prevent genocides, and it knew in advance that genocide was being planned and was on the verge of being executed. The Security Council, especially the five permanent members, could not plead ignorance; they knew it was coming. But they absolutely refused to accept the principle of accountability, and no apology was ever offered. As the world continues its March to Modernity, the Security Council faces the real danger of becoming a relic of history, representing a premodern culture of absolute rule rather than the culture of accountability of the modern age.

The world also needs to do more to strengthen the legitimacy of the council by strengthening the legitimacy of the "mother body" from which it gains its authority: the United Nations. If the United Nations were to crash and burn and disappear (together with the UN Charter), just like the League of Nations, the Security Council would crash with it.

Since the UN has become a constant object of ridicule in Western discourse, especially in the American media, and since many strategic thinkers are also beginning to despair over the prospect of improving global governance, I have a small practical suggestion to clear the doom and gloom. Please pick up a copy of the UN Charter and read it. The UN produces a tiny pocket volume, and it can be read in an hour or two.

It is a beautifully written document. Indeed, it was written by some of the best minds in the Western world and is rooted firmly in the Western intellectual and political tradition. The language is uplifting because its ideas come from Western ideals of universality of representation. Indeed it begins with the words "We, the peoples of the United Nations . . . "

In short, even in facing the challenge of global governance, we do not have to reinvent the wheel. We can tap the wisdom of the (Western) founding fathers of the UN, who, having just survived the scourge of World War II, put together a remarkable document that carefully balances the need to engage all of humanity while creating various organs (like the UN Security Council and the International Court of Justice) to handle specific issues. It is clear reading the UN Charter that all of its elements were meant to be a package deal. American efforts to use one part and ignore the rest could only kill the charter, one of the most valuable documents worked out in history. The legitimacy of the UN bodies flows from this charter. On its own, taken out of its context, the UNSC enjoys no legitimacy.

The UN Security Council is not the only global body that faces the danger of losing its legitimacy because of a deficiency of democratic legitimacy. The IMF and World Bank are in almost exactly the same situation. One of the strangest anomalies of our times is the practice that no Asian can lead either the IMF or the World Bank, the two leading global economic institutions. An unwritten but firm understanding since the founding of these institutions after World War II is that the head of the IMF should be a Western European and the head of the World Bank an American. Asians (as well as Africans and Latin Americans) are excluded. Any rule that disqualifies 88 percent of the world's population from leadership of a global economic institution is inherently unsustainable, especially when economic power is steadily shifting toward Asia. Indeed, this rule is an embarrassment to both the IMF and the World Bank.

The IMF and the World Bank have set up working groups to reconsider the process of selecting their leaders and to recommend changes. In theory, the solution should be easy to find, if they adopt the approach taken in the private sector. Most successful private organizations, including global corporations, research institutions, and universities, have thrived by implementing the principle of meritocracy. Organizations that have picked the strongest and most qualified individuals without regard to nationality, race, or creed—that is, the best human rather than the best connected human—have thrived. The stakeholders in these organizations demand that they adopt this performance-based approach. This also explains why so many Asians are rising to the top of many leading corporations, including McKinsey, Citibank, Standard Chartered Bank, and others.

All this would suggest a simple solution: adopt a clear and transparent process for selecting the heads of these organizations in which meritocracy and not nationality is the key consideration. However, certain harsh geopolitical realities will prevent meritocracy from being the key, let alone the sole, consideration in this selection process. Western Europe and to some extent the US are worried about their diminishing role and influence in global affairs. They are likely to fight a rear-guard action to retain their share of global influence.

Controlling the selection of leaders is not the only way North America and Western Europe dominate the IMF and the World Bank. They also dominate the voting power within these two institutions by controlling the allocation of quotas. An Australian Treasury working paper on IMF quotas published in November 2004 made a few pertinent observations. It noted that whatever measure is used to determine economic weight—GDP at market prices, GDP based on PPP—"a pattern of under-representation of China and Japan (and other countries in East Asia) emerges."[9] It then makes a profound observation: "It will be increasingly difficult for the IMF to present itself as a truly international institution if growing parts of the world economy do not have a voice in its governance commensurate with their true economic size."[10]

It is difficult to understand the IMF and World Bank quota systems because complex formulae are used. In theory, quota shares are meant to reflect share of the world GDP; in practice, they do not. Even though the quota shares of the G-7 and other advanced countries have diminished in relative terms, they continue to dominate the decision making on the board of directors. Professor Stephany Griffith-Jones of the Institute of Development Studies, University of Sussex, illustrates this point:

> Developed and developing countries that have joined the Bank in more recent years have received very different treatment. For example, when Switzerland joined in the mid 1990s, it was treated very well. By contrast, when China requested an increase in capital following the return of Hong Kong to Chinese sovereignty, it received only the same share as Canada—despite the vast difference in GDP between the two countries, not to mention the huge difference in population.[11]

(Note that China was a founding member of the IMF and the World Bank).

The managing director of the IMF, Rodrigo de Rato, is aware of the problems. As he says, "In a number of countries, Fund quotas have become increasingly out of line with economic weight. For example, Asia's share of world GDP was about 22 percent in 2003. This is about one third higher than its share in Fund quotas."[12] De Rato is currently seeking to have quotas better reflect economic size and importance, but in order to make any changes he requires the support of the IMF's major current shareholders—the United States and Western Europe. Their support for anything other than some modest changes is far from guaranteed.

Many believe that it is in some ways reasonable for North America and Western Europe to retain control of the IMF and the World Bank since they provide most of the money for these organizations. It is important, therefore, to emphasize that while this was true in the early days of the IMF and the World Bank, this is no longer true.

Griffith-Jones has explained how the World Bank, for example, depends less and less on contributions from rich developed countries. Her remarks are worth quoting at length, as they significantly undermine one key argument that apparently supports both North American and Western European domination of these organizations.

The governance of the IBRD [International Bank for Reconstruction and Development] today does not reflect current contributions to IBRD's capital. Initially, at the time of its foundation, IBRD's paid-in capital helped jump-start the institution. Over the decades, the Bank's equity grew fairly steadily, partly through additions to paid-in capital, but largely through additions to reserves out of substantial net income, which originates in the profits of loans made to developing countries. . . . Thus, the fiscal cost of the IBRD to its governments has fallen steadily over time; furthermore, the increase in reserves, as well as the virtual absence of defaults over fifty years, has meant that risks from potentially large contingent liabilities (the callable part of subscribed capital), have tended to zero. As a result, the financial case for strong developed country dominance on the World Bank Board has weakened considerably. To put it in other words, in the World Bank, voting power is aligned to ownership shares. At its founding, when ownership shares were closely related to financial contributions, this made sense. Today, however some major shareholders, especially the United States, exercise influence that is out of proportion to their current costs.[13]

One critical problem that both the World Bank and the IMF should be acutely aware of is their diminishing political credibility on the world stage. At one point they appeared invincible, invulnerable, and infallible. Now they appear to be incompetent and irrelevant in the eyes of many. Of the two, the World Bank still enjoys a more positive reputation, but even so, Lex Reiffel, a visiting fellow at the Global Economy and Development Center of the Brookings Institution, has recently argued that the World Bank should be shut down. In his words,

While shutting down the IMF would leave a serious gap in the international financial system, shutting down the World Bank would not. To remain relevant for another 60 years, the World Bank will probably have to move its headquarters out of Washington, disperse its staff to offices in the countries where it operates, select a non-American president, and untangle itself from the IMF. The Bank will be scarred by such reforms, however, if they are resisted by the United States.[14]

The IMF has still not fully recovered its credibility following its poor performance in the Asian Financial Crisis of 1997–1998. Any fair evaluation will show that the IMF did not do as bad a job as many of its critics allege. Still, there is no doubt that the widespread perception is that the IMF botched its handling of the crisis. This lack of confidence in the IMF is reflected in the reluctance of most developing countries to borrow from the IMF. Those that can repay all their loans to the IMF declare "independence." Even Latin American countries are doing this. Several Asian countries are guaranteeing their independence from the IMF by accumulating huge financial reserves, the largest ever seen in history. All this has created an acute problem for the IMF. With few countries taking their loans, the IMF income has dipped sharply. Suddenly the IMF needs the developing world at least as much as the developing world needs the IMF.

The time has come for America and Western Europe to ask whether maintaining the status quo in the IMF and the World Bank serves their real national interests. The dilemma they face is a simple one: Do they retain control and, in so doing, allow the legitimacy and credibility (and consequently effectiveness) of the IMF and the World Bank to diminish? Or do they open up the leadership positions and reshuffle voting rights toward emerging countries?

Any real answer to this dilemma requires a clear consensus on the role and purpose of these two institutions. The leftist critics of IMF and the World Bank have long attacked them for being instruments of capitalist exploitation of the poor in the Third World. Such allegations do not hold water, especially in an era when once poorer countries like China, India, Brazil, and South Africa have become strong champions of globalization as the leading industrial economies. These countries buy the argument that growing economic integration and accelerating globalization will benefit their economies and people. Having become stakeholders in the more optimistic Western vision of globalization, they are ready to participate in making more effective the global economic institutions that allow globalization to thrive.

Any debate on the future directions and roles of the IMF and the World Bank will have to be part of a larger debate on the role of the key multilateral institutions created in the aftermath of World War II. The victors of World War II declared, in the opening words of the UN Charter, that they were determined "to save succeeding generations from the scourge of war, which twice in our lifetime has brought untold sorrow to mankind."[15] The fundamental approach they took was to move the world toward a more rules-based order in which there would be greater respect both for the principles of international law and for the various multilateral institutions set up to promote and implement these principles.

President Harry Truman made it a point to emphasize that for a multilateral order to work the great powers had to set the example in accepting its rules: "We all have to recognize, no matter how great our strength, we must deny ourselves the license to do always as we please."[16] Sadly, America has in the intervening sixty years become deeply disillusioned with the UN as well as the Bretton Woods institutions, which were set up largely with the support of the United States. Many Americans now question the values and usefulness of these institutions.

America has often asserted that what it seeks to do is to reform and strengthen the Bretton Woods and UN institutions. John W. Snow, a former US Treasury Secretary, said, "Comprehensive, fundamental reform is needed if the IMF is to remain legitimate and relevant to its membership. . . . For this effort to succeed, members need to look beyond their immediate narrow interests."[17] In practice, however, there is a widespread perception that the American goal is not to strengthen but to weaken these institutions.

To complicate the picture even more, there is no solid consensus in the Washington establishment on what needs to be done with the UN and the Bretton Woods institutions. Lex Rieffel writes, "Pressure is building on G-7 finance ministers to act decisively this year [2006] to fix the International Monetary Fund, but the time is not ripe for one compelling reason: The IMF's major shareholder—the United States—the only one with a voting share large enough to block fundamental changes, is not ready to act and will not be ready until 2009."[18] Rieffel argues that the absence of any domestic consensus in America means that no reform is possible. He also acknowledges that any proposed changes to the IMF must "be seen as good not only for 300 million Americans but also for the other 6 billion co-habitants of this world."[19]

Rieffel means well with his comments, but he is probably unaware that his suggestion that the 6.3 billion other people of the world should wait for the 300 million Americans to be ready for reform will only confirm the growing perception of American insensitivity. We live in the time of greatest change ever seen in history. This clock of history will not stop just because the American political system is paralyzed. Indeed, it may move even faster.

The paradox is that North America and Western Europe together have been more responsible than any other powers in unleashing the forces of globalization. Now they are reluctant to confront the consequences and allow the principle of democracy to be the determining factor in the governance of key global organizations.

RULE OF LAW

The second fundamental principle underpinning global society is the rule of law. This hallowed Western principle, honored in theory and in practice, insists that no person, regardless of status, is above the law.

So why is America leading the opposition to a single rule of law for all nations? Many forces are at work. Americans are brought up to believe that their democracy is the best democracy in the world and that their Senate and House of Representatives are the best legislative institutions in the world. Nothing, they believe, can improve on them. So America gives itself the right to not be bound by any mandatory

provisions of any international law. This crude summary of a sophisticated American explanation ignores the central unspoken issue of
power. America refuses to accept any explicit constraints on its power
(even though in practice, America has been a remarkably law-abiding
country). It does not hesitate to walk away from international treaties
and conventions that command almost universal adherence.

Thus America has become simultaneously the model country in
implementing the rule of law at home and the international outlaw—
in the sense of refusing to recognize the constraints of international
law. Many Americans live comfortably with this contradiction. But
they also expect other countries to obey and abide by universally
accepted treaties and conventions, like the Nuclear Non-proliferation
Treaty (NPT). They react with horror when Iran tries to walk away
from the NPT. But Americans are unaware that the world is equally
shocked when their country abandons a universally accepted treaty
like the Comprehensive Test Ban Treaty (CTBT).

Bill Clinton has given the best justification for why it is in America's
interest to adhere to the international rule of law. By demonstrating
that the greatest power of the world today had voluntarily accepted the
multiple constraints of contemporary international law, he argued,
America would help to create a world order that would lead to the *next*
great power adhering to the same rule of law. Clinton did not mention
any country by name, but it was clear which country he was referring
to: China. Every loophole in the rule of law that America creates for
itself now will be available to China in the future. On 11 January 2007
China conducted an anti-satellite missile test and successfully destroyed
its own missile in space. The Western media reacted with horror. The
Economist's editors wrote, "Yet, it is hard to see the test other than as a
display of China's ability to challenge American space power. . . . The
test and the secrecy surrounding it will do nothing to reassure other
countries that China's rise is, as it frequently insists, peaceful and a
threat to no one. . . . 'If your opponent is of choleric temper, seek to ir-
ritate him,' said Sun Tzu, a Chinese military strategist whose writings

2,500 years ago are still often cited in China today. China has certainly mastered that axiom."[20] When the *Economist* made this comment, it did not emphasize that the US had begun the military space race. Instead, it confirmed the general perception that China was emerging as a dangerous power in militarizing space. When I met a senior Chinese colonel in Davos in January 2007, she told me that America had already begun deploying weapons in outer space, ignoring prevailing international opinion that outer space should be kept weapons-free. America set the precedent for China's behavior.

The Bush administration's decision to exempt itself from the provisions of international law on human rights is even more dangerous. For over a half century, since Eleanor Roosevelt led the fight for the adoption of the Universal Declaration of Human Rights, America has been the global champion of human rights. This may well have been a good ideological weapon to use in the Cold War: America the free versus the Soviet Union the unfree. This American championing of greater adherence to human rights standards was also a result of a strong ideological conviction that it was America's God-given duty to create a more civilized world. Most Americans have no idea how much shock the Bush administration has caused by walking away from universally accepted human rights conventions, especially on torture. Here too America has created a huge loophole for others.

Despite having abandoned several human rights provisions, America continues to produce an annual State Department report on the status of human rights in every country in the world except America. These reports are meant to be objective. Before 9/11, they were treated with some respect (although many questioned some obvious double standards). After 9/11, most sophisticated elites all over the world treat these reports with derision. The reaction of one senior Egyptian diplomat was particularly telling. He told me that each year the State Department report on human rights in Egypt would accuse the Egyptian authorities of using torture in their interrogation techniques. Yet, with regular frequency, an American military plane would land at Cairo airport to deliver a group of prisoners, who were hooded and manacled. American soldiers would hand over these prisoners to the Egyptian authorities and request that they be "interrogated." He asked, "If the State Department report criticizes Egypt for using torture in its interrogation techniques, why does America hand over prisoners to Egypt for interrogation? What represents America's real position: Does it approve or condemn torture?"

The fact that such a question could even be asked shows how far America has walked away from its role as a champion of human rights. Probably the most important provisions of any legal system are those that protect individual rights: protection from arbitrary detention, torture, and assassinations. In the past there was no doubt that America adhered to these fundamental protections of individual rights. In the 1960s and 1970s Congressional inquiries unearthed evidence of several CIA plots to eliminate foreign leaders, including the Cuban leader Fidel Castro. The Church Committee, for example, exposed eight distinct plots against Castro's life from 1960 to 1965. The CIA was also found to be active in many states in Africa and Latin America, working to undermine left-wing regimes hostile to the US. This prompted President Gerald Ford to issue Executive Order 11905 in February 1976—reissued by his successors, President Jimmy Carter (Executive Order 12306) and President Reagan (Executive Order 12333)—which forbids clandestine acts of targeted killings.[21] When Americans discovered that the CIA could have been carrying out a secret assassination program in violation of American principles, they were shocked. Widespread revulsion required the CIA to abandon the program. After 9/11, the political consensus in America changed sharply. Today many Americans quietly accept the fact that their country has begun to violate some of the fundamental principles of human rights. In private, they also believe that such violations are defensible because America has been attacked by terrorists. They believe that self-defense is justification for America violating its own principles.

The American electorate would not accept either a chief justice or an attorney general who broke his own laws from time to time. Yet the global body politic is expected to respect a custodian that has violated its own laws. This is clearly untenable.

There is a huge historical irony in America turning away from an international rule of law imposed equally on all nations. America was among the first modern societies to appreciate the functional virtues of the social contract that undergirds all laws. Having lived in New York City, I know that the police could do little if the more than one million residents of Harlem decided to violate the rule of law and began looting and destroying the rich homes of the few thousand wealthy citizens on Park Avenue. What effectively protects the Park Avenue residents is a social contract worked out between the rich and the poor: the poor agree not to violate the property of the rich, and in return the rich agree to abide by the same law as the poor. The rich agreed not to be exempted from the law because they were the primary beneficiaries of this social contract.

As the richest occupants of our global village, America should logically be at the forefront of pushing for a similar rule of law across the globe. Indeed, this would provide the best protection for the massive global interests of America (and also become a powerful weapon to be used against terrorists who clearly violate laws). However, for this to work, America—like the residents of Park Avenue—will also have to agree to be bound by the same laws.

Many Americans believe that their nation is powerful enough to insist on its exceptionalism. With time, as the world shrinks more and more, America will see the wisdom of applying to the rest of the world the same principles it applies to bringing social order at home: a single rule of law for all people and nations.

SOCIAL JUSTICE

Another key principle that explains the social order and stability of modern Western societies is the principle of social justice. Inequality is accepted as long as some kind of social safety net is created to help the very poor and dispossessed. Most Western European states also accepted this principle for functional reasons. They fought off the Marxist revolutions that could have engulfed them by creating democratic socialist societies, which gave even the most disadvantaged members of the society a stake in maintaining and supporting social order. America has disavowed socialism, but in its own way it has imbibed key elements of this Western European social contract. Indeed, the best philosophical justification for taking care of those at the bottom of any society is provided by an American philosopher, John Rawls. The world would be a far happier place if we could apply Rawls's principles universally.

Many in the West believe that they are applying the principle of social justice globally through the massive foreign aid they give to the developing world. Each year, according to OECD estimates, the OECD members give approximately US$103.9 billion to the developing world.[22] Many in the West claim that if the total amount of Western aid is added up, it shows that the West has made a massive transfer to the developing world. In short, their narrative becomes one in which the West tried nobly to help the poor countries of the world but the poor countries failed.

If the true story of Western aid to the developing world is told, however, it may well emerge as the story of the Big Lie. It is true that Western countries have put significant amounts of money into their Overseas Development Assistance (ODA) budgets. It is not true that the purpose of these ODA allotments is to help poor countries. Self-interest has almost always trumped altruism in how this money is spent. Its primary purpose is to serve the immediate and short-term security and national interests of the donors. In the case of the US, for a long time a few countries, like Israel and Egypt, have absorbed most of the money set aside for ODA. It is hard to make a case that these few countries represent the most deserving poor in the developing world. The secondary purpose of ODA is to support the domestic interests of the donors. My own estimate is that out of every US$10 that is allegedly spent in the Third World, US$8 returns to the donor country in the form of administration expenses, consultant fees, and contracts for donor country corporations. An emerging literature tries to explain why Western aid has failed. Some recent books include the former World Bank economist William Easterly's *The White Man's Burden: Why the West's Efforts to Aid the Rest Have Done So Much Ill and So Little Good*, and former UN Director Stephen Browne's *Do Donors Help or Hinder?* In short, the rich developed countries have failed to apply social justice globally.

The story of Asia shows that where Western ODA has failed to do the job, domestic good governance can succeed. As a result of Kofi Annan's Millennium Report, the UN General Assembly adopted a series of Millennium Development Goals (MDGs). One of the main MDGs was to halve global poverty by 2015. Against the poor record of development since the end of World War II, this appeared to be an ambitious target. Remarkably, this is one of the few MDGs that is likely to be realized. The reason is simple: China and India are succeeding. Both have made significant strides to reduce poverty. Since China and India have between them almost two-fifths of the world's population, their success (as well as that of other Asian countries) holds hope for reducing global poverty.

This is why the Asian March to Modernity can help to produce a more stable world order. It addresses the challenge of improving social justice globally. The West claimed that it tried and failed. The Asian countries have tried and succeeded. In so doing, they have made a massive contribution toward making the twenty-first century a peaceful century.

PARTNERSHIPS AND PRAGMATISM

The application of the three Western principles of democracy, rule of law, and social justice will go a long way toward creating a more stable world order. But the West will not be able to apply them on its own. The West represents only 12 percent of the world's population; it will have to learn to work with the remaining 88 percent to achieve the goal of global stability. Here is where the West may also have to break new ground. Hitherto the most successful partnerships have been West-West—for example, the Trans-Atlantic Alliance. Equally strong East-West partnerships must be created. But in working with partners from other cultures and civilizations, the West will have to curtail its ideological impulses and learn to be more pragmatic.

The most successful geopolitical partnership of recent times has been the Trans-Atlantic Alliance. It succeeded for many reasons: an overwhelming fear of the Soviet Union in the Cold War, benign America leadership, shared values, common interests, and common cultural origins. Despite the difficulties that surfaced from time to time (as in the Iraq War), the alliance has held. West-West partnerships have a natural glue.

By definition, East-West partnerships will be harder to create and sustain because of cultural differences. Here the good news is that some East-West partnerships are taking off. Across the Pacific, a sense of community is being developed. President Clinton labeled it the "new Pacific Community" when he hosted the first ever summit of APEC leaders in Blake Island, Seattle, in November 1993. The first transpacific links were also a result of cooperation with America against the Soviet Union in the Cold War. But they have since been sustained by the explosive growth in trade (and transpacific trade now far exceeds transatlantic trade), growing people-to-people contacts, and, most significantly, by the hundreds of thousands of Asians who have graduated from American universities. I have participated in several transpacific meetings in the past several decades. Over time I have observed how the personal chemistry across the Pacific has improved significantly. As people get to know each other, the cultural differences begin to matter less and less, even to evaporate. All this provides hope that we can create and sustain East-West partnerships.

While America has done a reasonable job of reaching out to partners outside its zone of cultural comfort, Europe appears to have greater difficulties doing so. This is curious. Europe has had longer and deeper connections with the East, although it is unclear whether the colonial contacts have helped or hindered the development of new partnerships. The record shows that the EU has failed to establish good partnerships outside the Christian heart of Europe.

I have experienced this problem myself. In the 1990s the Singapore government launched an initiative to bring Europe closer to East Asia. The rationale was simple. There were three major growth centers in the world: North America, East Asia, and Europe. In this triangular relationship, the transatlantic connection between North America and Europe was strong. So too was the transpacific connection between North America and East Asia. The missing link was the relationship between Europe and East Asia. Singapore Prime Minister Goh Chok Tong proposed that an Asia-Europe Summit Meeting (ASEM) be held to bring the two sides closer together.

Prime Minister Goh proposed this meeting in 1994. As permanent secretary of the Singapore Ministry of Foreign Affairs, I traveled to Europe and East Asia to sell the idea, but there was little selling needed. Everyone agreed that this was an idea whose time had come. So the first ASEM was held in Bangkok in March 1996, and there was good participation from Europe. As all EU heads of government attended the ASEM meetings, the ASEM process showed great promise.

Then came the Asian Financial Crisis in July 1997. The East Asian economies, which had been described as "miracle" economies in a 1993 report by the World Bank, suddenly looked like fragile dominoes. The rich European countries had offered to form a partnership with the East Asian countries on the assumption that the East Asian economies would be success stories. Once they began to fail, Europe lost interest.

The Asian Financial Crisis provided the EU a perfect opportunity to prove to the East Asian countries that it was *not* a fair-weather friend. But the EU failed to seize this opportunity. Instead it did the opposite, ditching East Asia at the first sign of trouble. The ASEM Summits continued to be held every two years, but the European participation was lackluster. At the second ASEM Summit in London in April 1998, fifteen EU heads of government participated in the meeting but with little conviction that ASEM would go anywhere.

This European tendency to treat non-European cultures and societies with disdain and condescension has become deeply rooted in the European psyche. In 1993–1994 I attended a meeting of ASEAN and EU senior officials in Luxembourg. The ASEAN team was led by Tan Sri Ahmad Kamil Jaafar, a distinguished Malaysian diplomat. The Luxembourg hosts invited us to lunch. Just as Tan Sri Kamil was about to greet his Luxembourg hosts, a young Luxembourg official asked him (in the presence and earshot of Tan Sri Kamil's Luxembourg counterpart) whether he had brought along his invitation. Since he had not done so, he was refused entry to the lunch at which he was supposed to be the guest of honor.

To understand the psychological impact of this incredible rudeness, remember the famous incident of Mahatma Gandhi being thrown out of a South African first-class train compartment even though he had a first-class ticket. It was a clear demonstration that Asians were meant to be second-class citizens. To be refused entry to a lunch at which one was supposed to be the guest of honor was more than a slight. The ease with which the Luxembourg officials delivered the insult revealed the disdain the European officials had for Asians.

This explains the EU's failure to establish any kind of meaningful partnership with its non-European neighbors, even across the Mediterranean. At its narrowest point, Europe is separated from North Africa by the Straits of Gibraltar, which is eight miles wide. Europe and North Africa have been meaningful neighbors for over two thousand years. Despite this geographical proximity, there is no real partnership between the two regions, even though one is badly needed.

There are several reasons. Cultural arrogance is just one of them. The European officials claim that they cannot have a real partnership with the North African states because they have not come up to European standards of democracy and human rights. Yet when America under President Bush violated some fundamental human rights provisions, Europe did not try to impose its human rights standards on America (and indeed there is growing evidence that some EU member states had participated in the infamous "rendition" program). This is also why the Indian commerce and industry minister, Kamal Nath, reacted with fury when he was told that India, the world's largest democracy, had to comply with European standards on democracy and human rights in any partnership agreement between the EU and India. The 500 million people in Europe were imposing conditionalities on 1.2 billion Indian people. And European officials thought that this was perfectly natural and justified.

The time has come for Europe to engage in some deep reflection on its failure to establish any meaningful East-West partnership. And if it fails to reach out to the Islamic world, it will over time generate serious problems. In trying to develop a new mindset to deal with the rest of the world, Europe could learn a lesson or two from China. Few seem to remember that for centuries, China was both insular and culturally arrogant in its dealings with the rest of the world, seeing no reason to engage the world. Now it is engaging with great gusto.

Europe has not been able to establish good partnerships outside its cultural cell, with North Africa, West Asia, the Balkans, or even Russia. By contrast, with the possible exception of Japan, China has successfully established win-win partnerships with all its neighbors. In some cases, China has been remarkably generous.

In theory, the ten states of ASEAN should not have a comfortable relationship with China. In the early Cold War days China even supported subversive Communist Party movements that were trying to overthrow the noncommunist ASEAN governments. Despite this troubled history and unequal relationships, the relations between ASEAN and China have never been better.

The most concrete proof of China's willingness to develop win-win partnerships with its neighbors is provided by trade figures. In 1990, at the end of the Cold War, China's trade with Japan was US$16 billion, South Korea US$3.8 billion, ASEAN US$7.1 billion, and India US$260 million. In 2005, fifteen years later, the figures were US$213.3

billion (Japan), US$111 billion (South Korea), US$130.4 billion (ASEAN), and US$20 billion (India).

The explosion of China's trade relations with all its neighbors as well as its distant trading partners is in itself a remarkable development. China's determination to increase its trade connectivity with the rest of the world stands in sharp contrast to the hitherto traditional civilizational impulse of China: to minimize trade relations. The famous American historian on China, J. K. Fairbank, writes about the traditional Chinese attitude toward trade:

> It seems anomalous that foreign trade could be considered in Chinese theory to be subordinate to tribute, but so it was. It was officially regarded as a boon granted only to the barbarian, the necessary means to his sharing in the bounty of China, and nothing more. No doubt this quixotic doctrine reflected the anti-commercial nature of the Chinese state, where the merchant was low in the social scale and beneath both the farmer and the bureaucrat who lived off the produce of the land. It was strengthened perhaps by the self-sufficiency of the empire which made supplies unnecessary from abroad. At all events, it was the tradition that foreign trade was an unworthy object for high policy, and this dogma was steadily reiterated in official documents down into the nineteenth century.[23]

China has had to overcome some of its cultural constraints to engage the world in a new fashion. Europe may have to do the same.

China's decision to open its markets and establish close partnerships with all its neighbors was undoubtedly driven by sound geopolitical considerations, including the prevention of any possible containment strategy by America. Despite its occasional and difficult relationship with Japan, China decided to increase its trade and economic interdependence with Japan as well. China remains Japan's investment country of choice in Asia: Japan invested US$4.6 billion in China in 2006.

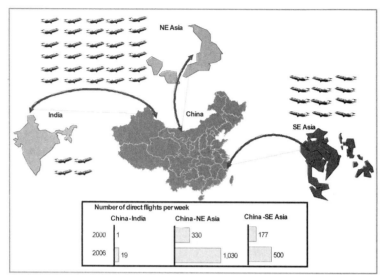

Figure 6.1   Over the Past Six Years, Flight Frequencies Have Grown Between China and Its Asian Neighbors, Brookings Institution Report, 2007
Source: McKinsey & Company analysis.

There have also been a remarkable number of people traveling between China and Japan. In 2005, Chinese students studying in Japan totaled 80,592, while 18,874 Japanese students studied in China. More than five million people traveled back and forth between Japan and China in 2007. In fact, in recent years flight frequency between China and other Asian nations has grown significantly. For example, in 2000 there was only 1 direct flight per week between China and India, while in 2006 there were 19. Between 2000 and 2006 the flights per week between China and Northeast Asia have increased from 330 to 1,030, and those between China and Southeast Asia have grown from 177 to 500 (see Figure 6.1).

This decision by China to create new partnerships with its neighbors has in turn triggered a virtuous spiral of competition among other countries to match China's offer. After China offered an FTA to ASEAN countries, Japan, South Korea, and India have made the same offer. The negotiations have not been completed, but trade flows have increased. These developments have created new patterns of trade and economic interdependence, and the trade and economic relationships have been complemented by a new pattern of political cooperation, which has been driven by ASEAN. Each year, ASEAN organizes a series of meetings, initially among the leaders of the ten member states. These meetings are then followed by the ASEAN+3 meetings (where China, Japan, and South Korea represent the +3) and then the East Asian Summit, which includes the previous thirteen countries and Australia, New Zealand, and India.

Many in the West treat these diplomatic gatherings as a big yawn. This is true of many summits. But sometimes, history is made at these meetings. With the center of the world's economic gravity shifting to East Asia, which is providing the rising new powers, it would have been quite natural to see increased political competition and tensions in the region. This was what American scholars expected. Instead, there has been growing cooperation. ASEAN's ability to drive this process has been nothing short of astonishing. EU should be taking lessons from ASEAN on diplomacy, not vice versa.

ASEAN's diplomatic leadership has not only yielded political dividends but also changed the chemistry of the region significantly and enabled cooperation to emerge in many new areas. ASEAN has helped the region to become more aware of its historical patterns of cooperation. A visionary proposal by the foreign minister of Singapore, George Yeo, has helped to rekindle old connections. From the seventh to twelfth centuries CE, Asia's leading university was in Nalanda, a town in what is now the Indian state of Bihar. Scholars from all over Asia used to go to Nalanda. The famous Chinese scholar Hsuen Tsang (or Xuanzang in today's Pinyin spelling), who visited India in 630 CE, undertook an epic journey from China to Nalanda that was recorded in his famous chronicles *A Record of the West Compiled During the Tang Dynasty (Ta Tang Si Yu Ki)*.

Nalanda was burned down by Turkish Muslim invaders under Bakhtiyar Khalji in 1197 and was forgotten for almost eight hundred

THE NEW ASIAN HEMISPHERE

years. Singapore's proposal to revive it was well-received by the East Asian Summit (EAS). Nalanda has a long way to go before it can be revived. But the sheer process of being involved in this project has helped to remind senior Chinese, Japanese, Korean, Indian, and ASEAN policymakers that the region has deep, meaningful, and mutually beneficial links.

The EU could put forward an equally visionary proposal by trying to revive the ancient centers of learning in the Arab world. From the time of the prophet Muhammad until 1924, the actual or nominal leadership of the Sunni Muslim community was held by successive caliphates in the Umayyad, Abbasid, and finally Ottoman empires. The Umayyad Caliphate, established in 661, lasted for about a century. During this time, Damascus became the capital of an Islamic world that stretched from the western borders of China to southern France. Not only did the Islamic conquests continue during this period through North Africa to Spain and France in the West and to Sind, Central Asia, and Transoxiana in the East, but the basic social and legal institutions of the newly founded Islamic world were established. The Abbasids, who succeeded the Umayyads, shifted the capital to Baghdad, which soon developed into an incomparable center of learning and culture as well as the administrative and political heart of a vast world. They ruled for over five hundred years. These Arab centers of learning preserved the great cultural fruits of Greek and Roman civilizations when Europe was then plunged into its Dark Ages. Europe rediscovered the Greek and Roman civilizations through the learning preserved and protected by the Caliphates. At a time when European minds are obsessed with the possible nightmare of a deep clash between Christianity and Islam, it would be a remarkably bold and generous gesture to offer to revive the ancient centers of learning in the Arab world.

Such a visionary move would help to achieve many goals. It would demonstrate Europe's generosity toward the Arab world. By reviving interest in the Greek and Roman learning preserved by Arabs, Europe would help to demonstrate that there are no fault lines between the Islamic and Christian worlds. In the past, both had benefited from close links. This would also undermine the claims of several fundamentalist Muslim thinkers that there are no common links between secular Europe and the religious Islamic world. It is also conceivable that a revival of interest in the caliphate of the twelfth century could trigger a new renaissance in the Arab and Islamic worlds. Europe cannot create such a renaissance, but it can generously lay the foundation. New partnerships will then be created between Europe and Muslim countries. It can be done.

PRAGMATISM

One of the key goals of this book is to restore Western optimism about the future of our world. Western minds can make one simple change to become more optimistic: they need to drop all the ideological baggage they accumulated in the several eras of Western triumphalism, and they must stop believing that they can remake the world in their own image. The world can no longer be Westernized. Naipaul was wrong; the West does not represent "universal civilization." There are many other successful civilizations, many of which are about to blossom again in the twenty-first century.

To achieve the optimistic outcomes we all desire, both the West and the rest of the world must rediscover the ancient virtue of pragmatism. Unfortunately, this word has fallen into some disrepute in the West. All too often, it is associated with a Machiavellian instinct of allowing noble ends to justify the use of unethical means. Yet, just as Machiavelli has been misunderstood throughout the ages, the virtues of pragmatism are often lost and forgotten in modern (especially Western) discourse.

We are moving into one of the most complex centuries in human history. There will be many successful societies and civilizations in several corners of the globe. There will also be many serious problems and challenges in all corners. Any kind of ideologically driven agenda will surely come to grief and indeed create real danger for the world, especially if it generates even greater misunderstanding, say, between Islam and the West. Therefore, I will end this book by suggesting how the application of pragmatism can lead to a better world.

Asia's biggest contribution to history has been to demonstrate how the March to Modernity can create a more stable, peaceful, and prosperous world. Most societies are ready to join this March to Modernity; the first big pragmatic decision that the West needs to make is to abandon all efforts to isolate or contain any society. Any such isolation prevents the entry of the March to Modernity.

Take the cases of Iran and Myanmar, two societies that the West has tried to isolate. Right now, no American policymaker would dare advocate that America establish diplomatic relations with Iran. This is because, by some strange process of political logic, the establishment of diplomatic relations is regarded as an act of political approval. This assumption in itself shows how unpragmatic America has become.

For over two thousand years, it has been accepted that the establishment of diplomatic relations conveys neither approval nor disapproval. This is why the Vatican, which takes moral values seriously, has established diplomatic relations with virtually all states. In the years that America was trying to isolate and cut off Libya, the Vatican maintained diplomatic relations with it.

In the Cold War, the Soviet Union was the major adversary of the United States and Western Europe. One reason why no major grief resulted in the Cold War was that all the adversaries kept talking to each other. At no time did either America or the EU say that its diplomatic relations with Moscow meant approval of the gulag-filled regime of the Soviet Union. This was the historical norm. In establishing diplomatic relations with all nations, both the United States and Europe will discover the virtues of pragmatism and common sense.

In 2007 the United States worked hard to turn back the nuclear ambitions of Iran and North Korea. It openly admitted that it had made progress with North Korea and less with Iran. Why did this happen? The simple answer is that China pragmatically engaged North Korea and spoke at length to it directly and forcefully. By contrast, America refused to talk directly to Iran. A simple pragmatic truth that Washington, DC, still finds hard to swallow is that engagement, not containment, will lead to a solution to the Iran problem.

The Persian civilization has been around for two thousand years. America has been around for only a little over two hundred years. We can safely bet that the Persian civilization will last as long as America into the future (and probably longer). Hence, one big pragmatic step that America could take is to peer beyond the veil of Islamic theocracy and try to develop a deep understanding of Persian culture and civilization. It should establish superficial diplomatic relations with the government and develop deep people-to-people relations with Iranian society. Iranian students should return to studying in America. American tourists should visit the rich archaeological sites in Iran. America should invest in Iran and even propose a free trade agreement.

To understand the impact that these policies could have on Iranian society, just compare the state of Chinese society in 1972 (when Nixon launched various exchanges with China) with Chinese society in 2002. The Chinese civilization remained intact. But the approach of Chinese society to the rest of the world changed dramatically. Instead of threatening the world, China began to engage deeply. Half a million Chinese students have studied in American universities. Hundreds of thousands of Americans have visited China. By 2005 America had invested more than US$18.06 billion in China.[24] Today, most Chinese people have one big dream: the American dream. They want peace; their own homes, TVs, and washing machines,; and to travel to Disneyland and study at Harvard. Without even trying to do so, America has completely transformed Chinese society. It can do the same with Iran.

To understand why containment fails, look at the case of Myanmar. America and the EU have isolated Myanmar for almost two decades. What has been accomplished by this isolation? Nothing! This has caused great anguish among the exiled Myanmar community overseas. After deep reflection, they have decided that isolation of Myanmar is hopeless. Instead, engagement with Myanmar society could eventually lead to change. A young Myanmar intellectual, Thant Myint-U, wrote in the *International Herald Tribune*:

> What outside pressure can bring about democratic change? And why, after nearly two decades of boycotts, aid cutoffs, trade bans and diplomatic condemnation, are Myanmar's generals apparently more in charge than ever before? Are we really looking at Myanmar—a country of 55 million people—in the right way? . . . Only liberal democracy can bring long-term stability to a country as diverse as Myanmar. The question is how to go from here to there, leave behind the rhetoric and look for practical measures based on a better understanding of the country's past.[25]

A similar application of the pragmatic spirit is needed in Washington, DC, if it is going to solve the number one problem in the minds of American policymakers: Iraq. The first step in any pragmatic analysis of Iraq is to acknowledge certain hard realities. Iraq cannot escape its history. There are three large communities in Iraq: 15 million Shiites (60 percent of Iraq's population of 27 million), 5.4 million Sunnis (nearly 20 percent of Iraq's population), and 4 million Kurds. The Sunni community has been politically dominant for centuries. Its ascendancy began under the Sunni Ottoman Turks, whose empire ruled the Middle East for nearly four hundred years—they conquered southern Mesopotamia in 1534. The Ottoman defeat in World War I did not end Sunni dominance. All previous Shiite attempts to gain power in Iraq have failed. I remember a conversation I had with the Tunisian and Moroccan ambassadors to the UN in New York just before the American invasion of Iraq in March 2003. One ambassador said to the other, "If America invades Iraq and introduces democracy in Iraq, it would finally enable the Shiites to gain political control of

Iraq, after waiting for centuries." They knew this as a basic fact. Astonishingly, those who engineered the American invasion of Iraq seemed to be unaware of the significance of what they were doing.

In "winner take all" democratic elections, the Shias naturally gained political power. Sunni resistance could have been easily predicted, as many did. Instead of using democratic elections to select the government of Iraq, America should work toward creating a new political bargain among the three communities, in which each feels that their rights and interests are protected.

The abandonment of democracy will be a bitter pill for America to swallow. It may well be seen as a step backwards. But America's most reliable friends among Iraq neighbors are all nondemocracies: Saudi Arabia, Jordan, the Gulf states, and even Egypt. America has worked well with them. Hence, the Saudi Arabia-nization or Jordan-ization of Iraq need not be a step backwards if it leads to stability for the people of Iraq and an end to the bitter civil war. Ironically, Iraq's only real democratic neighbor is Iran.

America did not know how to export democracy to Iraq. It will know even less how to construct a new political system in Iraq that is an acceptable political bargain among its three communities. It should leave this job to Iraqis and, equally importantly, to Iraq's neighbors, including Iran. Involving Iran may be another bitter pill for America to swallow, but America already began swallowing when it announced on 27 February 2007 that it will invite Iran to join Iraq and its neighbors. It is difficult for Americans to admit that they are being pragmatic, however. The remarks of White House spokesperson Tony Snow the next day illustrate the doublespeak the US has to engage in to justify pragmatism. When asked about Iran's participation, Snow responded, "There is no crack. A number of people have been characterizing U.S. participation in a regional meeting as a change in policy; it is nothing of the sort." When a reporter asked Snow why he was being "so defensive about going the diplomatic route," Snow replied, "We're not." "What we're trying to do is clarify," he said, adding that the United States had not dropped its condition that Iran must halt its nuclear work before engaging in direct talks. Asked directly whether he was ruling out one-on-one "sidebars" with Iran during the coming meetings, Snow said flatly, "Yes." His comments seemed not to comport entirely with Condoleezza Rice's upbeat tone a day earlier, when she spoke of a "new diplomatic initiative."[26]

America gave a huge gift to Iran when it invaded Iraq. For centuries, the Shia community had yearned for the Shias in Iraq to gain power. Where the Iranians failed, America succeeded. Now the Shia domination of Iraq (if it is wisely tempered with enough political space for the Sunni and Kurd communities) has become practically irreversible. America would like to consolidate the gains made by the democratization of Iraq; so does Iran. It is therefore in Iran's interest to work with America, rather than against it, in stabilizing Iraq. On ideological grounds, America should not cooperate with Iran. But if America were to take a pragmatic approach, Iran is a natural partner to achieve the stabilization of Iraq and an honorable exit for American troops from Iraq. Tehran may no longer have much to fear from those who rule Baghdad, but the chaos brewing within Iraq's borders makes Iranian rulers nervous. A failed Iraq—or worse, a warring Iraq infested with radical ideologies and ruled by violent militias—threatens Iran's stability. Kurdish autonomy or independence could disturb Iran's own delicate Kurdish situation.

The great irony about American reluctance to work with Iran is that Iran has an even greater vested interest than America in the stability of Iraq. An American nightmare is an unstable Mexico. Hence, in each financial crisis in Mexico, America has intervened decisively to stabilize Mexico to prevent a flood of refugees from Mexico to the US. Iraq is Iran's Mexico. Any instability in Iraq will lead to a huge outflow of refugees to Iran. If conflict continues, Iran will also have to provide resources to protect the interests of the majority Shiite community. This could be both expensive and difficult for Iran at a time when it has enough domestic problems to worry about. In addition, like Turkey, Iran has a strong vested interest in Iraq *not* splintering into three states. An independent Iraqi Kurdistan would be as big a nightmare for Iran as it is for Turkey. Hence, Iran would clearly prefer to have a stable Iraq at its doorstep, a stable Iraq that is a result of a new grand political bargain among the three communities.

America succeeded for over two centuries because of its common sense. In contrast to Europe, which had huge burdens of history and a resistance to change, America leapt ahead because of its willingness to challenge conventional wisdom and to try new approaches. America's strength had always been its down-to-earth and common-sensical approach to solving problems. Fortunately, these common-sense traditions still exist in America. When President Bush set up the Iraq Study Group (ISG) under the bipartisan leadership of James Baker and Lee Hamilton, the ISG came up with sensible approaches to solving the Iraq problem. One of their recommendations clearly said that America would have to talk to Iraq's neighbors, including Iran. Recommendation 9 of the ISG Report states that "under the aegis of the New Diplomatic Offensive and the Support Group, the United States should engage directly with Iran and Syria in order to try to obtain their commitment to constructive policies toward Iraq and other regional issues. In engaging Syria and Iran, the United States should consider incentives, as well as disincentives, in seeking constructive results."[27] Unfortunately, the instinctive response of the Bush administration was to react ideologically. It initially rejected the ISG report but gradually agreed to implement some of its recommendations, including the inclusion of Iran in the discussions.

The point of this story is that there is an Iraq problem in Baghdad. But there is an even bigger Iraq problem in Washington. Like any other problem, it is possible to find pragmatic solutions, but to find them it is necessary to have an open mind and rid oneself of one's ideological preconceptions. Here I often sympathize with American diplomats. They have a hard enough time negotiating with America's competitors and adversaries overseas. But they *spend* more of their time negotiating with their competitors and adversaries in Washington. By the time they come to negotiate overseas, they are already exhausted from their internal negotiations. They also arrive shackled with rigid negotiating positions. This too explains why it is difficult for America to be pragmatic in its external policies.

To the best of my knowledge, America is the only country to actually have a philosophical school called "Pragmatism." I studied philosophy in both Singapore and Canada in what might best be called the British approach to studying philosophy. We studied British and European philosophies; scant attention was paid to the Pragmatist school of America. Pragmatism was not deemed to be serious philosophy because it did not try to find or suggest absolute truth, in a way that a Kant or a Hegel would. Because it had a more open attitude toward truth, pragmatism was treated with disdain by the British and European schools of philosophy.

At the beginning of the twenty-first century, as we enter into one of the most intense periods of change experienced by humanity, America is abandoning its pragmatist streak when it needs it most. We are moving into very uncertain political and economic terrains. It would be foolish to assume that the Western ideological assumptions of the nineteenth and twentieth century will necessarily work in the twenty-first century. It would be wiser to keep an open mind and to challenge every ideological assumption embedded in our minds. Pragmatism is the best guiding spirit we can have as we venture into the new century. It is therefore only appropriate to quote once again the greatest pragmatist of the twentieth century, Deng Xiaoping: "It does not matter whether a cat is black or white; if it catches mice, it is a good cat."

NOTES

INTRODUCTION

1. Daniel Mandel, "The Churchill Doctrine," FrontPageMagazine.com, 26 January 2005, http://www.meforum.org/article/673.

2. "President Bush discusses terror plot upon arrival in Wisconsin," White House press release, http://www.whitehouse.gov/news/releases/2006/08/20060810 -3.html.

3. Interview given by M. Michel Barnier, Minister of Foreign Affairs, France, to Res Publica, 18 February 2005, http://www.ambafrance-us.org/news/standpoint/ stand109.asp.

4. Michael Wilson, Canadian Ambassador to the United States, "Notes for a Briefing to the House International Relations Committee Subcommittee on the Western Hemisphere," 25 May 2006, http://geo.international.gc.ca/can-am/washington/ ambassador/20060525-en.asp.

5. Henry Hyde, "Perils of the Golden Theory," statement from the International Affairs Budget Request, before the International Relations Committee, US House of Representatives, 26 February 2006, http://commdocs.house.gov/ committees/intlrel/hfa26078.000/hfa26078_0f.htm.

CHAPTER 1

1. "The Big Election Offer—Free Colour TVs," *Straits Times* (Singapore), 30 December 2006.

2. Robert Kagan, *Dangerous Nation* (New York: Alfred A. Knopf, 2006), 328.

3. Anand Giridhardas, "Poor Rural India? It's a Richer Place," *International Herald Tribune*, 19 October 2005.

4. Michael Breen, *The Koreans: Who They Are, What They Want, Where Their Future Lies* (London: Orion Business Books, 1998), 5.

5. Joseph Kahn, "A Textbook Example of Change in China," *New York Times*, 31 August 2006.

6. Kanchan Lakshman, "More Muscle to Pakistan's madrassas," *Asia Times* (online), 25 April 2007.

7. Eric Pfanner and Raymond Bonner, "Doctor at Heart of Terror Case in Britain," *International Herald Tribune*, 4 July 2007.

8. "A Progressive Islam, Open to the World," excerpt from a speech by Dr. Yaacob Ibrahim, Minister for the Environment and Water Resources and Minister-in-Charge of Muslim Affairs, at the Hari Raya get-together on November 3, 2006, at the Istana, *Straits Times*, 7 November 2006.

9. Remarks of Lawrence H. Summers, Charles W. Eliot University Professor of Harvard University, at the World Economic Forum, Davos, Switzerland, 24–28 January 2007.

10. "Report: China to Complete First Stage of Modernization by 2015," *English People's Daily* (online), 29 January 2007.

11. Shashi Tharoor, "Meanwhile: India's Cellphone Revolution," *International Herald Tribune*, 2 February 2007.

12. Kevin Sullivan, "For India's Traditional Fishermen, Cellphones Deliver a Sea Change," *Washington Post*, 15 October 2006.

13. "To Do with the Price of Fish," *Economist*, 10 May 2007.

14. "Can Cell Phones Fix World Poverty? Author Nick Sullivan and Grameen-Phone Co-Founder Iqbal Quadir Discuss at the Aspen Institute," February 21, 2007, http://www.aspeninstitute.org; Nicholas Sullivan, *You Can Hear Me Now: How Microloans and Cellphones Are Connecting the World's Poor to the Global Economy* (San Francisco: Jossey-Bass, 2007), 145.

15. "Can Cell Phones Fix World Poverty?"

16. Johan Norberg, "American and European Protectionism Is Killing Poor Countries and Their People," *CATO Journal*, 4 September 2003, http://www.cato.org/pub_display.php?pub_id=3226.

17. Thomas H. Hoenig, "The Global Economy," Northern Colorado Summit on National Economic Issues, Loveland, Colorado, 15 September 2005.

18. Opening remarks by H. E. Nitya Pibulsonggram, Minister of Foreign Affairs of Thailand, at the international conference "Foreign Ministries: Adaptation to a Changing World," 14 June 2007.

19. "Global Economic Prospects: Managing the Next Wave of Globalization," World Bank, 2007.

20. John K. Veroneau, "Introduction," *Benefits of Trade, Costs of Protection*, eJournal USA, USInfo.State.Gov, 18 January 2007, http://usinfo.state.gov/journals/ites/0107/ijee/introduction.htm.

21. Ibid.

22. US Census Bureau, Foreign Trade Statistics, "Trade in Goods (Imports, Exports and Trade Balance) with China," 2005.

23. The APEC Forum was founded in Canberra, Australia in 1989 and had seventeen members in November 1993. They were: Australia, Brunei Darussalam, Canada, China, Hong Kong (China), Indonesia, Japan, Republic of Korea, Malaysia, Mexico, New Zealand, Papua New Guinea, the Philippines, Singapore, Chinese Taipei, Thailand, and the United States. Since then, several new countries have joined. They are: Chile, Peru, Russia, and Vietnam.

24. Fred Bergsten, "Plan B for World Trade," *Financial Times*, 15 August 2006.

25. David Hencke, "So That's Where the 100 Billion Euros Went," *Guardian*, 22 January 2007.

26. Nicola Smith, "Cost in Translation," EU Commission (online), January–February 2007, http://ec.europa.eu/commission_barroso/orban/news/docs/55-57multilingualism.pdf.

27. Niranjan Rajadhyaksha, *The Rise of India: Its Transformation from Poverty to Prosperity* (Singapore: Wiley & Sons (Asia), 2007), 13.

28. Paul Krugman, "The Trade Tightrope," *New York Times*, 27 February 2004.

29. John F. Kennedy, Special Message to the Congress on Foreign Trade Policy, 25 January 1962, http://www.presidency.ucsb.edu/ws/index.php?pid=8688.

30. Edward Gresser, "Is 'Free Trade' Working? Testimony before the Senate Commerce Committee, Subcommittee on Interstate Commerce, Trade and Tourism," 18 April 2007, http://www.ppionline.org/ppi_ci.cfm?knlgAreaID=108&subsecid=206&contentid=254256.

31. David Hale, "The Best Economy Ever," *Wall Street Journal*, 31 July 2007, A15.

32. Ibid.

33. "How the Money Is Spent, Inside Europe," BBC News, http://news.bbc.co.uk/2/shared/spl/hi/europe/04/money/html/agriculture.stm.

34. Alexei Barrionuevo and Keith Bradsher, "Have Farm Subsidies Outlasted Usefulness?" *International Herald Tribune*, 7 December 2005.

35. Based on US Department of Agriculture (USDA) statistics provided by the Environmental Working Group: http://farm.ewg.org/farm/progdetail.php?fips=00000&progcode=total&page=district.

36. Daniel Drezner, "The New New World Order," *Foreign Affairs*, March–April 2007.

37. Francis Fukuyama, "The End of History," *National Interest*, Summer 1989.

38. Michael Wines, "An Ailing Russia Lives a Tough Life That's Getting Shorter," *New York Times*, 3 December 2000.

39. Vladimir Popov, "Russia Redux," *New Left Review*, 44, March–April 2007.

40. Amy Chua, *World on Fire: How Exporting Free Market Democracy Breeds Ethnic Hatred and Global Instability* (New York: Anchor Books, 2004), 5, 11, 16.

41. Ibid., 15.

42. J. M. Roberts, *The Triumph of the West* (Boston: Little, Brown, 1985), 289.

CHAPTER 2

1. Angus Maddison, *The World Economy: A Millennial Perspective* (Washington, DC: Brookings Institute Press, 2007).

2. Dominic Wilson and Roopa Purushothaman, "Dreaming with BRICs: The Path to 2050," Global Economics Paper No. 99, Goldman Sachs, 1 October 2003, http://www2.goldmansachs.com/insight/research/reports/report6.html.

3. "Overview: China at a Glance," *People's Daily* (online), http://english.people.com.cn/china/19990914A113.html.

4. "The Great Leap Forward, 1958–60," US Library of Congress, http://countrystudies.us/china/88.htm.

5. World Development Indicators, World Bank, 2005.

6. Andy Mukherjee, "Viewpoint: India's Vision Problem," *International Herald Tribune*, 15 March 2007.

7. "Shenzhen Focuses on Efficiency over GDP," China Yearbook 2003–2004, http://www.china.org.cn/english/government/118413.htm.

8. Michael Schuman, "The Birth and Rebirth of Shenzhen," *Time*, 14 August 2006.

9. Hu Jintao, "Why China Loves Globalization," *Globalist*, 7 June 2005.

10. Gao Shangquan, *China's Economic Future: Challenges to U.S. Policy*, Joint Economic Committee, 104th Congress (August 1996), S. Prt. 104–62.

11. Hannah Beech, "Asia's Great Science Experiment," *Time*, 23 October 2006.

12. Yojana Sharma, "In the Know," *South China Morning Post*, 27 February 2007.

13. Kanta Murali, "The IIT Story: Issues and Concerns," *Frontline* 20, no. 3, 1–14 February 2003.

14. Ibid.

15. Celia W. Dugger, "Web Moguls' Return Passage to India," *New York Times*, 29 February 2000, http://partners.nytimes.com/library/tech/00/02/biztech/articles/29india.html.

16. Jason Overdof, "India's Weapon: Its Diaspora," *Newsweek International*, 13 November 2006.

17. Amy Yee, "Vital Role for Indian Abroad," *Financial Times* (Asia-Pacific), 9 January 2007.

18. Raghunath A. Mashelkar, "India's R&D: Reaching for the Top," *Science*, 4 March 2005, http://www.sciencemag.org/cgi/content/full/307/5714/1415.

19. Ibid.

20. Beech, "Asia's Great Science Experiment."

21. "Global Economic Prospects: Managing the Next Wave of Globalization," World Bank, 2007.

22. Thomas Friedman, "Laughter and Tears," *Straits Times*, 24 May 2007.

23. Nicolas Kristof, "The Educated Giant," *New York Times*, 28 May 2007.

24. Anand Giridharadas, "An Economist's Rise Defies Caste System," *International Herald Tribune*, 11 October 2005.

25. Manjeet Kriplani, "Bihar's Tiny School Is Churning Out IIT-ians," *BusinessWeek*, 16 August 2006.

26. Michael E. Marti, *China and the Legacy of Deng Xiaoping: From Communist Revolution to Capitalist Evolution* (Washington, DC: Brassey's, 2002), 40.

27. "The Brezhnev Era," US Library of Congress, http://countrystudies.us/russia/14.htm.

28. "After Brezhnev: Stormy Weather," *Time*, 23 June 1980.

29. Zheng Yongnian and Lye Liang Fook, "Elite Politics and the Fourth Generation of Chinese Leadership," *Journal of Chinese Political Science* 8, nos. 1–2 (Fall 2003).

30. Ibid.

31. Alastair McIndoe, "100 Years On, Political Clans Still Reign in Philippines," *Straits Times*, 13 June 2007.

32. Goh Keng Swee, "Public Administration and Economic Development in LDCs," in Linda Low, ed., *Wealth of East Asian Nations: Speeches and Writings by Goh Keng Swee* (Singapore: Federal Publication, 1995), 128–45.

33. Goh Keng Swee, "The Vietnam War: Round 3," in Low, ed., *Wealth of East Asian Nations*, 313–32.

34. Simon Elegant and Michael Elliot, "Lee Kuan Yew Reflects," *Time Asia*, 5 December 2005.

35. Deng Xiaoping, Nanxun Jishim, p. 232, quoted in Michael Richardson, "'Mini-Singapore' Project Is Off and Running in China: Mr. Li and Mr. Lee Talk Business," *International Herald Tribune*, 21 May 1994.

36. Marti, *China and the Legacy of Deng Xiaoping*, 103.

37. Richard K. Betts, "Wealth, Power and Instability," *International Security* 18, no. 3 (Winter 1993–94): 64.

38. Aaron L. Friedberg, "Ripe for Rivalry," *International Security* 18, no. 3 (Winter 1993–94): 7.

39. Russell Mokhiber and Robert Weissman, "New US Treasury Secretary's Famous Remarks as World Bank Chief," Alternative Information and Development Centre, http://www.aidc.org.za/?q=book/view/130.

40. Joshua Ramo, "The Three Marketeers," *Time*, 15 February 1999.

41. Stephen I. Schwartz, ed., *Atomic Audit: The Costs and Consequences of U.S. Nuclear Weapons since 1940* (Washington, DC: Brookings Institution Press, 1998).

42. World Development Indicators, World Bank, 2005.

43. Dennis Bloodworth, *An Eye for the Dragon: Southeast Asia Observed: 1954–1970* (New York: Farrar, Straus and Giroux, 1970), xiv–xv.

44. Simon Elegant, "Disorder in the Courts," *Time*, 31 March 2007.

45. See Zheng Yongnian, *Will China Become Democratic? Elite, Class and Regime Transition* (Singapore: Marshall Cavendish International, 2004), 56.

46. For a discussion of this, see Martin G. Hu, "WTO's Impact on the Rule of Law in China," Mansfield Dialogues in Asia, 2001, www.mansfieldfdn.org/programs/program_pdfs/08hu.pdf.

47. From the *Complete Collection of Laws, Regulations and Rules in China* (Beijing: Beijing University Press for the Center of Legal Information and the Beijing Zhongtian Software Company, 1997).

48. Zhenmin Wang, "The Developing Rule of Law in China," *Harvard Asia Quarterly*, vol. 4, http://www.asiaquarterly.com/content/view/88/40.

49. Ibid.

50. *Democracy and Law* (Shanghai), no. 1 (1995): 6. The information in the previous two paragraphs comes from Gillian H. L. Goh, "Democratic Practice, Civil Society

and Rule of Law in China: Two Steps Forward One Step Back from Tiananmen to Falun Gong," unpublished manuscript.

51. Elegant, "Disorder in the Courts."

52. Jim Yardley, "A Young Judge Tests China's Legal System," *International Herald Tribune*, 28 November 2007.

53. Ashwinie Kumar Bansal, "Burden of Backlog," *The Tribune* [Chandigarh, India], 20 May 2007.

54. "Global Economic Prospects."

55. Statistics from the Ministry of Education of the People's Republic of China, http://www.moe.edu.cn/english/international_2.htm.

56. "More Talents Return Home From Overseas," *People's Daily* (online), 6 September 2000, http://english.peopledaily.com.cn/english/200009/06/eng20000906_49877.html.

57. Edward Tse, "China's Five Surprises," *Strategy + Business* (in-house publication of Booz-Allen-Hamilton), 16 January 2006, http://www.strategybusiness.com/resilience/rr00028.

58. Open Doors Report 2006, Institute for International Education, 2006, http://opendoors.iienetwork.org/?p=89251.

59. "Indian Students Return Home from US," *Economic Times*, 17 August 2005.

60. Tse, "China's Five Surprises."

61. John Sudworth, "Indians Head Home in 'Brain Gain.'" BBC News, 27 August 2006, http://news.bbc.co.uk/2/hi/south_asia/5290494.stm.

62. "It's a Reverse Brain Drain to India Now!" *Indian Express*, 23 December 2006, http://www.expressindia.com/fullstory.php?newsid=78613.

63. Sudworth, "Indians Head Home."

64. Robyn Meredith, "Back to India," *Forbes Asia*, 23 July 2007.

65. Harsh Kabra, "India's IT Prodigals Return Home," BBC News, 29 April 2005, http://news.bbc.co.uk/2/hi/south_asia/4447833.stm.

66. Kabra, "India's IT Prodigals."

67. Jane Perlez, "Chinese Move to Eclipse US Appeal in Southeast Asia," *New York Times*, 18 November 2004.

68. Chip McCorkle, "China Grants Yale Access to Market," *Princetonian*, 8 May 2006, http://prince-web1.princeton.edu/archives/2006/05/08/news/15574.shtml.

69. Speech by Yale President Richard C. Levin, "Creating Global Universities: From Student Exchanges to Collaboration," 12 November 2003, http://www.yale.edu/opa/outreach/china/20031112_levin_naea.html.

70. Kevin Cool, "China 101: Peking University Is Stanford's Latest Overseas Partner," September–October 2004, http://www.stanfordalumni.org/news/magazine/2004/sepoct/features/101.html.

71. "US-China University Collaboration for Training Government Officials," *Chinese News*, 19 January 2002, http://news.tsinghua.edu.cn.

72. Kristof, "The Educated Giant."

73. "A Thousand Chinese Desires Bloom," *BusinessWeek*, 22 August 2005, http://www.businessweek.com/magazine/content/05_34/b3948531.htm.

74. Tse, "China's Five Surprises."

75. David Cohen, "India Special: The Silicon Subcontinent," *New Scientist*, 19 February 2005.

76. APJ Abdul Kalam, "Golden Moments: 2006," *India Today*, 3 July 2006.

77. Jo Johnson and Joe Leahy, "Ambitions of India's Retail Revolutionary," *Financial Times*, 20 October 2006.

78. Alex Perry, "Bombay's Boom," *Time*, 18 June 2006.

79. Niranjan Rajadhyaksha, *The Rise of India: Its Transformation from Poverty to Prosperity* (Singapore: John Wiley & Sons, 2007), 20.

80. Fareed Zakaria, "India Rising," *Newsweek*, 6 March 2006.

CHAPTER 3

1. George F. Kennan, "America and the Russian Future," *Foreign Affairs*, April 1951.

2. Statistics from Stockholm International Peace Research Institute Yearbook 2007, http://yearbook2007.sipri.org. Numbers are in constant 2005 US dollars.

3. "United States Aircraft Carriers," Worldwide Military, http://www.worldwide military.com/Navy%20ships/US%20Carriers/USA_Carriers_EN.htm.

4. "Exclusive: Ex-British Ambassador to Uzbekistan Craig Murray on Why He Defied UK Foreign Office by Posting Classified Memos Blasting US, British Support of Torture by Uzbek Regime," *Democracy Now!* 19 January 2006, http://www .democracynow.org/article.pl?sid=06/01/19/1452237.

5. Chinmaya R. Gharekhan, *The Horseshoe Table: An Inside View of the UN Security Council* (New Delhi: Dorling Kindersley, 2006), 201.

6. Ibid.

7. Editorial, "Punishment Please," *Economist*, 25 August 2005.

8. World Development Indicators (WDI), World Bank, 2005. The "West" is here and in all other WDI statistics considered to be all OECD EU states plus the United States, Canada, Australia, New Zealand, and Switzerland.

9. World Development Indicators, World Bank.

10. Ibid.

11. *Fortune* Global 500, CNNMoney.com, 24 July 2006, http://money.cnn.com/ magazines/fortune/global500/2006.

12. "Who Will Pay Money for US-Planned 'Toppling Saddam'?" Consulate-General of the People's Republic of China, 13 March 2003, http://houston.china-consulate .org/eng/nv/t52449.htm.

13. *Fortune* Global 500, CNNMoney.com.

14. Ibid.

15. Robert Angel, "The Japan Lobby: An Introduction," Japan Policy Research Institute Working Paper No. 27, December 1996, http://www.jpri.org/publications/ workingpapers/wp27.html.

16. Ibid.

17. "The Top 1000 World Banks 2006," *The Banker*, 3 July 2006, http://www.the banker.com. These rankings are derived from the list of top ten banks by tier one capital, which is the core measure of a bank's financial strength from a regulator's point

of view. It consists of the types of capital considered the most reliable and liquid, primarily equity. To measure the largest banks by assets is more complicated, as some banks have large asset management arms, including mutual funds and fixed income portfolios.

18. Ibid.

19. Joshua Ramo, "The Three Marketeers," *Time*, 15 February 1999.

20. J. M. Roberts, *The Triumph of the West* (Boston: Little, Brown, 1985), 278.

CHAPTER 4

1. Nishikawa Shunsaku, "Fukuzawa Yukichi," *Prospects: The Quarterly Review of Comparative Education* 23, no. *3/4* (1993): 8. The quote by Fukuzawa is from the article "Datsu-A Ron" (Leaving Asia) published in *Jiji-shimpo*, 16 March 1885. The translation is by Sinh Vinh in *Fukuzawa Yukichi nenkan* [Annals], vol. 11 (Mita, Tokyo, Fukuzawa Yukichi kyokai, 1984), http://www.ibe.unesco.org/publications/ThinkersPdf/fukuzawe.pdf.

2. "Ataturk: His Legacy Is Still Alive," Turkses, http://www.turkses.com/index.php?option=com_content&task=view&id=508&Itemid=31.

3. *Sun Zhongshan quanji*, vol. 1, p. 278, quoted in Kishore Mahbubani, "India: Emerging as Eastern or Western Power? India Can Follow in the Footsteps of Japan or China—or Even Forge Its Own Path," *YaleGlobal*, 19 December 2006, 278.

4. Amartya Sen, *The Argumentative Indian: Writings on Indian History, Culture, and Identity* (London: Penguin Books, 2005), 107.

5. Ibid.

6. Singh Amardeep, "Teaching Journal: Katherine Mayo's Mother India (1927)," Lehigh University, 7 February 2007, http://www.lehigh.edu/~amsp/2006/02/teaching-journal-katherine-mayos.html.

7. Quoted in Vai Ramanathan, "English Is Here to Stay: A Critical Look at Institutional and Educational Practices in India," *TESOL Quarterly* 33, no. 2 (Summer 1999): 211–31.

8. Quoted in Sen, *Argumentative Indian*, 107.

9. Quoted in "Europe Looks at India: The Modern Dilemma," 1946, http://www.oldandsold.com/articles11/europe-india–8.shtml.

10. Karl Kaiser, "Big Power Relations in the 21st Century," *Global Paradigm Shift. Political, Security and Economic Dimensions*, YBM-Si-sa, 2008, 16–33.

11. "Inside Europe: How the Money Is Spent: Foreign Aid," BBC News, http://news.bbc.co.uk/1/shared/spl/hi/europe/04/money/html/foreign.stm.

12. Professor Wu Zengding, "The Era of Globalization and Chinese Civilization," Shaanxi Normal University, 23 February 2006.

13. Ibid.

14. World Development Indicators, World Bank, 2005.

15. Bethan Brookes and Peter Madden, "The Globe-Trotting Sports Shoe," http://www.saigon.com/~nike/christian-aid.htm.

16. "Chinese Travelers Changing the World's Tourism Pattern," *People's Daily* (online), 15 June 2007, http://english.people.com.cn/200706/15/eng20070615_384645 .html.

17. Edward Friedman and Bruce Gilley, *Asia's Giants: Comparing China and India* (New York: Palgrave Macmillan, (2005), 175–76.

18. John Thornton, "Assessing the Next Phase of a Rising China," Brookings Trip Report, Brookings Institution, 22 December 2006.

19. Guy de Jonquieres, "Why Asia Needs a More Active Market in Ideas," *Financial Times*, 30 August 2006.

20. Lu Yiyi, "West Must View China through Clearer Lenses," *Straits Times*, 3 January 2007.

21. Mark Rowe, "China's New Cultural Revolution," *Independent*, 18 February 2007.

22. Ying Zhu, "Yongzheng Dynasty and Chinese Primetime Television Drama," *Cinema Journal* 44, no. 4 (Summer 2005): 3–17.

23. Joseph Kahn and Daniel Wakin, "Western Classical Music Made and Loved in China," *International Herald Tribune*, 2 April 2007.

24. Daniel Wakin, "Chinese Musicians Hitting a High Note in the West," *International Herald Tribune*, 3 April 2007.

25. Clement Crisp, "China Makes Dramatic Strides," *Financial Times*, 5 January 2007.

26. "An Analysis of the World Muslim Population by Country/Region," Invest East, http://www.factbook.net/muslim_pop.php.

27. Text of Mahathir Mohammad's speech at OIC summit, 20 October 2003, http://www.bernama.com/oicsummit/speechr.php?id=35&cat=BI.

28. King Abdullah address to the Nineteenth Summit of the League of Arab States, Royal Embassy of Saudi Arabia (Washington, DC), 28 March 2007, http://www .saudiembassy.net/2007News/Statements/SpeechDetail.asp?cIndex=686.

29. Claude Salhani, "Analysis: Breath of Fresh Air in Arab World," *UPI*, 9 April 2007.

30. Patricia Martinez, "Muslims First, Malaysians Second," *Straits Times*, 21 August 2006, 10. It should also be noted that 97 percent said that it was acceptable for Muslims to live alongside non-Muslims and 80 percent believed that Muslims should learn about other religions.

31. See the website of Terror Free Tomorrow: http://www.terrorfreetomorrow.org.

32. The Pew Global Attitudes Project, "The Great Divide: How Westerners and Muslims View Each Other," Pew Research Center, 22 June 2006, http://pewglobal.org/ reports/display.php?ReportID=253.

33. Arab Human Development Report, United Nations, 2002, p. 113.

34. Marwan Bishara, "Three Conflicts, Two Mind-Sets, One Solution," *International Herald Tribune*, 7 August 2006.

35. David Brooks, "A War of Narratives," *New York Times*, 8 April 2007.

36. Fawaz A. Gerges, "Disowned by Mentor, Bin Laden Seeks New Pastures," *YaleGlobal* (online), 19 September 2007, http://yaleglobal.yale.edu/article.print ?id=9681.

37. Sen, *Argumentative Indian*, 286.

38. Tariq Ramadan, "The Pope and Islam: A Struggle over Europe's Identity," *International Herald Tribune*, 21 September 2006.

39. Michael Vatikiotis, "Reality Check on Islam in Indonesia," *Jakarta Post Opinion and Editorial*, 14 April 2007, http://www.thejakartapost.com/yesterdaydetail.asp?fileid=20070414.F03.

40. Fareed Zakaria, "Hassle and Humiliation," *Newsweek*, 26 February 2007.

41. Darshan Singh Maini, "US Doublethink: Terrorism and Human Rights," *Tribune*, 25 February 2000.

42. M. S. N. Menon, "Uncle Sam's Double-Standards Well-Known, but Not Its Janus Face," *Tribune*, 16 March 2003.

43. Sen, *Argumentative Indian*, 283.

44. Ibid., 284.

45. Ibid., 136.

46. Jawaharlal Nehru, *The Discovery of India*, 5th ed. (London: Meridian Books, 1960), 80.

47. Sen, *Argumentative Indian*, 287.

48. Vincent A. Smith, *Akbar the Great Mogul 1542–1605*, 2nd ed. (Oxford: Clarendon Press, 1902), 226.

49. Shashi Tharoor, "A Glossary of Indianness—The 'B' List," *Times of India*, 29 April 2007.

50. "Bollywood Stars and Hyderabadi Biryani for Musharraf," rediff.com, 17 April 2005, http://www.rediff.com/news/2005/apr/16mush11.htm.

51. Jack G. Shaheen, "Hollywood's Muslim Arabs," *Muslim World*, Spring 2000, 23.

52. Jack Shaheen, "Hollywood Widens Slur Targets to Arab and Muslim Americans since September 11," *Pacific News Service*, 27 February 2002.

53. Bridget Johnson, "Hollywood's Last Taboo," *OpinionJournal*, 13 July 2005, http://www.opinionjournal.com/la/?id=110006954.

CHAPTER 5

1. John Jay, The Federalist No. 2, "Concerning Dangers from Foreign Force and Influence," 31 October 1787, http://www.constitution.org/fed/federa02.htm.

2. Lee Kuan Yew, "Global War against Terror Can Be Won," speech accepting Woodrow Wilson Award for Public Service, 17 October 2006, http://www.wilson center.org/index.cfm?fuseaction=awards.item&news_id=205466.

3. Michael Massing, "The Storm Over the Israel Lobby," *New York Review of Books* 53, no. 10, 8 June 2006.

4. Saad Eddin Ibrahim, "The 'New Middle East' Bush Is Resisting," *Washington Post*, 23 August 2006.

5. "IPCC Reports Quick Action Can Avert Worst Climate Impacts," Environment News Service, 4 May 2007, http://www.ens-newswire.com/ens/may /2007–05–04–01.asp.

6. Gwynne Dyer, "Paying for the Sins of Emissions," *Straits Times*, 25 June 2007.

7. "Climate Change: You Will Have Many Vector-Borne Diseases," Interview with Rajendra Pachauri—Part III, rediff.com, 7 June 2007, http://www.rediff.com/news/2007/jun/07inter.htm.

8. Deep K. Datta-Ray, "Don't Tempt the Hawks," *Straits Times*, 12 June 2007.

9. Daniel Esty, "Is China Turning Green?" *Fortune*, 4 May 2007.

10. Statistics provided by the Embassy of Japan, Singapore, 14 February 2007.

11. Ma Kai, "China Is Shouldering Its Climate Change Burden," *Financial Times*, 4 June 2007.

12. "IPCC Reports Quick Action Can Avert Worst Climate Impacts."

13. James Carroll, "60 Years of Faulty Logic," *International Herald Tribune*, 13 March 2007.

14. "Strategic Defense Initiative," RonaldReagan.com (The Official Website), http://www.ronaldreagan.com/sdi.html.

15. Ibid.

16. George Shultz, *Turmoil and Triumph* (New York: Scribner's, 1993), 770–73.

17. Mohamad ElBaradei, "Towards a Safer World,"*Economist*, 18 October 2003, 47–48.

18. Anne-Marie Slaughter, and G. John Ikenberry, "Forging a World of Liberty under Law," Princeton Project on National Security, 27 September 2006, http://www.wws.princeton.edu/ppns/report/FinalReport.pdf.

19. President George W. Bush, Address to a Joint Session of Congress and the American People, 20 September 2001, http://www.whitehouse.gov/news/releases/2001/09/20010920-8.html.

20. Zuraidah Ibrahim, "Iran's Many Personalities Will Intrigue the Observer," *Straits Times*, 22 March 2007.

21. Fareed Zakaria, "What Iranians Least Expect?" *Newsweek*, 2 October 2006.

22. Richard Nixon, Toasts of the President and Premier Chou En-Lai of the People's Republic of China at a Banquet Honoring the President in Peking, 21 February 1972, http://www.presidency.ucsb.edu/ws/print.php?pid=3748.

23. Scheherazade Daneshkhu, "The West Must Stop Meddling in Iran's Affairs," *Financial Times*, 30 August 2006.

24. Nassrine Azimi, "Do Not Neglect Culture," *International Herald Tribune*, 8 May 2007.

25. "Ahmadinejad's Letter to Bush," *Washington Post*, 9 May 2006, on http://www.washingtopost.com/wp-dyn/content/article/2006/05/09/AR2006050900878.html.

26. Mark Lilla, "The Politics of God," *New York Times*, 19 August 2007.

27. Ibid.

28. Nicholas Kristof, "Diplomacy at Its Worst," *New York Times*, 29 April 2007.

29. Agence France-Presse, "Chirac Warns of Flood of Africans," *Straits Times*, 15 July 2006.

30. Associated Press, "Egypt Blasts Group of Middle East Peacemakers to Criticize Israel," *International Herald Tribune*, 31 May 2007.

31. Kishore Mahbubani, "Review Essay—Charting a New Course," *Survival* 49, no. 3, Autumn 2007.

32. John Cherian, "A Guarded Engagement," *Frontline* 15, no. 26, 19 December 1998–1 January 1999.

33. Ibid.

34. Lee Kuan Yew, "Post–9/11 Balance of Influence in Asia-Pacific," *Forbes*, 18 June 2007.

35. Speech by Premier Wen Jiabao of the State Council of the People's Republic of China at the Japanese Diet, 12 April 2007, http://www.mfa.gov.cn/eng/zxxx/t311107.htm.

36. Michael E. Marti, *China and the Legacy of Deng Xiaoping: From Communist Revolution to Capitalist Evolution* (Washington, DC: Brassey's, 2002), 154.

37. Cynthia Watson, Testimony to the U.S.–China Commission, 21 July 2005, p. 2, http://www.uscc.gov/hearings/2005hearings/written_testimonies/05_07_21_22wrts/watson_cynthia_wrts.pdf.

38. Stephen Johnson, "Balancing China's Growing Influence in Latin America," Heritage Foundation No. 1888, 24 October 2005.

39. Abraham McLaughlin, "Trade Drives Political Role Ahead of Zimbabwe's Elections," *Christian Science Monitor*, 30 March 2005.

40. Antoaneta Bezlova, "China's Soft-Power Diplomacy in Africa," *Asia Times*, 23 June 2006.

41. "The G7 in Washington," *Economist*, 4 October 2004, available on http://www.economist.com/agenda/displayStory.cfm?story_id=3258391.

42. Richard Halloran, "China's Decisive Role in the Asian Financial Crisis," Global Beat Issue Brief No. 24, 27 January 1998.

43. Ibid.

44. Gideon Rachman, "Walk Softly and Carry a Big Purse," *Straits Times*, 23 February 2007.

45. Sheng Lijun, "China-ASEAN Free Trade Area: Origins, Developments and Strategic Motivations," Institute of Southeast Asian Studies Working Paper, International Politics & Security Issues Series No. 1 (2003).

46. Beverly Crawford, "The Impact of EU Enlargement on the Euro-Med Partnership," Jean Monnet/Robert Schuman Paper Series Vol. 5 No. 23, July 2005.

47. Kevin Byrne, "Euromed: An Economic Failure?" Cafebabel.com, 28 November 2005, http://www.cafebabel.com/en/article.asp?T=A&Id=1545.

48. Niveen Wahish, "On the Wrong Foot," *Al-Ahram* (online), 28 April–4 May 2005, Issue No. 740, http://weekly.ahram.org.eg/2005/740/ec3.htm.

CHAPTER 6

1. Dr. Manmohan Singh, prime minister of India, speech to the LSE Asia Forum 2006,7 December 2006, http://www.lse.ac.uk/collections/LSEAsiaForum/pdf/ManmohanSingh_OpeningAddress.pdf.

2. Yongjin Zhang, *China in International Society since 1949: Alienation and Beyond* (New York: St. Martin's Press, 1998).

3. World Bank Development Indicators, World Bank, 2005.

4. US Census Bureau estimate (as of 1 July 2006).

5. Pascal Lamy, *Towards World Democracy* (London: Policy Network, 2005), 21–22.

6. Shamshad Ahmad, "No More of This Global Carnival," *Dawn*, 2 December 2007.

7. Deniz Ulke Aribogan, "The Summit of Divided Nations," *Aksam*, 15 September 2005.

8. Gyorgy Fodor, "Mirror Tell Me," *Magyar Hirlap*, 19 September 2005.

9. Karen Taylor et al., "IMF Quotas, Representation and Governance," Australian Government Treasury Working Paper, November 2004, 11.

10. Ibid., 12.

11. Stephany Griffith-Jones, "Governance of the World Bank," paper prepared for the UK Department for International Development, 2002, 11.

12. Rodrigo de Rato, "The Changing Role of the IMF in Asia and the Global Economy," speech given to the National Press Club, Canberra, Australia, 13 June 2006.

13. Griffith-Jones, "Governance of the World Bank," 2.

14. Lex Rieffel, "Don't Rush to Reform the Fund (and the Bank)," *Examiner*, 23 March 2006.

15. Preamble, 1945 Charter of the United Nations.

16. Cited by Joe Klein, "The Truman Show," *New York Times*, 11 June 2006, http://www.nytimes.com/2006/06/11/books/review/11klein.html.

17. Celia Dugger, "Donor Nations to Focus on Growing States," *New York Times*, 24 April 2006.

18. Rieffel, "Don't Rush to Reform the Fund (and the Bank)."

19. Ibid.

20. Editorial, "Stormy Weather," *Economist*, 27 January 2007.

21. Barton Gellman, "CIA Weighs 'Targeted Killing' Missions," *Washington Post*, 28 October 2001. See also William Horsley, "Fighting a 'Dirty War,'" BBC News, 21 September 2001.

22. "Development Aid from OECD Countries fell by 5.1% in 2006," OECD website, http://www.oecd.org/document/17/0,3343,en_2649_33721_38341265_1_1_1_1,00.html.

23. J. K. Fairbank, "Tributary Trade and China's Relations with the West," *Far Eastern Quarterly* 1 (1942): 139.

24. "Foreign Investment in China," *US-China Business Council*, April 2006, http://www.uschina.org/info/chops/2006/fdi.html.

25. Thant Myint-U, "Don't Force Democracy in Myanmar," *International Herald Tribune*, September 30–October 1, 2006.

26. Richard A. Oppel Jr. and Helene Cooper, "Iran to join US at Iraq Talks," *International Herald Tribune*, 28 February 2007.

27. The Iraq Study Group Report, http://www.usip.org/isg/iraq_study_group_report/report/1206/iraq_study_group_report.pdf.

INDEX

Abbasids, 271
Abdullah, King, 152–153
Abel Prize, 12–13
ABM. *See* Anti-Ballistic Missile treaty
Abu Ghraib, 159. *See also* Iraq
Administrative Litigation Act, 87–88
Administrative Service Officers (AOs), 73
Afghanistan
  Japanese support for US in, 118
  NATO in, 106
  occupation of, 161
  Soviet Union in, 114
  Taliban in, 106, 162
  Western solidarity in, 3
Africa
  China and, 225–226
  China-Africa Business Council and, 226
  economic development in, 216–217, 232–234, 237, 266
  EU and, 216–217, 232–234, 237, 266
  G-7 and, 123–124
  migration from, 237
  population/age distribution for, 218f
"After Brezhnev: Stormy Weather," 71
Aggregate Measurement of Support (AMS), 31–32
Agriculture
  subsidies for, 27, 32–33, 38, 130, 232
  UR and, 27, 29–31

Ahmadinejad, Mahmoud, 207–208, 212–216
AIDS. *See* HIV/AIDS
AIPAC. *See* American Israeli Public Affairs Committee
Akbar, 169–170. *See also* India
All-India Scheduled Castes Federation, 68
Ambani, Mukesh, 97–98
Ambedkar, Bhimrao, 67
American Dream, 97, 274
American Israeli Public Affairs Committee (AIPAC), 182–183
Americans for Peace Now, 182–183
Amnesty International, 166
Amorim, Celso, 246
AMS. *See* Aggregate Measurement of Support
Annan, Kofi, 250, 263
Anti-Americanism
  Bush and, 131, 167
  in Latin America, 108
  in Turkey, 130–131, 156
  in world, 226–227
Anti-Ballistic Missile treaty (ABM), 198
AOs. *See* Administrative Service Officers
APEC. *See* Asia-Pacific Economic Cooperation

KISHORE MAHBUBANI is Dean and Professor in the Practice of Public Policy of the Lee Kuan Yew School of Public Policy at the National University of Singapore. He has had a distinguished diplomatic career and is the author of *Can Asians Think?* and *Beyond the Age of Innocence.* In 2005, *Foreign Policy* magazine included him among the top hundred intellectuals in the world.

PublicAffairs is a publishing house founded in 1997. It is a tribute to the standards, values, and flair of three persons who have served as mentors to countless reporters, writers, editors, and book people of all kinds, including me.

I. F. STONE, proprietor of *I. F. Stone's Weekly*, combined a commitment to the First Amendment with entrepreneurial zeal and reporting skill and became one of the great independent journalists in American history. At the age of eighty, Izzy published *The Trial of Socrates*, which was a national bestseller. He wrote the book after he taught himself ancient Greek.

BENJAMIN C. BRADLEE was for nearly thirty years the charismatic editorial leader of *The Washington Post*. It was Ben who gave the *Post* the range and courage to pursue such historic issues as Watergate. He supported his reporters with a tenacity that made them fearless and it is no accident that so many became authors of influential, best-selling books.

ROBERT L. BERNSTEIN, the chief executive of Random House for more than a quarter century, guided one of the nation's premier publishing houses. Bob was personally responsible for many books of political dissent and argument that challenged tyranny around the globe. He is also the founder and longtime chair of Human Rights Watch, one of the most respected human rights organizations in the world.

.   .   .

For fifty years, the banner of Public Affairs Press was carried by its owner Morris B. Schnapper, who published Gandhi, Nasser, Toynbee, Truman, and about 1,500 other authors. In 1983, Schnapper was described by *The Washington Post* as "a redoubtable gadfly." His legacy will endure in the books to come.

Peter Osnos, *Founder and Editor-at-Large*